JOHN FREELY'S ISTANBUL

JOHN FREELY'S ISTANBUL

In Memory of Hilary Sumner-Boyd

S
C
A
L
A

in association with
ARCHAEOLOGY AND ART PUBLICATIONS

First published in 2005 by
Scala Publishers Ltd, Northburgh House,
10 Northburgh Street, London EC1V 0AT

In association with
Archaeology and Art Publications
Hayrye Cad. ÇORLU Apt. 3/4
80060 Galatasaray, Istanbul

ISBN 1 85759 306 5
ISBN 975-6561-64-5

Vintage prints on pages 18, 31, 41, 48, 54 (below), 66, 74, 80, 184
and 196 kindly supplied by Antony Baker.

Series editors: Brian Johnson and Nezih Başgelen

Edited by Howard Watson
Designed by Anikst Design, London
Produced by Scala Publishers
Index by Diana LeCore

Printed in Turkey by Ofset Yapimevi

10 9 8 7 6 5 4 3 2 1

Cover: The skyline of the old city of Istanbul, seen from the
Golden Horn.

Title page: The Golden Horn, c. 1808. French School.
(Photograph printed courtesy Yanni Petsopoulos.)

Contents page (from top to bottom): The mosques of the old
city illuminated in the evening; the prayer room in the
Mosque of Ahmet I; an old man in the courtyard of the
Mosque of the conqueror; Yeni Valide Camii, Uskudar;
Heybeliada, the second largest of the Princes' Islands; the
Galata shore of the Golden Horn after a snowstorm.

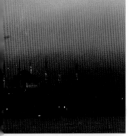

CONTENTS

PROLOGUE

What follows are my impressions of Istanbul, based on half a lifetime of living in the city during three separate intervals from 1960. It was then that I began teaching at the old Robert College, now the University of the Bosphorus, to which I returned in 1993 and where I continue to teach today.

My early impressions of the city appeared in *Strolling Through Istanbul*, co-authored with the late Hilary Sumner-Boyd and first published in 1972. Later editions of this work and of my *Blue Guide Istanbul* updated the descriptions of the city's Byzantine and Ottoman monuments and the antiquities in its museums. But at the same time, in each successive edition of these books, some old layers of the local color of Istanbul were stripped away – as when the buildings along the shore of the Golden Horn were demolished by Mayor Bedrettin Dalan, or when Nazmi's Café in Bebek was replaced by an apartment house, or when the painter Aliye Berger passed away and her apartment on the old Grande Rue de Pera was closed – so that there was no longer any reason to describe these places in my guide books.

I am reminded how much Istanbul has changed when I look in my *Stamboul Sketches*, published in 1974 with photographs by Sedat Pakay. This book has never been reissued, and so my essays and Sedat's photos remain as an unaltered record of what the city was like at that time, although even then some of the subjects I wrote about had already disappeared and existed only as fond memories. As I wrote in the introduction to *Stamboul Sketches*:

These sketches were written over the course of the dozen years during which we have lived in Istanbul, and so many of them may now seem somewhat dated. For the scene has changed, and many of the characters have departed, some never to return. You will search in vain for the Albanian Flower-Peddler; Nazmi's Café and the Taverna Boem have closed their doors forever; and some of our street-poets and wandering minstrels now sing and play here no more. Nevertheless I have made no attempt to update the sketches, for they and the photos by Sedat Pakay are a picture of the city we knew and loved in years past, the old Stamboul of our memories.

Both in my guide books and in *Stamboul Sketches* I have frequently quoted from the seventeenth-century Turkish chronicler Evliya Çelebi. Evliya is the author of the *Seyahatname*, or *Narrative of Travels*, which contains a lengthy, detailed and frequently fabulous description of Istanbul during what was apparently the most colorful period of Ottoman history. I have done the same in the present book, and for the same reasons that I gave in the introduction to *Stamboul Sketches*:

Evliya Efendi appears and reappears throughout these sketches, for in his Seyahatname he touches on virtually every aspect of the city's life. So in my own wanderings through Stamboul I have constantly had him by my side, he comparing his town with mine, like an eccentric companion guide. And I have often interwoven my narrative with that of Evliya Efendi, trying to bridge the gulf of years that separates his time from ours, so as to reveal something of the continuity of human experience which seems to exist in this ancient city.

Turkish Spelling and Pronunciation

All letters have one and only one sound. Turkish is very lightly accented, most often on the last syllable, but all syllables should be clearly and almost evenly articulated.

Vowels have their short Continental value as in French, German and Italian, i.e. **a** as in f**a**ther, **e** as in g**e**t, **i** as in s**i**t, **o** as in d**o**ll, **u** as in b**u**ll. (In modern Turkish pronunciation there is little distinction between long and short vowels.) Note **ı** (undotted) is between **i** and **u**, as the final **a** in Anna; **ö** as in German or the **u** in f**u**rther, **ü** as in German or French **u** in t**u**.

Consonants are as in English, except:
c as **j** in **j**am: e. g. *cami* (mosque) = **j**ahmy
ç as **ch** in **ch**urch: e. g. *çeşme* (fountain) = **ch**eshme
ğ is always hard as in **g**ive, never soft as in **g**em
g is almost silent; it tends to lengthen the previous vowel
s is always unvoiced as in **s**it, never like **z**
ş as **s** in **s**ugar: e. g. *çeşme* = che**sh**me

1

EMINÖNÜ

The skyline of historic Istanbul has hardly changed in my time, or for centuries before. This is a major miracle, considering how much of the old city has been destroyed in the years that I have known it, particularly the picturesque wooden houses of the late Ottoman era that were demolished in the last third of the twentieth century to make way for concrete apartment blocks and commercial buildings. But the skyline has survived in all of its splendor, the domes and minarets of imperial mosques crowning six of the seven hills of the old city – Greek Constantinople, ancient Byzantium – when viewed from the Bosphorus, the Golden Horn, or the Sea of Marmara. These are the three waterways to which the historian Procopius was referring, when in the sixth century AD he described Constantinople as being encircled by "a garland of waters."

The French antiquarian Petrus Gyllius, writing in the mid-sixteenth century, called the Bosphorus "the strait that ends all straits, for

The skyline of the old city of Istanbul, seen from the Golden Horn

with one key it opens and closes two worlds, two seas." The two worlds he was referring to are Europe and Asia, which the Bosphorus separates as it flows for some 32 kilometers between the Black Sea and the Sea of Marmara. At its southern end, the Bosphorus is joined on its European side by the Golden Horn, a scimitar-shaped inlet fed at its upper end by two streams known in times past as the Sweet Waters of Europe. The Bosphorus and the Golden Horn then flow together into the Marmara, passing between the old city of Istanbul and its Asian suburbs. The Golden Horn divides the European part of the city, with the port quarter of Galata on its north, from the old city to the south, which some of us still refer to as Stamboul.

Gyllius was the first to number the seven hills of the old city. The First Hill is at the apex of the old city, a roughly triangular peninsula that forms the southeasternmost projection of the European continent, rising above the confluence of the Bosphorus and the Golden Horn. The next five hills rise in succession from the ridge that parallels the Golden Horn, while the Seventh Hill rises above the Marmara shore in the southwestern part of the peninsula.

The original Greek city-state of Byzantium, founded c. 660 BC by Byzas the Megarian, comprised little more than the First Hill, encircled by a defense wall. When in AD 330 the emperor Constantine the Great shifted his capital to Byzantium, renaming it Constantinople, he built a defense wall that enclosed four hills. Then in 447 Theodosius II built a new line of walls a mile further out into Thrace, extending for more than four miles from the Golden Horn to the Marmara and enclosing seven hills, the same as in old Rome. This was of great symbolic importance, for Constantinople was "the second Rome," capital of what modern historians call the Byzantine Empire, the Christian continuation of the ancient Roman Empire.

The Byzantine Empire reached its peak during the reign of Justinian (r. 527–65), whose realm extended around the Mediterranean and rivaled that of Augustus at the height of the old Roman Empire. Justinian's supreme monument was the great church of Haghia Sophia, which still stands on the First Hill, dominating the skyline of the city when viewed from ships approaching on the Sea of Marmara.

Constantinople was captured and sacked in 1204 by the knights of the Fourth Crusade and the Venetians, who occupied the city until it was recaptured by the Byzantines in 1261. By that time the Byzantine Empire was only a small fragment of what it had been in the days of Justinian, though in its latter years it flourished in a brilliant renaissance.

The Byzantine Empire came to an end on May 29, 1453, when, after a seven-week siege, Constantinople fell to the Ottoman Turks under Mehmet II, who was thenceforth known to his people as Fatih, or "the Conqueror." The city then came to be known as Istanbul, a corruption of the Greek *eis stin poli,* meaning "in (or to) the city."

Immediately after the Conquest, Fatih began to rebuild the city to suit its role as the new capital of the Ottoman Empire. He brought in both Turks and non-Muslims to resettle the city, which had become depopulated during the last years of Byzantium. He built a huge mosque complex named Fatih Camii on the Fourth Hill, on the site of the former Church of the Holy Apostles. Then, c. 1465, he began erecting an imperial palace on the First Hill, which came to be called Topkapı Sarayı.

The pinnacle of the Ottoman Empire arrived with the sovereignty of Süleyman the Magnificent (r. 1520–66), who in a dozen successful campaigns extended the bounds of his realm from the Danube to north Africa and from the Adriatic to the Caucasus and western Persia. His crowning architectural achievement is the Süleymaniye, the superb mosque complex that he built on the Third Hill, overlooking the Golden Horn.

The Ottoman Empire began its long and inexorable decline after Süleyman's reign; nevertheless it lasted until 1923, when the new Republic of Turkey was created by Atatürk and his followers, with its capital at Ankara. Thus the ancient city at the confluence of the Bosphorus and the Golden Horn relinquished its role as the capital of a world empire for the first time in sixteen centuries, though the splendid monuments on its seven hills were there as a reminder of its imperial past.

The city has grown tremendously since 1923, when its population was about half a million, numbering today more than 10 million, its metropolitan limits extending for miles along both the European and Asian shores of the Marmara and up the Bosphorus to within sight of the Black Sea. Its ethnic composition has changed dramatically as well since the beginning of the Turkish Republic, when only about half the city's population was Muslim Turkish, the principal minority being Greek Orthodox. Today the population is almost entirely Turkish, the Armenian and Jewish minorities numbering several tens of thousands, the Greeks less than two thousand. But this is still a very diverse city ethnically, for the Turkish citizens represent people from all over the once vast dominions of the former Ottoman Empire, drawn to Istanbul by the same forces that made Constantinople a world center in times past.

The port quarter of Galata on the north side of the Golden Horn is linked with Stamboul by two bridges, the lower one known as the Galata Bridge and the upper as the Atatürk Bridge. The Galata Bridge is the main crossing-point for pedestrians, taking one from Karaköy in Galata to Eminönü in the old city.

Eminönü has been a market quarter since the earliest days of the city, for the original harbor of Byzantium was on the Golden Horn, below the First and Second Hills. The ancient harbor, which has long since been filled in, extended from the present Galata Bridge to the western slope of the First Hill. This part of the Golden Horn still has the appearance of a harbor, particularly on the Stamboul shore, for it is lined with the *iskeles,* or piers, of the various ferry lines, with boats continually going to and from the Bosphorus and the Asian suburbs, as well as the stations on the upper Golden Horn.

The pedestrians on the Galata Bridge run a gauntlet of peddlers hawking their wares above the roar of traffic and the shrill whistles of the ferry boats. Amateur fishermen line the railings of the bridge, many of them, from the looks of them, having no other source of food than their daily catch. The professionals sell their catch from fish markets on the shore beside the two ends of the bridge, where one can dine on fried fish sandwiched between the two halves of a loaf of bread. The first time that I crossed the Galata Bridge, in late September 1960, I had a fried-fish sandwich for lunch aboard a rowboat on the Eminönü shore, and now in the early years of the twenty-first century I occasionally still do the same, pleased that at least this aspect of life in Istanbul has not changed in my time.

In fact, the scene in Eminönü has not changed in its essentials since at least the days of Evliya Çelebi, the seventeenth-century Turkish chroni-

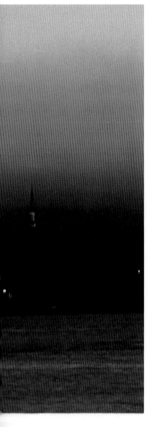

above
The mosques of the old city illuminated in the evening

left
The Stamboul shore of the Golden Horn, with the mosque of Süleyman the Magnificent on the summit of the Third Hill

cler, whose *Seyahatname,* or *Narrative of Travels,* is largely devoted to a description of Istanbul and its way of life. The most colorful part of this work is an account of the Procession of the Guilds, a public muster ordered in 1638 by Murat IV, who, in preparation for a campaign against Baghdad, wanted to see for himself what were the resources of Istanbul. The parade lasted for three days, as representatives of all the city's 735 guilds passed before the Alay Kiosk, trying to amuse and amaze the sultan with their displays and antics. Among them were the guilds of fishermen and fish-cooks, who, as Evliya writes in describing their activities in the procession, had their meeting-place on the Stamboul shore of the Golden Horn, where they still have a market today.

The famous tulip motif on an Iznik tile

The establishment of the fishermen is outside the Flour Hall, at the old fish market on the Golden Horn. The fishermen adorn their shops on litters with many thousand fish, amongst which many monsters of the sea are to be seen. They exhibit dolphins on chains, sea-horses, whales, and other kinds of fish of great size, which they catch a couple of days before the procession and load onto wagons drawn by seventy-eight buffaloes. They pass, crying "Hi!" and "Ho!," to the great amazement of the beholders. The enfranchised fishermen also collect various insects of the sea, and a great number of them carry in their hands halberds, harpoons, muskets, and artificial trees.

The fish cooks are all infidel Greeks who cook fish in different ways, some with olive oil and some with linseed oil; they also cook mussel pilaf, oysters and a soup of kefal-fish. They also have oysters called lakoz, which are very strengthening. If eaten quickly, they taste like a green slime, but they are very invigorating, and are therefore wholesome to men who wish to please their wives; in short it is a delicacy for debauchees … In the public processions, the fish cooks pass singing songs and making jests. They are a comical set of fellows and make the sultan laugh much, he being of a very merry disposition.

The imposing Yeni Cami, the New Mosque – or, as it is more fully known, the New Mosque of the *Valide Sultan,* or Queen Mother – dominates the chaotic square at the end of the Galata Bridge in Eminönü. The mosque was originally commissioned by the *valide sultan* Safiye, mother of Mehmet III, in 1597. But Safiye had to abandon the project when her son died in 1603, and work was not resumed until 1660, when the *valide sultan* Turhan Hadice, mother of Mehmet IV, decided to complete the construction of the mosque, which she dedicated on November 6, 1663.

Yeni Cami was the center of a *vakıf,* or foundation, whose institutions together form a complex known as a *külliye,* a feature typical of the larger Ottoman mosques in Istanbul. Besides the mosque itself, the *kül-*

liye of Yeni Cami initially incorporated a primary school (*mektep*), a fountain (*çeşme*), a fountain-house (*sebil*), a hospital (*darüşşifa*), a mausoleum (*türbe*), a public bath (*hamam*), and a market (*çarşı*), the revenue from the latter two contributing to the upkeep of the complex. Most of the facilities remain, but the school, the public bath and the hospital have gone.

The attractive L-shaped building, to the right of the mosque when viewed from the Galata Bridge, is the market of the Yeni Cami complex. Known in English as the Spice Bazaar, it is actually called the Mısır Çarşısı, or Egyptian Market. The shop owners in the Mısır Çarşısı were organized into eight separate guilds, as Evliya notes in describing their passage in the imperial procession, the most notable being the Egyptian Grocers and the Merchants of Musk Sherbets.

The Egyptian Grocers pass armed on wagons filled with baskets of ginger, pepper, cardamum, cinamum, cloves, rhubarb, spikenard, and aloes, forming altogether three thousand items ... The Merchants of Musk Sherbets pass exposing to public view every kind of sherbet made of rhubarb, ambergris, roses, lemons, tamarinds, etc., of different colors and scents, which they distribute among the spectators.

The area around Yeni Cami is the principal street market in Istanbul, particularly on Sunday, when the poor of the city throng to buy cut-price goods of every sort from peripatetic peddlers, themselves poor. The peddlers, none of whom has a license, are continually fleeing from the ineffective raids of the market police, who usually give up exhausted after a short chase. The merchants lay out their wares on tarpaulins around the mosque, in the underpasses leading to the Galata Bridge, and on the quays along the Golden Horn, where blind composers and musicians play tapes of their latest works at ear-splitting volume, though not drowning out the staccato fusillades of toy helicopter gunships circling their electronic commanders. Except for the electronics and the underpasses, the scene has not changed in its essentials since I first set foot in Eminönü, as I was reminded when I re-read my description of the peddlers here in my *Stamboul Sketches,* published in 1974: "These peddlers have the mobility of magpies and the seasonal sense of migratory birds, scurrying after a group of gullible peasants here, fleeing from the market police there, producing umbrellas for sale when rain threatens and sunglasses when the weather clears."

The courtyard in the angle of the L of the Spice Bazaar has always been the city's market for birds, which in Evliya's time would have included nightingales, who still serenade us from valleys along the

Bosphorus in April and May. Evliya tells us that in his time there were 500 nightingale merchants in Istanbul, and he describes them as they pass in the imperial procession.

They furnish great men and barber shops with nightingales, which by their melodies enrapture the soul. They have some precious cages set with onyxes and pearls; some of these cages are worth a thousand piastres and are only given as presents to kings. In these cages, the nightingales, excited by the noise of the crowd, sing loudly and merrily, vying with each other in their warbling notes. In other cages talking parrots and chattering parakeets are seen, some of which recite the Sura Ikhlas and other prayers.

The end of the courtyard opposite the south entrance to Yeni Cami has always been the place of the public letter-writers, who are much used by illiterate peasants from Anatolia. They were known in Evliya's time as "petitioners," since most of the letters they wrote were petitions to the Divan, the supreme council of the Ottoman Empire. The public letter-writers outside Yeni Cami have kept up with the times, and in the years that I have observed them here I have seen them make the transition from old-fashioned mechanical typewriters to laptop word processors and e-mail.

The area opposite the mosque is also the station of the seal-engravers and sign-painters, both of whom still use the old cursive Ottoman script. When I first came to Istanbul one would also find here one or two sellers of leeches, but I have not seen one of these in years. There was also an old man who told fortunes using a white rabbit, which at a signal from its master would duck its head into a box of folded-up pieces of paper, like those used in Chinese fortune cookies, and present one to the paying customer, usually with a pithy bit of advice on the future, such as "Think before you act!" I had not seen one of these fortune-tellers for years either, but not long after the beginning of the new millennium I saw a dark-skinned young man standing behind Yeni Cami with *two* white rabbits, both of which were busy picking out folded-up pieces of advice for a crowd of peasants. When I walked over to take a closer look, the fortune-teller addressed me in French, telling me that he was an Algerian from Carcassonne, and that he had come to Istanbul with no other resources than his two divinatory rabbits, which I thought augured well for the future of our eternally surprising old city.

Hasırcılar Caddesi, the Avenue of the Mat-Makers, starts at the west gate of the Spice Bazaar and leads up the Golden Horn parallel to the shore highway, passing through the quarter known as Küçük Pazar, or the Little Market. Evliya Çelebi would have known this street well, since his father's house was at the far end of this street and its extensions, beside Sağrıcılar Camii, the Mosque of the Leather-Workers, which still stands beside the approach to the present Atatürk Bridge. Evliya was born there in 1611, in a house that has long since disappeared, but whose garden survives as a tiny graveyard. There are only two graves there, one of them being that of Evliya's ancestor Yavuz Ersinan, who built the mosque in 1455, and the other being that of Horoz Dede, or "Grandfather Rooster." Yavuz Ersinan was one of Fatih's standard-bearers during the siege in 1453, and Horoz Dede was his companion in arms. Horoz was so named because during the siege he roused the Turkish troops each day before dawn with the fanfare of his rooster call. When he died he was buried beside Yavuz Ersinan's mosque, with Fatih himself leading the devotions of the mourners.

Hasırcılar Caddesi is the last surviving stretch of the original Turkish market area that was built along the Golden Horn after the Conquest. Many of its shops are in the outer arcades of old Ottoman *hans,* or inner-city caravansarais. The oldest of these *hans* is Balkapan, the Honey Store, whose vast substructure dates back to Byzantine times. It was probably used by the Venetians when they had their concession here in the late Byzantine era, those of other Italian city-states being farther down the Golden Horn.

About 150 meters along Hasırcılar Caddesi from the Spice Bazaar, the right side of the street is bordered by the lower arcade of Rüstem Paşa Camii, one of the most elegant of the grand vezirial mosques in the city, renowned for its exquisite Iznik tiles. The mosque was built in 1561 by the great Mimar Sinan (c. 1492–1588), chief architect of Süleyman and his two immediate successors, Selim II and Murat III. The founder was Rüstem Paşa, twice grand vezir under Süleyman the Magnificent and husband of Mihrimah Sultan, the sultan's only daughter.

below left
Yeni Cami, the New Mosque of the Valide Sultan, on the Stamboul shore of the Golden Horn

below right
The prayer room of Yeni Cami

The main market area for fruit and vegetables was on the shore of the Golden Horn just upstream from the present Galata Bridge, where, up until the early 1970s, huge wooden caiques used to unload their cargoes at Yemış Iskelesi, the Pier of Dried Fruits, those that were no longer seaworthy serving as floating restaurants, teahouses and taverns. But then all of the ancient market quarter between the shore highway and the Golden Horn was demolished by Mayor Bedrettin Dalan, most of the area now serving as a parking lot, saddening those of us who remember what it once was.

Those who worked in this now vanished market were well represented in the imperial procession, in which, according to Evliya, the fruit merchants put on a particularly spirited performance to dramatize the scene that took place when caiques unloaded at Yemış Iskelesi.

The Fruit-Merchants pass on wagons adorned with all kinds of fruits. They also make artificial trees of apples, apricots, and other kinds of fruits, each carried on poles by eight or ten men. Others make kiosks with fountains playing, the four sides of which are festooned with fruit. Their boys, who are seated in these kiosks, bargain with the spectators and throw fruit to them. Some dress in robes made of chestnuts, reciting verses from the Kuran while holding prayer beads of dried raisins. They also build artificial ships, which are full of fruit, each ship being towed by a thousand men. The sails, prow, and stern of each of these ships are ornamented with fruit skins and nut kernels. Merchants flock in crowds to enter these fruit-ships to fill their baskets. With the greatest noise and quarreling arising from these simulated sales, they pass the Alay Kiosk. This is a faithful representation of what occurs at the port on the arrival of every fruit-ship at Yemiş Iskelesi.

One of Sedat Pakay's photos in my *Stamboul Sketches* shows some of the floating restaurants, teahouses, and taverns around Yemış Iskelesi not long before the destruction of the market quarter on the Golden Horn. In the foreground lies the entrance to the Sea Museum of Yaşar Kasım, a dwarf who is shown with his pet pelican. The museum consisted principally of the pelican and two senile seals, creatures unknown to the Anatolian peasants who paid a single copper coin to enter. When a few paying customers had assembled, Yaşar would whistle, whereupon the pelican flapped its wings and the seals in their tub of water clapped their flippers to the applause of the audience. At the end of the day Kasım would feed his seals and lock up his museum, after which he and his pelican would waddle home across the Galata Bridge, a scene engraved in my memory as a reminder of an Istanbul that we will never see again.

Among the few structures that remain on the site of the ancient market quarter is a tall medieval structure known as Zindan Kulesi, the Prison Tower, one of the bastions of the Byzantine sea-walls along the Golden Horn. This is the infamous Bagno, used in both Byzantine and Ottoman times as a prison for galley slaves. The tower is now a shrine of the Muslim saint known as Cafer Baba, who, according to tradition, came to Constantinople early in the ninth century as an envoy of Harun al Rashid, the Caliph of Baghdad, but was imprisoned in the Bagno and died there. Cafer's grave was restored following its rediscovery after the Turkish Conquest in 1453, as Evliya writes:

Cafer Baba is buried in a place within the prison of the infidels, where to this day his name is insulted by all the unbelieving malefactors, debtors, murders, etc., imprisoned there. But when (God be praised!) Istanbul was taken, the grave of Cafer Baba in the tower of the Bagno became a place of pilgrimage, which is visited by those who have been released from prison and who call down blessings in opposition to the curses of the unbelievers.

Near the tower there are the exiguous remains of an ancient gateway, one of the portals in the Byzantine sea-walls. Because of its proximity to the Bagno, the gateway is known in Turkish as Zindan Kapı, the Prison Gate, a name that was applied to the surrounding quarter, which up until the early 1970s was mostly occupied by maritime enterprises such as ship chandlers and naval supply stores. The original identity of this gate remains unclear, but it is possible that it was the Porta Hebraica, since it led to the Jewish quarter in the area now occupied by Yeni Cami. That quarter was inhabited by the schismatic Karaite Jews, who were evicted when the mosque was built and then relocated at Hasköy on the north shore of the Golden Horn, where their descendants still live. At the beginning of the Ottoman era, local Greeks called the gateway Porta Caravion, the Gate of the Caravels, because of the large number of ships moored at the nearby Yemış Iskelesi, which was known to the Italians as the Scala de Drongario.

Petrus Gyllius reports that there was a ferry service across the Golden Horn at this point since the earliest days of the city. Yemış Iskelesi is still used by the little motor boats that serve as ferries across the Golden Horn, patronized by old-timers such as myself who are too lazy to walk across the bridge, and who prefer to sit back and gaze at the skyline of the old city and its encircling garland of waters.

Next to the ruined gateway, there is an abandoned and dilapidated mosque known as Ahi Çelebi Camii, founded some time before 1523. It is of interest principally by virtue of its connection to Evliya Çelebi and the dream in which the Prophet Mohammed assured him that he would become a great traveler and chronicler, a miraculous incident that he relates in the opening book of the *Seyahatname*. When Evliya was about twenty years old, he tells us, he began making excursions in the vicinity of Istanbul and consequently decided to become a traveler.

It was in the time of the illustrious reign of Murat IV that I began to think of extensive travels, in order to escape from the power of my father, mother, and brethren. Forming a design of traveling over the whole earth, I entreated God to give me health for my body and faith for my soul. I sought the conversations of dervishes, and when I heard a description of the seven climates and of the four quarters of the earth, I became still more anxious to see the world, to visit the Holy Land, Cairo, Damascus, Mecca, and Medina, and to prostrate myself on the purified soil of the places where the Prophet, the glory of all creatures, was born and died.

With that hope, Evliya prayed for divine guidance, a request that was eventually granted to him on his twenty-first birthday. He writes that he fell asleep that night in his father's house and dreamt that he was in the nearby mosque of Ahi Çelebi. No sooner had he arrived there, in his dream, than the doors of the mosque opened and a brilliant crowd entered, all saying the morning prayer. Evliya tells us that he was lost in astonishment at the sight of this colorful assembly and that he looked upon his neighbor and said: "May I ask, my lord, who you are, and what is your illustrious name?" His neighbor answered and said that he was Sa'd Vakkas, one of the ten evangelists and the patron of archers. Evliya kissed the hands of Sa'd Vakkas and asked further: "Who are the refulgent multitude on my right hand?" "They are all blessed saints and pure souls, the spirits of the followers of the Prophet," answered Sa'd Vakkas, who then told Evliya that the Prophet himself, along with his grandsons Hasan and Hüseyin, were expected in the mosque at any moment to perform the morning service.

below left
The port of Istanbul
on the Golden Horn.
Print by Thomas
Allom, c. 1838

right
The Galata Bridge
across the Golden
Horn, with Galata in
the background

No sooner had Sa'd Vakkas said this than flashes of lightning burst from the doors of the mosque and the room filled with a crowd of saints and martyrs. "It was the Prophet!" Evliya writes,

Overshadowed by his green banner, covered by his green veil, carrying his staff in his right hand, his sword girt on his thigh, with the Imam Hasan on his right side and the Imam Hüseyin on his left. As he placed his right foot on the threshold he cried out "Bismillah!" and throwing off his veil, said "Health unto thee, O my people!" The whole assembly answered, "Unto thee be health, O prophet of God, Lord of the Nations!"

Evliya tells us that he trembled in every limb, but still he was able to give a detailed description of the Prophet's appearance, saying that it agreed

exactly with that given in the *Hallyehi Khakani:* "The veil on his face was a white shawl and his turban was formed of a white sash with twelve folds; his mantle was of camel's hair inclining to yellow; on his neck he wore a woolen shawl. His boots were yellow and in his turban was stuck a toothpick."

Evliya then tells us that the Prophet advanced to the *mihrap,* the niche indicating the direction of Mecca, struck his knees with his right hand, and commanded Evliya to take the lead in saying the morning prayers. Evliya did so and the Prophet followed by reciting the *Fatihah,* the first chapter of the Kuran, along with other verses. After other prayers were pronounced by Evliya and Belal, the first *müezzin* of Islam, the morning prayer was concluded. "The service was concluded with a general cry of 'Allah!' which very nearly woke me from my sleep," Evliya writes. He goes on to tell of how Sa'd Vakkas took him by the hand and escorted him into the Prophet's presence, saying, "Thy loving and faithful servant Evliya entreats thy intercession." Evliya, weeping in his excitement and confusion, kissed the Prophet's hands and received his blessings, along with the assurance that his desire to travel would be fulfilled. The Prophet then repeated the *Fatihah,* followed by all of his sainted companions, after which Evliya went round and kissed their hands, receiving from each his blessings.

Their hands were perfumed with musk, ambergris, spikenard, sweet basil, violets, and carnations; but that of the Prophet himself smelt of nothing but saffron and roses, felt when touched as if it had no bones, and was as soft as cotton. The hands of the other prophets had the odor of quinces, that of Abu Bekr had the fragrance of lemons, Omar's smelt like ambergris, Osman's like violets, Ali's like jasmine, Hasan's like carnations, and Hüseyin's like white roses ... Then the Prophet himself pronounced the parting salutation from the mihrap, after which he advanced towards the door and the whole illustrious assembly, giving me various greetings and blessings, went out of the mosque.

The last to leave was Sa'd Vakkas, who took the quiver from his belt and gave it to Evliya, saying, "Go, be thou victorious with thy bow and arrow; be in God's keeping, and receive from me the good tidings that thou shalt visit the tombs of all the prophets and holy men whose hands thou hast now kissed. Thou shalt travel through the whole world and be a marvel among men." Sa'd Vakkas then kissed Evliya's hands and departed from the mosque, leaving Evliya alone at the end of his dream.

As Evliya writes of his awakening:

When I awoke I was in great doubt whether what I had seen was a dream or reality, and I enjoyed for some time the beatific contemplations which filled my soul. Having afterwards performed my ablutions and offered up the morning prayer, I crossed over from Constantinople to the suburb of Kasım Pasha and consulted the interpreter of dreams, Ibrahim Efendi, about my vision. From him I received the comfortable news that I would become a great traveler, and after making my way through the world, with the intercession of the Prophet, would close my career by being admitted to Paradise. I then retired to my humble abode, applied myself to the study of history, and began a description of my birthplace, Istanbul, that envy of kings, the celestial haven and stronghold of Macedonia.

And so Evliya began the travels that eventually took him all over the Ottoman Empire, which at that time extended from central Persia through the eastern Mediterranean and from Egypt to the frontiers of Russia. He tells us that he traveled for forty years, passed through the countries of eighteen monarchs, and heard 147 languages. His last journey took him on a pilgrimage to Mecca, and then to Cairo, where he died around 1680, in what would have been his seventieth year.

I always think of Evliya when I stroll through the Küçük Pazar quarter, for he would have walked this way in his youth on his way between his father's house and Eminönü. The scene here has changed greatly since his day, as it has even in my own time, but there are human elements that are the same as they were when I first came to Istanbul, some of which remain unchanged since Evliya's time. I once again became aware of this recently when I walked along Hasırcılar Caddesi in early evening, when the scene brought to mind what I had written of this quarter in *Stamboul Sketches* three decades ago. From the teahouses there still comes the slap of playing cards and the click of tavlı counters. The debates of the unelected parliaments are as noisy as ever. The fruit shops continue to lure us in with their succulent displays, and fishmongers still produce their artistic arrangements of the daily catch, while the dramatically lit barbershops provide an element of street theater. And the framed calligraphic inscription on the barber's wall announces that his shop is under the protection of Selman, barber to the Prophet, of whom it was said, according to Evliya, that "Paradise longs for Selman every day and every night three times."

top
A wickerwork shop on Hasırcılar Caddesi

above
A spice seller in the Egyptian bazaar

Itinerant sellers of water, ayran, and boza minister to the thirst of the milling crowds, and street-peddlers rally to sell one more useless item to pay for their supper. Hopeful peasants crowd round the fortune-teller with his divinatory rabbit. Snow-bearded ancients file out of the mosque and take leave of one another in the ritual Islamic manner. Young girls rattle with their amphorae and buckets to a baroque street fountain, while housewives haul up the evening's groceries with line and basket, calling out to their children to come home. Street vendors enrich the air with the smells of hot corn and roasting chestnuts, while bakeries incense the neighborhood with the sacramental odor of freshly baked bread.

Eventually the crowd dwindles to a few stragglers and the market streets grow gradually quiet. Fruit sellers put away their produce with as much care as when they set it out twelve long hours before, now and then looking down the street in the hope that one last customer will appear. The fish market closes and cats appear from everywhere to scavenge the cobbles. One-by-one metal shop-fronts come clang-

A shop in the Spice Bazaar

ing down along the market streets, and watchmen's whistles answer one around the darkening quarter. Off in the distance I can hear the cracked voice of an old boza-seller as he proclaims to the empty streets that his boza is exceptionally fine.

Heading homeward myself, after seeing that the Eminönü I first knew is still, even at the beginning of the twenty-first century, the epicenter of Stamboul's daily life, I recall once again the words that Evliya wrote as he watched the last of the imperial procession go by: "Such is the crowd and population of that great capital Istanbul, which may God guard from all celestial and earthly mischief till the end of the world. Amen!"

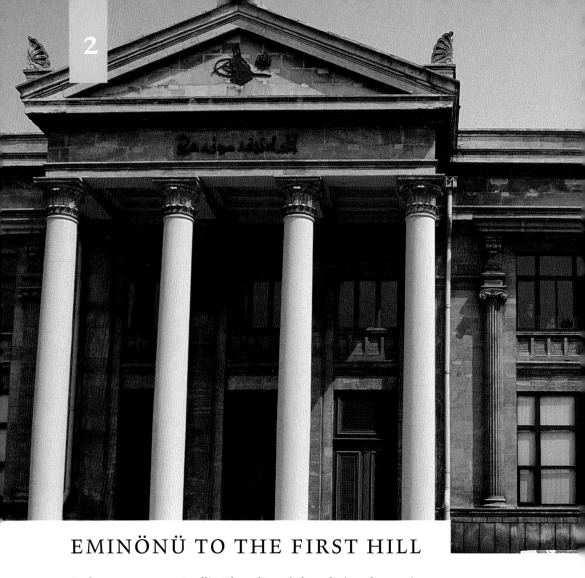

2

EMINÖNÜ TO THE FIRST HILL

As the name suggests, *Strolling Through Istanbul* was designed as a series of walks that took the reader through the streets of the city to see the historic monuments in its various quarters. The main emphasis of the book is on the antiquities of Istanbul, although, as I noted in the Preface, "the ancient monuments are described in the context of the living modern town of which they are an integral part," since it is "that intimate juxtaposition of old and new which makes Istanbul such a fascinating city." The present book covers some of the same areas as *Strolling Through Istanbul,* to which the reader may wish to refer for detailed description of monuments, but takes more the form of a series of impressions, drifting back and forth between present and past, including both my own memories and those of Evliya Çelebi, who is always with me as an invisible companion.

The area around Yeni Cami Meydanı, the market square between the

The Istanbul
Archaeological
Museum

mosque and the Spice Bazaar, is frequented by professional beggars, who usually station themselves near the front and side entrances to the mosque. Seeing them there over the years, I have noticed that the profession is passed along from one generation to the next, for they are indeed skilled professionals. Evliya tells us that the guild of the beggars also marched in the third section of the imperial procession, each group gathering around their sheikh.

The Sheiks of the Beggars (Dilenci) number seven thousand. Relying on the text of the Kuran, "Alms are for the poor (fakirs), and the wretched (meskin)," they pass in great crowds of strange figures with woolen cloth, and turbans of palm leaves, crying "Ya fettah", "O all-opening"; some blind, some lame, some paralytic, some epileptic, some having lost a hand or foot, some naked and barefoot, and some mounted on asses. They place their sheikh in the center, and after his prayer is performed, they all cry together "Allah, Allah, Amin," the cry of thousands of tongues rending the sky. This prayer is performed for the sultan's health immediately under the Alay Kiosk, where they receive alms. They are under the patronage of Sheikh Hafi, whose loins were girded by Selman the Persian, who received alms from the returning Muslim victors by saying "Sheien lillah," "Something for God's sake." He is buried at Medina.

The *sebil* of the Yeni Cami complex is one block east of the mosque on Hamidiye Caddesi. A *sebil* is a covered fountain, designed to provide free water for the parched. To endow a *sebil*, which means "way" or "path," was to pave the way to Paradise for the founder, with each cup of water taking him a step further on the way to eternal salvation. Around eighty Ottoman *sebils* remain in Istanbul, and although none of them continues to offer free water, some serve as cafés or as shops selling drinks, as in the Yeni Cami *sebil*. There are even a few mobile *sebils* to be seen, as I noticed in a recent stroll around Yeni Cami, just an aluminum tank carried by a porter who offers free cups of water to pedestrians and a sign identifying the name of the donor, who is thus progressing toward Paradise.

The portable *sebils* are not to be confused with the *saka,* the picturesquely dressed vendors of water who make their way through the market streets around Yeni Cami, just as they did in Evliya's time. Evliya notes that the *saka* marched in the sixth section of the imperial procession, organized into three separate guilds, the first being those attached to the Janissaries, the second those who carried water on horseback from the public fountains to dry neighborhoods, and the third the peripatetic water-vendors whom one still sees today.

Seven hundred Water-Carriers (Saka) are attached to the service of the hundred and sixty-two regiments of Janissaries. Their leather jacks are carried by gray Arabian horses, whose tails and manes they adorn with various ornaments in honor of Hassan and Hüseyin, the martyrs of Kerbala (who perished from want of water), and attach to their heads white plumes of feathers. They themselves wear black boots and leather jackets, and on their head white heron plumes; to the spectators on both sides they distribute water, crying, that it is in honor of the martyrs of Kerbala.

One block farther along Hamidiye Caddesi, on either side of the first turning on the right, there are two shops of the famous confectionery of Şekerci Hacı Bekir, founded here in 1771. The founder, Hacı Beker, was Chief Confectioner (*Baş Helvacı*) in the reign of Abdul Hamit I, renowned for his creation of *lokum,* or Turkish Delight, which was first sold in these shops along with numerous types of *helva,* a sweet prepared with sesame oil, various cereals, and syrup or honey. Evliya writes that the confectioners made up the thirteenth section of the imperial procession, marching in five different guilds, the last and most numerous of whom were the Helvacıs of Galata.

The Helvacis of Galata expose to public view different conserves of sugar such as almonds, pistachios, ginger, hazelnuts, orange peel, aloe, coffee, and so on, preserved in sugar of different colors in fine crystal bottles, hanging their shops with various kinds of tapestry of silk, satin and brocade. They are for the greatest part Greeks from Chios or Franks [western Europeans], great masters in their handicraft, and also deeply versed in medicine; they are five hundred men, established in sixty shops. They produce at this public exhibition trees of sugar, with fruits upon them, an admirable show! Behind them walk the chief confectioners of the Saray and of the town, with their troop of confectioners in pointed caps with their eightfold Turkish music.

At the next corner to the right is the *türbe* of Abdül Hamit I (r. 1774–89). Buried alongside Abdül Hamit is his mad son Mustafa IV, who was deposed on July 28, 1808, and executed three months later.

The next crossing is Ankara Caddesi, with Sirkeci Station, the last stop for trains from Europe to Istanbul, on the left. The station was completed by the German architect August Jachmund in 1889 as the terminus for the Orient Express, which that year made its first through journey from Vienna to Istanbul. During our early years in Istanbul, when travel was still a romantic adventure rather than a grim ordeal, my wife and I often traveled to and from Vienna on the Orient Express.

About 400 meters straight along we follow the tramline as it tuns right on to Alemdar Caddesi, which follows the outside of the outer defense wall of Topkapı Sarayı, erected by Fatih c. 1465. Further along to the right is the well-known Sublime Porte, a grand decorative gateway with a projecting canopy in the Turkish baroque style. In days gone by it led to the palace and offices of the Grand Vezir, the administrative center of the Ottoman Empire from the mid-seventeenth century. Over time the gateway became a symbol of the Ottoman government, and ambassadors were accredited to the Sublime Porte, in the same way as they still are to the Court of St. James in London. The current structure was built c. 1843 and is now the back entrance to the Vilayet of the Istanbul province.

The Alay Kiosk, the Review or Parade Pavilion, is a tall polygonal gazebo situated in an angle of the palace wall, opposite the Sublime Porte. The sultan could use this vantage point to see who was visiting the palace of the Grand Vezir, or, like the mad Murat IV, to fire at passing pedestrians with his crossbow. The existing kiosk was built by Mahmut II in 1819, but there had long been a Review Pavilion here, allowing the sultan to review the great official parades that took place in the Ottoman Empire up until the eighteenth century. The procession of the guilds, a sort of itinerant review of the city's trade and commerce, proved to be the most colorful. It was held about every fifty years until 1769, the last one taking place under Mustafa II.

As they passed the Pavilion, the guildsmen would have put on their most spirited show for the sultan. Evliya describes with illuminating detail the procession of the guilds that was held in 1638 under Murat IV:

All these guilds pass on wagons or on foot, with the instruments of their handicraft, and are busy with great noise at their work. The carpenters prepare wooden houses, the builders raise walls, the woodcutters pass with loads of trees, the sawyers pass sawing them, the masons whiten their shops, the chalk-makers crunch chalk and whiten their faces, playing a thousand tricks ... the toy-makers of Eyüp exhibit on wagons a thousand trifles and toys for children to play with. In their train you see bearded fellows and men of thirty years of age, some dressed as children with hoods and bibs, some as nurses who care for them, while the bearded babies cry after playthings or amuse themselves with spinning tops or sounding little trumpets ... The bakers pass, working at their trade. They also make for this occasion immense loaves, the size of the cupola of a hamam, covered with sesame and fennel; these loaves are carried on wagons which are dragged along by seventy to eighty pair of oxen. No oven being capable of holding loaves of so large a size, they bake them in pits made for that purpose, where the loaf is covered from above with cinders, and from the four sides baked slowly by the fire. It is worthwhile to see it ... These guilds pass before the Alay Kiosk with a thou-

The south aisle of
Haghia Sophia

*sand tricks and fits, which it is impossible to describe, and behind them walk their
Sheikhs followed by their pages playing the eightfold Turkish music.*

Another *sebil*, standing outside the precinct wall of a mosque, is further
up Alemdar Caddesi at the next corner on the right. This *sebil* was built
in 1778 as part of the *külliye* of Abdül Hamit I, whose *türbe* I mentioned
earlier in this chapter. The *sebil* originally stood next to the *türbe,* but it
was moved to its present site when the roadway was widened in the
1950s. Like several other *sebils* elsewhere in town, the one here serves as a
little stand-up café, serving sandwiches and non-alcoholic drinks.

The mosque is Zeynep Sultan Camii, founded in 1769 by a daughter of
Ahmet III, the Tulip King. The mosque was built by the architect Mehmet
Tahir Ağa in the Turkish baroque style which he introduced from France,
and of which this is one of the prettiest examples in the city.

The foundress is buried in the little graveyard behind the mosque,
along with members of her family and court. The tombstones are beautifully carved in low relief, surmounted with representations of the headdress of the deceased, indicating their sex and station. The tombstones
of the men are topped with stone turbans, by which one can identify the
deceased as a grand vezir, a sheikh of one of the dervish orders, a
kapacibaşı (chief doorkeeper), or a *kapıağaşı* (chief white eunuch). The
funerary stones of the women are topped with archaic headdresses reminiscent of *The Arabian Nights,* those of Zeynep Sultan and other princesses
surmounted by tiaras carved with stars, the façades decorated with floral
reliefs; the number of roses symbolize the children that she bore.

Directly opposite Zeynep Sultan Camii on the other side of Alemdar
Caddesi is the main entrance to Gülhane Park. This public park was cre-
ated on what in Ottoman times were the lower gardens of Topkapı
Sarayı, which were enclosed by the outer defense walls of the palace.

The Saray walls are believed to follow the same course as the original
defense walls of the Greek city-state of Byzantium, probably dating from
the fifth century BC. The walls enclosed the area around the First Hill,
whose summit formed the acropolis, or upper city of Byzantium, while
the lower city would have been the area that is now Gülhane Park. When
Byzantium was besieged in 340–339 BC by the Macedonians under Philip
II of Macedonia, father of Alexander the Great, the lower city was captured but the defenders in the acropolis held out for eighteen months
until the siege was lifted. These walls were destroyed when the Roman
emperor Septimius Severus captured and sacked Byzantium in AD 196,
slaughtering most of the surviving townspeople. A side road to the right

inside the entrance gate leads up to the First Court of Topkapı Sarayı, on the acropolis of ancient Byzantium. *En route* it passes the entrance to an enclosed terrace that houses the Archaeological Museum, the Museum of the Ancient Orient and the Çinili Köşkü, the latter being the oldest extant building of Topkapı Sarayı, dated 1472.

One of the only two monuments that have survived *in situ* from the ancient Greek city-state of Byzantium, and then only from its last years, is the Goths' Column, an honorific column standing 15 meters high on the hillside at the northern end of the park. The brief inscription at the bottom of the column gave rise to its name: "To Fortune, who returns by virtue of the defeat of the Goths." It is generally believed that the column was erected in honor of the Roman emperor Claudius II (r. 265–70), who won a notable victory over the Goths, for which he came to be called "Gothicus." The Byzantine historian Nicephorus Gregoras claims that there used to be a statue of Byzas the Megarian, the city's founder, on top of the column.

During our first years in Istanbul, my wife, Dolores, myself and our

three children often came here on Saturday afternoons in spring to have a picnic on the hillside by the Goths Column, overlooking Saray Burnu, the point at the confluence of the Bosphorus and the Golden Horn. When I come here today I see Turkish families with their picnic lunch spread out on the hillside beneath the column, and I think back to our early days in Istanbul, remembering what life was like in the city then, when it was still hardly touched by those aspects of the modern world that would ravage it in the last decades of the twentieth century: the high-rise buildings erected to house the millions who came here from Anatolia, the traffic, the pollution, and the dehumanization generated by this population explosion, which in the end led us to leave Turkey.

But at the beginning of the twenty-first century we were back in Istanbul, and I was standing once again beneath the Goths' Column on the First Hill, seeing Anatolian families enjoying a picnic just as we did in times past, and my heart lifted at the realization of how deep and strong were the roots of memory that tied me to this ancient city.

right
The Goths' Column.
Print by William
Bartlett, c. 1838

left
The Alexander
Sarcophagus, Istanbul
Archaeological
Museum

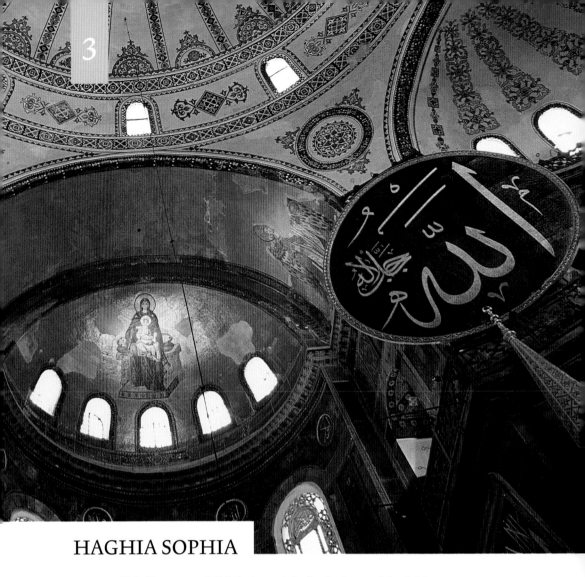

3

HAGHIA SOPHIA

A steep cobbled lane named Söğuk Çeşme Sokağı, the Street of the Cold Fountain, leads uphill from the entrance to Gülhane Park along the outer defense walls of Topkapı Sarayı. This must be one of the very old-est streets in the city, leading as it does along a line of walls built c. 1465, which apparently follow the same course as the original fifth-century BC walls of ancient Byzantium.

When we first came to Istanbul the houses along this street, most of which were built up against the Saray walls in the nineteenth century, were in utter ruins and on the point of collapse. But since then they have been superbly restored by the Turkish Touring and Automobile Club under the direction of Çelik Gülersoy, who converted them into the Ayasofya Pansionlar, a luxury hotel complex beautifully decorated and furnished in late Ottoman style. One of the restored houses is now the Istanbul Library of the Çelik Gülersoy Foundation, an incomparable collection of old books, paintings, prints, and maps dealing with Istanbul. When anyone complains about the neglect and destruction of Istanbul's historic houses, I always remind them of the work of Çelik Gülersoy, who in the last decades of the twentieth century has done more than all others combined to preserve the city's architectural heritage.

Midway along Soğuk Çeşme Sokağı there is a right turning along Caferiye Sokaği, which goes past the west side of what was once the atrium of Haghia Sophia. The street takes its name from Cafer Ağa, chief white eunuch in the reign of Süleyman the Magnificent. Halfway along the street on its right side, an alleyway leads into the central courtyard of Cafer Ağa's *medrese,* built for him by the great Sinan. After Cafer's death in 1557 the project was continued by his brother Gazanfer Ağa, who succeeded him as chief white eunuch, completing the building in 1560. Cafer Ağa's *medrese* has recently been restored as a market for old Ottoman crafts; it also houses a café, where I often stop for a drink when strolling around the First Hill, for this beautiful Ottoman cloister is a haven completely cut off from the noise of the modern city around it.

The entrance to the Ayasofya Meydanı, the great square beside Haghia Sophia, is immediately to the left at the end of the street.

Haghia Sophia was the first monument I visited in Istanbul, on my first free day after our arrival. I had been reading about it since my youth, and I could hardly contain my excitement when I finally walked into the vast nave and stood under the great dome, echoes of all the historical events that I knew had taken place here resonating in my mind, while I tried to comprehend its architecture in the soaring vaults and towering colonnades around me.

Mosaic of the Virgin and Child in the apse of Haghia Sophia, and to its right one of the huge *levhas* inscribed with the name of God in Arabic, Allah

The first church on this site, dedicated to Haghia Sophia, the Divine Wisdom, was completed c. 360 by the emperor Constantius, successor to his father, Constantine the Great. On June 9, 404, during a riot by the supporters of the patriarch John Chrysostom who had been dismissed by the empress Eudoxia, wife of the emperor Arcadius, the church was burnt down. A new church was subsequently built on the site by Theodosius II, Arcadius' son and successor, who dedicated it to Haghia Sophia on October 10, 415. This church was in turn destroyed by fire on January 15, 532, the first day of the Nika Revolt, when the factions of the Hippodrome nearly overthrew Justinian, before his general Belisarius slaughtered 30,000 of them to end the insurrection on January 23. Justinian began work on the present church just a month later, appointing as his chief architects Anthemius of Tralles and Isidorus of Miletos, the two greatest mathematical physicists of the age. Anthemius died during the first year of construction, leaving Isidorus to complete the project under his sole direction.

The new church was dedicated to Haghia Sophia on December 26, 532, by Justinian and his wife, Theodora, whose names appear together as co-founders in the imperial monograms of the capitals on the colonnades in the nave. The church was designed as a domed basilica, preceded on the west by an exonarthex and narthex, the outer and inner vestibules. The central area of the nave is covered by the great dome, with a mean diameter of 32 meters, with its crown 56 meters high - the approximate height of a fifteen-story building. Forty ribs branch out from the crown of the dome, separating a ring of forty windows above the cornice. The dome is supported by four huge piers standing on the corners of a square 31 meters on each side. Four great arches spring from these piers to support the cornice of the dome, with spherical triangles known as pendentives making the transition from square to circle. The nave is extended to east and west by semidomes, supported by the main piers and pairs of secondary piers at either end. The tympanum walls filling the central arches to north and south are pierced by two courses of windows.

At the eastern and western ends, semicircular exedrae curve between the main and secondary piers, with two porphyry monoliths below and six of verd-antique above, on which rest smaller semidomes. Beyond the subsidiary piers at the eastern end, a semicircular apse, covered by a small semidome, pushes out beyond the wall of the building.

In the north and south, four massive verd-antique columns support galleries that extend around all sides of the nave except the east. Six further columns of verd-antique in the north and south galleries support the tympana.

The structure was damaged by a series of earthquakes between 553 and 557, and on May 7, 558, the eastern sector of the dome collapsed, along with the arch and semidome on that side of the church. Isidorus of Miletos was no longer alive, so Justinian assigned the task of rebuilding the church to the architect's nephew Isidorus the Younger, who completed the project in 563, less than two years before the death of Justinian.

A series of earthquakes in the ninth and tenth centuries damaged the building further and caused cracks to appear in the dome, until finally in 989 part of the dome and the western arch collapsed. Basil II entrusted the reconstruction to the Armenian architect Trdat, and on May 13, 996, the church was once again reopened.

Haghia Sophia was looted and profaned by the Latins during their sack of Constantinople in April 1204. During the Latin occupation of

Constantinople, 1204–61, Haghia Sophia was served by Roman Catholic clergy under the Venetian cardinal Thomas Morosini. When the Byzantines recaptured Constantinople, the emperor Michael VIII Palaeologos made his triumphal entry into the city on August 15, 1261, and rode straight to Haghia Sophia, where he escorted the Greek Orthodox patriarch Arsenius to the throne once occupied by St. John Chrysostom.

During the last century of Byzantine rule, Haghia Sophia fell into disrepair, part of the general decay of the dying city noted by travelers to Constantinople in that period. The Spanish ambassador Clavijo, who visited Constantinople in 1403, wrote that, "Everywhere throughout the city there are great palaces, churches and monasteries, but most of them are now ruined ... The outer gates of Haghia Sophia are broken and fallen."

On Monday, May 28, 1453, the eve of the city's fall to the Turks, the last Greek Orthodox service in Haghia Sophia began, continuing throughout the night and on into the next morning, when word came that the city had been captured. The congregation then barred the doors, but within hours the Turkish soldiers forced their way into the church, a scene described by the Greek chronicler Kritoboulos of Imros in his *History of Mehmed the Conqueror.*

Going into the largest church, that of the Holy Wisdom, they [the Turkish soldiers] *found there a great crowd of men, women and children taking refuge and calling upon God. Those they caught as in a net, and took them all in a body and carried them captives, some to the galleys and some to the camp*

Sultan Mehmet II, now known as Fatih the Conqueror, rode to Haghia Sophia after making his triumphal entry into the city in the afternoon of Tuesday, May 29, 1453. After dismounting at the door of the Great Church he picked up a handful of earth, sprinkling it over his turban in a symbolic gesture of humility. Fatih then surveyed the building and gave orders that it be immediately converted into a mosque.

The conversion of the church into a mosque required the erection of a minaret for the *müezzin* to give the call to prayer, and also some internal constructions, including the *mimber,* or pulpit, and the *mihrap,* the niche that indicates the *kible,* the direction of Mecca. This done, Fatih attended the first Islamic service in what was now known as Aya Sofya Camii Kabir, the Great Mosque of Haghia Sophia, which occurred with the noon prayer on Friday, June 1, 1453.

The first minaret was a temporary wooden structure erected over the southeast buttress. Fatih soon replaced this with the present brick

minaret at the southeast corner of the building. Selim II built the stone minaret at the northeast corner in 1574, and the two stone minarets at the northwest and southwest corners were added a year or two later by his son and successor, Murat III. All three of these stone minarets are works of the architect Sinan, who also restored all of the buttresses and the fabric of the building. Otherwise the edifice that one sees today is essentially that of Justinian's time, except for the buttresses on the north and south sides, added in the late Byzantine period and rebuilt in the Ottoman era.

The last major reconstruction of Haghia Sophia in Ottoman times was commissioned by Sultan Abdül Mecit and carried out in 1847 by Swiss architects, the brothers Gaspare and Giuseppe Fossati. During the course of this restoration, the surviving figurative mosaics were cleared of the whitewash and plaster with which they had been covered earlier in the Ottoman period. When the project was complete, the mosaics were covered over once again, after which they were recorded by the Fossatis so that they could be located in the future.

Haghia Sophia continued to function as a mosque until 1932, nine years after the end of the Ottoman Empire, when it was closed to convert the building into a museum, which opened in 1934. In April 1932 Thomas Whittemore and other members of the Byzantine Institute began the task of uncovering and restoring the figurative mosaics, some of which had disappeared since the Fossatis had recorded them. Since then there have been other repair projects, the most recent of which – a restoration of the mosaics and Islamic calligraphy in the dome – has necessitated the erection of scaffolding in the nave.

The first two figurative mosaics uncovered by the Byzantine Institute, both in 1933, were in the narthex and the porch beyond its southern end, the so-called Vestibule of the Warriors. According to the *Book of Ceremonies,* the manual of court ceremonies written by Constantine VII Porphyrogenitos (r. 913–59), the imperial bodyguard waited here while the emperor was in the church, and hence the name of the vestibule.

One of the two mosaics uncovered in 1933 is above the door leading from the porch into the narthex. It portrays the Blessed Virgin with the newborn Christ in her lap as she receives two emperors, both identified by inscriptions in Greek. "Constantine the Great Emperor among the Saints," on the right, offers her a model of a walled town representing Constantinople, while on the left, "Justinian the Illustrious Emperor" presents her with a model of a domed church symbolizing Haghia Sophia. This and the mosaic in the narthex are both dated to the last quarter of the tenth century. These and all of the other surviving mosaics in Haghia

Sophia are from after the Iconoclastic Period, c. 717–845, when figurative images were banned from the churches of Byzantium, while virtually all of those dating from before that era were destroyed.

previous pages
Haghia Sophia viewed
from the south

The emperor and his party, in approaching the interior of the church from the Vestibule of the Warriors, would have followed the directions given in the *Book of Ceremonies*: "The princes remove their crowns, kiss the holy Gospel carried by the archdeacon, greet the patriarch, and proceed to the Imperial Gate. Bearing the candles and bowing thrice, they enter the church after a prayer is pronounced by the patriarch."

Nine doorways on the east side of the narthex lead into the nave, the largest of these, at the center, being the Imperial Gate. The lunette above the Imperial Gate contains the other mosaic rediscovered in 1933. Christ is represented upon a jeweled throne with his feet upon a footstool. His right hand is raised to give a blessing, while his left holds a book with this inscription: "Peace be with you. I am the light of the world." The mosaic has been dated to the period of emperor Leo VI's reign (886-912) and it is thought that he is represented by the imperial figure prostrating himself before Christ, on the left.

The use of the Imperial Gate was a privilege of the emperor and his entourage. On both sides of the entrance to the nave, there are grooves worn into the pavement. The *Book of Ceremonies* tells us that in the Byzantine era, the imperial *praepositii* stood here flanking the entryway, and nine centuries of their presence left these hollows as a reminder of the great antiquity of this building.

Whenever I pass through the Imperial Gate, I remember the first time I did so, when I was the only one in the Great Church except for a drowsy watchman at the entrance. My initial and abiding impression was that of an immense enclosed space, penetrated by beams of dust-speckled sunlight coming from the circlet of windows below the dome, the only sounds being the echoing murmur of doves and the occasional flutter of their wings from the vaults above. Walking forward into the nave, I could see the whole of the vast interior at once and admire its profound grace and grandeur: here was the famous dome, which the Byzantines thought of as being hung from Heaven by a golden chain, and here, the tremendous nave, winged by the two-tiered colonnade that led Procopius to compare it to the lines of dancers in a chorus. It seemed that all the disparate features of this huge building blended together in perfect harmony. I remembered thinking that this was the greatest building in the world, and I feel the same today; and while I can no longer have its sublime beauty to myself, I can always fall back on my first memory, in which I am utterly alone in this sacred place.

Few of the mosaics that once adorned the nave have survived. The most beautiful of those that have been preserved – and the largest – is in the conch of the apse, and depicts the Blessed Virgin with the Christ Child on her knees. There is a colossal figure of the Archangel Gabriel on the south side of the arch that frames the apse opposite; on the north side of the arch, there sadly remain only a few feathers from the wings of the Archangel Michael.

Three other mosaic portraits can be seen from the nave, in niches at the base of the north tympanum wall. They portray three bishops of the early church: St. Ignatius the Younger (in the first niche from the west), St. John Chrysostom (in the second), and St. Ignatius Theophorus of Antioch (in the fifth). The remaining mosaics that can be seen from the nave are the six-winged seraphim or cherubim in the eastern pendentives. (The mosaics in the western pendentives are the Fossati brothers' imitations completed during their 1847–9 restoration.) Dated to the mid-fourteenth century, perhaps replacing older mosaics of the same subject, they have never been entirely obscured. Sometimes the faces have been covered, as they were by the Fossatis' gold-starred medallions. Evliya thought that they were moribund talismans, as his *Seyahatname* reveals: "Before the birth of the Prophet these four angels used to speak, and gave notice of all the dangers which threatened the empire and the city of Constantinople, but since his Highness [the Prophet Mohammed] appeared all talismans have ceased to act."

The other mosaics are in the galleries, which are approached by an inclined labyrinth leading up from the northern end of the narthex. The earliest of them is in the north gallery, high on the east face of the northwest pier. It depicts the emperor Alexander, who succeeded his elder brother, Leo VI, in May 912. Two other imperial mosaic portraits are in the east end of the south gallery, an area that may have been set aside for the royal family as a private place of prayer.

The earliest in date of these panels depicts Christ flanked by the empress Zoe (r. 1042) with Constantine IX Monomachus (r. 1042–55), her third husband. (Zoe had previously been married in turn to Romanos III and Michael IV, and her adopted son Michael V had ruled in the years 1041–2.) One oddity of this mosaic is that alterations have been made to the three heads and the two inscriptions concerning Constantine, probably at the beginning of his reign. It has been suggested that the mosaic originally showed Zoe with her first husband, Romanos III. The faces were destroyed during the reign of Michael V, an enemy of Zoe, but when she returned to power in 1042, she may have had them restored, substituting that of Romanus with her third husband, Constantine, and changing the inscriptions.

The other mosaic shows the Virgin and Child between an imperial couple. The mosaic continues at a right angle onto the thin panel of side wall, where there is the figure of a young prince. The three figures are the emperor John II Comnenos (r. 1118–43), his wife, Eirene, daughter of King Ladislaus of Hungary, and Prince Alexios, their eldest son. The date of the main panel corresponds to the year of John's accession, 1118, and the portrait of Alexios to four years later when he became co-emperor with his father, only to die soon afterwards.

The most recent of the gallery mosaics is on the east wall of the west buttress in the south gallery. This is the magnificent Deesis, or Intercession of the Virgin and St. John the Baptist before Christ. The features of the three figures in the composition are still intact, even though most of the mosaic is now missing. One of the greatest works of art that has survived from Byzantium, the mosaic is dated to the latter half of the thirteenth century, saliently illustrating the renaissance that occurred during the last two centuries of the empire under the Palaeologues, the last dynasty to rule the Byzantine Empire. I first saw this mosaic in the early 1960s, before the galleries were opened to the public, when my friend Robert van Nice was making measurements there for his book on the architecture of Haghia Sophia. I spent the last hour of daylight on an afternoon in late December looking at the Deesis, which had only a few years before re-emerged from the plaster and whitewash that had occulted it for nine centuries, an enduring symbol of the last Byzantine renaissance.

A sarcophagus lid inscribed with the name Henricus Dandolo is set into the pavement opposite the Deesis. Dandolo, Doge of Venice, was nearly ninety years old and almost completely blind when he commanded the Venetian fleet in the Latin conquest of Venice on April 13, 1204. He ruled as Despot of the Venetian share of the dismembered Byzantine Empire until his death on June 16, 1205. He was then buried in Haghia Sophia, but after the Greeks recaptured Constantinople in 1261 they opened Dandolo's grave and threw his bones to the dogs.

Nothing now remains of the structures associated with the Christian liturgy in Haghia Sophia, for that was all stripped away when Fatih had the building converted into a mosque. The structures associated with the mosque are the donations of various sultans, notably Mahmut I's library built beyond the south aisle in 1739, and, to the left of the apse,

Haghia Sophia as a
mosque. Print by
Thomas Allom, c. 1838

the imperial loge designed for Abdül Mecit by the Fossatis, who are also
responsible for the present *mihrap* and *mimber*. When Haghia Sophia was
converted into a mosque, the original *mihrap* and *mimber* were oriented
toward Mecca, which is some ten degrees south of the direction in which
the church was oriented. The raised floor of the apse, reoriented to line up
with the *mihrap,* is thus askew with the longitudinal axis of the building.

The Fossatis were also responsible for the eight huge green *levhas,* or
painted wooden plaques, that hang at gallery level. The calligraphy,
bearing in golden letters the Sacred Islamic Names of Allah, the Prophet
Mohammed, the first four Caliphs – Abu Bekr, Omar, Othman, and Ali –
and the first Imams, Hasan and Hüseyin, sons of Ali, is by Mustafa Izzet
Efendi. He also inscribed the dome with a quotation from the Kuran,
reading: "In the name of God the Merciful and Pitiful: God is the light
of Heaven and Earth. His light is Himself, not that which shines
through glass or gleams in the morning star or glows in the firebrand."

41

Evliya writes extensively in his *Seyahatname* of Haghia Sophia, which he ranks first among the imperial mosques of the city. At one point Evliya served as a *müezzin* in Haghia Sophia, and it was here that he first met Murat IV. Evliya's description of Haghia Sophia as a mosque in the days of Murat IV indicates that the ancient building once more contributed its grandeur to an imperial age, just as it had during the reign of Justinian over a thousand years earlier.

This mosque, which has no equal on earth, can only be compared to the tabernacle of the seventh heaven, and its dome to the tabernacle of the ninth. All of those who see it remain lost in contemplating its beauties; it is the place where heavenly inspiration descends into the minds of the devout and which gives a foretaste even here

right
The Deesis mosaic, with the Virgin on the left, viewed from the east bay of the south gallery

below
Detail of the Deesis mosaic in the south gallery of Haghia Sophia, with St. John the Baptist looking pleadingly toward Christ

below of the Garden of Eden. Sultan Murat IV, who took great delight in this incomparable mosque, erected a wooden enclosure within it near the southern door, and when he went to prayer on Friday caused cages containing a great number of singing birds, and particularly nightingales, to be hung there, so that their sweet notes, mingled with those of the müezzins' voices, filled the mosque with a harmony approaching to that of paradise. Every night in the month of Ramazan, the two thousand lamps lighted there and the lanterns containing wax tapers perfumed with camphor pour forth streams of light upon light, and in the center of the dome a circle of lamps in letters as finely formed as those of Yakut Musa'sime, that text of the Kuran: "God is the light of the heavens and of the earth."

For more than nine centuries Haghia Sophia served the devout Christians of Constantinople; then, for nearly five centuries it served the faithful Muslims of Istanbul. These words, which Evliya wrote as an encomium for Haghia Sophia, apply equally to the building in either period, as a church or mosque: "Aya Sofya is in itself peculiarly the place of God. It is always full of holy men, who pass the day there in fasting and the night in prayer. Seventy lectures well pleasing to God are given there daily, so that to the student it is a mine of knowledge, and it never fails to be frequented by multitudes every day."

The lectures are now given by guides and the multitudes are tourists, and so now I tend to visit Haghia Sophia only on the days when it is officially closed, if I am given special permission by the museum director. On those days I usually wander around for a while before standing at the rear of the nave, looking down between the two-tiered colonnade toward the apse and then up at the dome, taking in the sublime beauty of the building as I did when I first saw it. And when I do so, I recall the lines written more than a thousand years ago by an anonymous Russian monk, who had come to Constantinople as an envoy of Prince Vladimir of Kiev:

We know not whether we were on Heaven or on Earth. For on Earth there is no such splendor or beauty, and we are at a loss how to describe it. We only know that God dwells there among men, and their service is fairer than the ceremonies of other nations. For we cannot forget that beauty.

4

TOPKAPI SARAYI

After Haghia Sophia, Topkapı Sarayı was the second monument that I visited after our arrival in Istanbul, and I kept coming back to it again and again, for there was so much to see there and it was so steeped in secret history. At that time there were very few visitors and a large part of the palace was not yet open to the public, including the Harem, which was still being restored, and after I came to know the guards they let me wander around on my own. Thus I came to know it quite intimately, knowledge that I used in writing *Inside the Seraglio, Private Lives of the Sultans in Istanbul,* published in 1999, in which I tried to describe what life was like in this extraordinary palace, particularly the innermost part known as Dar-üs Saadet, the House of Felicity.

After his conquest of the city in 1453, Fatih discovered that the palaces of the former Byzantine emperors were now uninhabitable. As a result, he chose an overgrown area on the Third Hill on which to build

above
The pavilions and gardens of Topkapı Sarayı, and in the background the hills on the Asian side of the lower Bosphorus

right
Haghia Eirene, the former Church of the Divine Peace, in the First Court of Topkapı Sarayı

an imperial residence. This came to be called Eski Saray, or the Old Palace, because within just a few years, by 1459, he had built an even newer palace at the northern end of the First Hill, the site of the acropolis of ancient Byzantium. He began by ringing the acropolis with an imposing defense wall, which extended from the Byzantine sea-walls along the Marmara to those along the Golden Horn. Eventually, this new palace took its name from the main sea gate in this wall – Topkapı, or the Cannon Gate – because it was flanked by two enormous cannon; thus it came to be called Topkapı Sarayı.

The outer wall of Topkapı Sarayı was completed by 1465, according to Kritoboulos, although inscriptions indicate that work on its various pavilions went on for another thirteen years. Apparently Fatih at first intended Topkapı Sarayı to be principally his administrative center, keeping his harem in the Old Palace on the Third Hill.

Giovanni Maria Angiolello, an Italian captive in the Ottoman service, says that the palace had three courts, to which a fourth was later added, and that it was surrounded by a high wall. He also notes that within the grounds there were both botanical and zoological gardens, as well as a lake stocked with fowl, where the sultan enjoyed shooting.

With the exception of the Fourth Court and the Harem, the plan of the palace as it stands today was laid out by Fatih in the years 1469–75. The present Harem was added in the third quarter of the sixteenth century, with extensive developments in the mid-seventeenth and mid-eighteenth centuries, while the remote pavilions of the Fourth Court are from several eras. In 1574, 1665, and 1856 catastrophic fires damaged much of the palace. While the three main courts remain in essence as arranged by Fatih, many of the original buildings have either disappeared (as is the case with most of those in the First Court) or been reconstructed.

Throughout the palace's history, Bab-ı Hümayun, the Imperial Gate facing the northeast corner of Haghia Sophia, has been the main entrance. To the right of the gate is the grandest and most handsome of all the street-fountains in Istanbul, built by Ahmet III in 1728 in the Turkish rococo style. The fountain can be seen in many nineteenth-century prints showing imperial processions issuing from the Imperial Gate of Topkapı Sarayı, the mounted sultan followed by a brilliant array of his guards and retainers, usually on the occasion of his progress to one of the imperial mosques of the city for the Friday noon prayer.

The Imperial Gate leads to the First Court, with Haghia Eirene, the former church of the Divine Peace, on its lefthand side. The present Haghia Eirene was built at the same time as Justinian's Haghia Sophia,

45

in the years 532–7, replacing an earlier church of the same name that dated back to the ancient town of Byzantium. The church was never converted to a mosque, and up until the dissolution of the Janissaries in 1826 it was used by them as a storehouse for their weapons. Later it served as an archaeological storehouse and still later as a museum of Ottoman cannon, an ironic fate for a church dedicated to the Divine Peace. Today the building is only open to the public for concerts and art exhibits, which is a pity, since it is one of the most beautiful and historic structures remaining from the Byzantine era. When we first came to Istanbul, the building was wide open and we were able to explore it at will, even climbing out on its roof and up onto its main dome, where we once enjoyed a picnic with champagne that cost two and a half Turkish liras a bottle. Those were the days!

The large building beyond Haghia Eirene is the Darphane, the former Ottoman Mint, which included the Outer Treasury of Topkapı Sarayı, now used for occasional exhibits. The other buildings around the First Court, none of which has survived, included storerooms, workshops, the palace bakery, the infirmary, the palace waterworks, latrines, a small mosque, and barracks for artisans and domestics of the Outer Service, those whose duties did not take them into the Inner Palace.

The portal at the far end of the First Court is Bab-üs Selam, the Gate of Salutations, also known as Orta Kapı, or the Middle Gate. This is the entrance to the Inner Palace. Only the sultan was allowed to ride beyond this point; everyone else had to dismount. Set into the wall beside the gate is the infamous Executioner's Fountain, where the executioner cleaned his hands and sword after a beheading. Beside the gate there are two marble niches known as Example Stones, since they were used to display the severed heads of notable rebels or criminals to set an example.

The rooms within the gatehouse were used to house the chief gatekeeper and his men. The room on the left side of the gate was reserved for the chief executioner, who was also the chief gardener. A cubicle beside his room housed prisoners awaiting execution.

The executioners also had their place in the procession of the guilds, and Evliya describes them as they pass in the second section of the parade, led by their chief Kara (Black) Ali.

The Chief Executioner of Sultan Murat IV, Kara Ali, was girded with a fiery sword, wore in his girdle all the instruments of torture and of his profession, nails, borers, matches, razors for scorching, steel plates, different powders for blinding, clubs for breaking the hands and feet, hatchets, and spoons, and was followed by his ser-

*vants carrying the rest of the seventy-seven instruments of torture. Then followed
other servants with gilt, well carved, well greased, and well perfumed pales [for
impaling], with ropes and chains on their waists, and drawn swords in their
hands. They pass with great vehemence, but no light shines from their faces, for
they are a dark set of people.*

The Middle Gate leads into the Second Court. Although it once also had
several fountains, it still remains very much as it was when Fatih
designed it – a peaceful, generously proportioned cloister with plane
trees and cypresses.

The three gateways in the east portico of the Second Court provide
access to a narrow courtyard running the whole length of the area. The
former palace kitchens, which now house the Saray's Porcelain
Collection, are off from the east side of this courtyard, with the mosque
of the culinary staff and the storerooms opposite, the latter now containing the Saray's Silver and Glass Collections.

The earliest description of the kitchens is by Giovantonio Menavino, a
Genoese captive who served as a page in the Saray in the years 1505–14, during the reign of Beyazit II. According to Menavino, in Beyazit's time the
kitchens were divided into two sections, one for the sultan and the other
for the household of the palace and those who attended meetings of the
Divan, or imperial council, together staffed by about 160 cooks, bakers, and
other servants. The number of kitchen staff increased considerably in the
century after Beyazit's reign, when the population of the palace reached its
peak. The number of confectioners alone rose to as many as 600 in the late
sixteenth century. The confectioners made up a separate branch of the
kitchen service, distinguished from the other cooks by their tall white hats
"rising to a pretty height somewhat to the resemblance of a sugar-loaf,"
according to Jean Baptiste Tavernier, who was with the French embassy in
Istanbul during the tears 1629–37. Tavernier writes of the privileged position of the confectioners and how they abused it.

*For whereas they are the only Persons who have the freedom of going in and coming
out of the Seraglio, they set double the price on everything they buy. But their most
considerable gain proceeds from the infamous commerce of those young Lads, whom
they bring into their Masters, and whom they cunningly slip into the Infirmary,
after they have put them into habits like their own.*

Ordinarily the palace kitchens served two meals a day, but in the summer months a late supper was also prepared for the sultan and the

women of his harem, who dined after the last prayer, about two hours past sunset. A double line of some 200 waiters formed between the kitchens and the sultan's apartment, with those in one row handing along the various courses as they were prepared and those in the other line passing back the empty dishes.

The Second Court was also known as the Court of the Divan, the imperial council, which met inside the domed chamber under the tower at the far left of the courtyard. The Divan and the Inner Treasury beyond it are the only buildings in the courtyard, with the remainder of the periphery consisting of colonnaded porticoes. The entire right side of the courtyard beyond the colonnade is occupied by the kitchens, while beyond the walls to the left are the royal stables, a mosque, and the dormitories of the halberdiers.

The Divan met here four times a week, and at those times the courtyard was filled with a tremendous mass of people, some 5,000 on ordinary days and perhaps twice that number for special occasions. Despite

Bab-üs Saadet, the Gate of Felicity, the entrance to the Third Court of Topkapı Sarayı. Print by Thomas Allom, c. 1838 such numbers, an almost total silence prevailed throughout the court-yard, a fact commented on by a number of foreigners. The Venetian *bailo* Andrea Gritti, who would later become Doge, describes the scene that he observed in 1503, when he came for an audience with Beyazit II:

I entered into the court, where I found on one side all of the Janissaries on foot and on the other side all the persons of high esteem, and the salaried officials of His Majesty, who stood with such great silence and with such beautiful order that it was a marvelous thing not believable to one who had not seen it with his own eyes.

The main entrance to the Harem, the Carriage Gate, is under the tower beside the council chamber. The gate takes its name from the fact that the women of the Harem passed through it in closed carriages on their rare excursions from the palace.

There was no need to include a harem in the original Topkapı Sarayı as designed by Fatih, as he kept his women at the Old Saray on the Third Hill. This arrangement continued until the time of Süleyman the Magnificent, who allowed the famous Roxelana, his wife Haseki Hürrem, to set herself up in Topkapı Sarayı. Their son Selim II (r. 1566–74) spent virtually his entire reign in the women's quarters of Topkapı Sarayı, as did his son and successor Murat III (r. 1574–95), who is responsible for the oldest extant structures in the Harem, as well as the Has Oda, or Royal Hall, and his own magnificent apartments in the Selamlık. The palace archives credit Murat with twenty-four sons and thirty-two daughters, a record for the Ottoman dynasty. The record is all the more impressive in that all but the first two of these children were born in the last twelve years of Murat's life, when he seems to have done little other than serve as the royal stud.

The reign of Selim II began a period in Ottoman history known as Kadınlar Sultanatı, the Sultanate of Women, in which a series of powerful women in the Harem exercised considerable influence over affairs of state. The most powerful woman in the Harem was the *valide sultan,* mother of the reigning sultan. Her principal rival was often the *birinci kadın,* literally "first woman," mother of the sultan's eldest son, the heir apparent. This rivalry was the source of some of the bloodshed that stains the history of the harem, particularly following the deaths of Selim II and Murat III, when in each case the successor, aided by his mother, slaugh-tered all of the other sons of the deceased sultan so that they would not contest the throne. This was justified by the Ottoman law of fratricide, first codified by Fatih, who after killing his own half-brother had quoted appropriate verses from the Kuran, such as "The execution of a prince is preferable to the loss of a province," and "Death is better than disquiet."

This fratricide for the most part ended in 1617, when with the death of Ahmet I the law of succession was changed; thenceforth a sultan was succeeded by the oldest living male in the imperial line, all of the younger males, after they reached puberty, being confined to a prison in the inner palace, the infamous *Kafes,* or Cage. Some of those imprisoned eventually succeeded to the throne as old men, after decades in the Cage had left them incompetent to rule.

Ahmet I was succeeded his brother Mustafa, who was so deranged that he was deposed after a reign of only ninety-six days and confined to the Cage. Ahmet's eldest son then came to the throne as Osman II, although he was only thirteen and a half. He ruled for only a little more than four years before an insurrection by the Janissaries overthrew him on May 18, 1622, and later that same day he was brutally executed. Osman was the first Ottoman sultan to be assassinated by his own people, which some foreign observers took to be a sign of the decline of the Ottoman Empire. As the English ambassador Sir Thomas Roe wrote in a letter home when he heard the news of Osman's execution: "At this instant I am advised that the newe great vizier Daout bassa, by the command of the newe emperour, hath strangled Osman, sent to prison butt fower howers agoe: The first emperour that they ever laid violent hands on; a fatal signe, I think, of their declynation."

The following day the Janissaries released Mustafa from the Cage and placed him on the throne. Mustafa's second reign lasted longer than the first, but his inability to rule once again became so evident that all parties eventually agreed that he must be removed. And so on September 10, 1623, the *ulema,* the supreme council of clerics, issued a *fetva,* or official opinion, stating that Mustafa was mentally unfit to be sultan. Mustafa was thus duly deposed, to be replaced by his nephew, who that same day came to the throne as Murat IV, just twelve days after his fourteenth birthday. Murat sent his uncle Mustafa to the Old Saray, where he was confined for the rest of his days. Murat's mother, Kösem, thus became *valide sultan,* acting as regent for her son Murat until he came of age.

The portal at the far end of the Second Court, Bab-üs Saadet, the Gate of Felicity, is the entrance to the Third Court, the forecourt to the strictly private and residential areas of the inner palace, the House of Felicity. The gate was guarded by the white eunuchs, whose chiefs bore the title of *kapı agaşı,* or agha of the gate.

The building directly inside the Gate of Felicity is the Arz Odası, or

Audience Chamber. After each meeting of the Divan the grand vezir and other members were received here by the sultan to ask for his final approval of their decisions. Foreign ambassadors were also brought here to be presented to the sultan on their arrival and departure.

Most of the other buildings in the Third Court were devoted to the famous Palace School, founded by Fatih to train promising youths for a career in the Ottoman military and the civil service. Initially, the only pages who went to the school came from the Christian minorities, taken as prisoners of war or recruited in the *devşirme,* and raised as Muslims, although in time Turkish youths also were enrolled. The extraordinary success of the Ottoman state during its early centuries derived largely from the excellence of the Palace School, whose graduates rose to the highest positions in the empire, including a large number of grand vezirs.

The pages in the Palace School were supervised by the white eunuchs, under the direction of the *kapı ağaşı.* Until the last quarter of the sixteenth century, the chief white eunuch was the most powerful official in the Inner Service, notable examples being Cafer Ağa and his brother Gazanfer Ağa. But thenceforth the chief black eunuch, known as the *kızlar ağası,* the agha of the girls, was the dominant figure, a change brought about by the greatly increased size and importance of the Harem, in which the women were guarded by the black eunuchs.

At the southwest corner of the Third Court, a portal known as Kuşhane Kapısı, the Bird-House Gate, leads into the Harem. This and the Carriage Gate in the Second Court were the only entrances to the Harem, other than a private entryway from the Privy Chamber, the sultan's apartments in the Selamlık. The Harem occupied the area to the west of the Second and Third Court, extending northward from the Tower of the Divan as far as the middle of the Third Court. The Privy Chamber and the rest of the Selamlık extended from there to the northern end of the palace and the Fourth Court, which was really a garden with kiosks on several levels.

The various branches of the Palace School were housed in the buildings around the Third Court, one of which now contains the Imperial costume collection, the famous Treasury of the Topkapı Sarayı, the Exhibition of Turkish and Islamic Art, with its incomparable miniatures collection, and the Pavilion of the Holy Mantle, which contains the sacred relics of the Prophet Mohammed. The latter pavilion originally housed the pages in the Has Oda, the branch of the Palace School that trained pages who personally waited on the sultan. The Has Oda itself, the Royal Hall, was the great throne room of the Selamlık, where the sultan was

attended by those pages who served as his intimate companions. Evliya, who served as a page in the Has Oda during the reign of Murat IV, tells of how on his first day there he impressed Murat with his numerous talents.

The sultan now made his appearance, like the rising sun, by the door leading to the inner harem. He saluted the forty pages of the inner chamber and the Musahib [intimate companions], *who returned the salutation with prayers for his prosperity. The sultan having with great dignity seated himself on one of the thrones, I kissed the ground before it, and trembled all over. The next moment, however, I complimented him with some verses that most fortunately came into my mind. He then desired me to read something. I said, "I am versed in seventy-two sciences, does your majesty wish to hear something of Persian, Arabic, Romaic, Hebrew, Syriac, Greek, or Turkish? Something of the different tunes of music, or poetry in various measures?"*

Evliya then took up a tambourine and "danced like a dervish before the throne." Following this, he recited other poems for the sultan, one of

which reduced him to tears, for it was about his late *musahib* Musa, who had been killed by the Janissaries when Murat first came to the throne. When Murat recovered his composure, he immediately ordered that Evliya be admitted into the company of his *musahibs*, "in the place of the deceased Musa." This singular audience ended when the call to prayer was heard, whereupon, as Evliya writes, "The sultan, ordering me to assist the *müezzin*, I flew like a peacock to the top of the staircase and began to exclaim, 'Ho, to good works!'"

Most of the sultan's audiences were in the Has Oda, and Evliya gives a list of Murat's weekly schedule there as well as mentioning his conduct of state affairs.

During the winter he regulated his audiences as follows: on Friday he assembled all the divines, sheikhs, and the readers of the Kuran, and with them he disputed till morning on scientific subjects. Saturday morning was devoted to the singers who sang the Ilahi, the Na't, and other spiritual tunes. Sunday evening was appropriated to poets and reciters of romances. On Monday evening he had the dancing boys and the Egyptian musicians. This assembly sat until daybreak and resembled the musical feast of Hüseyin Bukhara. On Tuesday evening he received the old experienced men who were upwards of seventy and with them he used to converse in the most familiar manner. On Wednesday he gave audience to the pious saints, and on Thursday to the dervishes. In the mornings he attended to the affairs of the Muslims. In such a manner did he watch over the affairs of the Ottoman states, that not even a bird could fly over them without his knowledge. But were we to describe all his excellent qualities we should fill another volume.

Evliya was also able to observe Murat at play, as in his account of an amusing encounter he had with him one day outside the sultan's bath.

One day the Sultan came out covered with perspiration from his hamam near the throne room, saluted those present, and said, "Now I have had my bath." "May it be to your health," was the general reply. I said, "My sultan, you are now clean and comfortable, do not therefore oil yourself for wrestling today, especially since you have already exercised yourself with others and your strength must be considerably reduced." "Now, have I no strength left?" said he. "Let us see," whereupon he seized me like an eagle, raised me over his head and whirled me about as children do a top. I exclaimed. "Do not let me fall, my emperor, hold me fast!" He said, "Hold fast yourself!" and continued to swing me around, until I cried out, "For God's sake, my sultan, cease, for I am quite giddy!" He then began to laugh, released me, and gave me forty-eight pieces of gold for the amusement which I had offered him. The Sultan subsequently stripped himself and wrestled with his Sword-Bearer, Melek Ahmet Agha, and Musa Agha, both remarkably stout men, and took them by their belts, lifted them over his head, and flung one of them to the right and the other to the left. It was I who on such occasions read the wrestler's prayer.

Evliya seems to have been constantly at the Sultan's side during his tenure as *musahib,* and in his *Seyahatname* he gives a detailed account of how Murat spent his days in the Selamlık. But he makes no mention of the Harem, for that was closely guarded by the black eunuchs and forbidden even to the sultan's companions.

The only buildings in Topkapı Sarayı erected by Murat IV are two handsome kiosks on the terrace of the Fourth Court overlooking the Golden Horn. These are called the Erivan Köşkü and the Baghdad Köşkü, names commemorating Murat's two great victories. During the last years of his reign, Murat spent much of his time in the Baghdad Köşkü, and when I visit this kiosk I can in my mind's eye see Murat there seated on a *divan,* surrounded by his *musahibs,* including Evliya, who is singing the mournful love song that reduced the sultan to tears: "I went to meet my beloved Musa; he tarried and came not./ Perhaps I missed him on the way; he tarried and came not."

When Murat died in 1640, he was succeeded by his mad brother Ibrahim, whose mother, Kösem, the *valide sultan,* was the power behind the throne, since her son was incapable of ruling on his own. At the time of his accession Ibrahim was the only surviving male in the imperial Ottoman line. He had been confined in the Cage throughout much of Murat's reign, living in constant fear that he would be executed by his brother. When Ibrahim finally succeeded to the throne, he showed no interest in women, and there were fears that he was impotent and the imperial line would thus come to an end.

Kösem took it upon herself to solve the problem by finding beautiful concubines for Ibrahim's harem, who were supplied to her from the slave market by a confidant named Pezevenk, or the Pimp. But when her son showed no interest in these women, she consulted his tutor Cinci Hoca, who dosed Ibrahim with aphrodisiacs and brought him illustrated pornographic books. The treatment worked, and Ibrahim soon began enjoying himself in the Harem. Fears for the dynasty were put to rest on January 2, 1642, when his concubine Turhan Hadice gave birth to a son, the future sultan Mehmet IV. Ibrahim's concubines eventually bore him a total of eighteen children, nine boys and nine girls, including two more future sultans, Süleyman II and Ahmet II.

Ibrahim's madness caused such chaos in the empire that all factions agreed that he would have to be removed. He was overthrown by the Janissaries on August 7, 1648, and on the following day his eldest son was raised to the throne as Mehmet IV, though he was only six and a half years old, the youngest sultan in the history of the Ottoman Empire. His mother, Turhan Hadice, was only twenty-three, and although she was now *valide sultan* the imperial council passed her over and appointed Kösem as regent for her grandson Mehmet IV, naming her *büyük* (great) *valide sultan,* the only woman in Ottoman history to ever have that title.

During the next three years Turhan Hadice secretly gathered support to undermine Kösem, her principal ally being the chief black eunuch Süleyman Ağa. Turhan Hadice made her move on September 2, 1651, when she had Süleyman Ağa and his men assassinate Kösem, who fought her assailants tooth and nail before she finally succumbed, ending the most remarkable career in the history of the Harem.

Mehmet IV ruled for thirty-nine years, one of the longest reigns in Ottoman history, ending when he was deposed on November 8, 1687. By that time the Ottoman Empire was in full decline, as evidenced by the failure of the Turkish siege of Vienna four years earlier. Nevertheless, the empire lasted for another 236 years before it finally collapsed in the aftermath of World War I, to be replaced in 1923 by the Turkish Republic.

Topkapı Sarayı was virtually abandoned in the mid-nineteenth century, when sultan Abdül Mecit moved to the new palace of Dolmabahçe on the European shore of the Bosphorus. During the last years of the Ottoman Empire the Harem of Topkapı Sarayı was inhabited only by the women of deceased sultans and their servants, some of whom continued a shadowy presence there into the early years of the Turkish Republic.

A decree of the Grand National Assembly of the Turkish Republic in April 1923 gave over Topkapı Sarayı to the administration of the museums of Istanbul. Years of restoration followed before the various parts of the palace could be opened to the public as the Topkapı Sarayı Museum. The last section of the palace to be opened was the Harem, although there are still parts of that ancient labyrinth that have not yet been completely restored and made available to visitors.

One of the palace buildings that is still closed is the Hall of the Favorites, a large barracks above a courtyard at the northern end of the Harem, overlooking the Golden Horn. When I first visited Topkapı Sarayı, in the autumn of 1960, the Harem was not yet open, but a friendly guard let me in anyway, and I spent the whole of an afternoon wandering through the women's quarters, ending up in the Hall of the

Haghia Eirene, seen from the southeast in the First Court of Topkapı Sarayı

Favorites. The windows were shuttered and the rooms in almost total darkness except for occasional beams of light penetrating through holes in the walls and ceilings; an old brass bedstead under a tottering canopy was shrouded in cobwebs, the remnants of its mattress giving off an odor of sepulchral decay. Through the deepening shadows, the mirror of a baroque dressing table reflected the dark image of a deserted bedroom, evoking the ghosts of those who once spent their sequestered lives here, in the Harem of the House of Felicity.

5

ISTANBUL: THE FIRST HILL

Long before I came to Istanbul, I read about the famous Hippodrome of Constantinople. So on the same day that I first visited Haghia Sophia I walked over to look at the site of the Hippodrome, in the park in front of the mosque of Sultan Ahmet I. I knew from reading Mamboury's guide to Istanbul that this was the oldest monument in the city, although all that remains is its *sphendone,* the massive semicircular retaining wall at its southern end, where the First Hill slopes steeply down to the Marmara.

The original Hippodrome was built, or at least begun, c. AD 200 by the Roman emperor Septimius Severus, who in 196 had captured Byzantium after a long siege and then destroyed the city. It was apparently completed by Constantine the Great, who dedicated it together with the city of Constantinople on May 11, 330. During the early Byzantine period the Hippodrome was the focal point of the city's public life, and the mobs who came there to watch the chariot races often got

out of hand, most notably in the Nika Revolt in January 532, which nearly cost Justinian his throne.

The Hippodrome had arched entryways at its straight northern end, with tiers of seats on its two straight sides and around the curved *sphendone* at its southern end. Estimates of the seating capacity vary, some authorities putting it as high as 100,000. The western side of the Hippodrome was demolished c. 1520 to make way for the Palace of Ibrahim Paşa, while what remained of the eastern side was destroyed in 1609, when construction began on the mosque of sultan Ahmet I. The site of the Hippodrome then became a public square known as the At Meydanı, the Place of Horses, an appropriate name for the ancient chariot racecourse, whose course is followed by the modern street that runs around its periphery.

Three ancient monuments still remain standing along the southern half of the Hippodrome's *spina,* or longitudinal axis. The two closest to the southern end, the so-called Colossus and the Serpent Column, were probably put in place by Constantine the Great when he dedicated the city in 330, while the third, the Egyptian Obelisk, was erected in 390 by Theodosius I.

The Colossus is an obelisk of squared stones, some 32 meters in height, near the south end of the Hippodrome. It takes its name from the Greek inscription on its base, which compares it to the Colossus of Rhodes. Evliya considered the three ancient monuments on the *spina* of the Hippodrome to be talismans, magical objects that had since antiquity protected the city from various evils, some of them having curative or prophetic powers. He numbered the Colossus as the fifteenth of the city's talismans, although he says nothing of its magical powers.

The Serpent Column took its name from the three intertwined bronze snakes that formed its shaft, which was originally the base of a golden trophy erected in the temple of Apollo at Delphi. The trophy had been presented to the temple by the thirty-one Greek cities that together overcame the Persians at the Battle of Plataea in 479 BC. The three serpent heads were broken off and lost after the Turkish Conquest in 1453; part of one of them was found in the mid-nineteenth century and is now in the Archaeological Museum. Evliya numbers the column seventeenth in his list of talismans, noting that it was erected "in the Hippodrome in order to destroy all serpents, lizards, scorpions, and suchlike creatures."

The Egyptian Obelisk, commissioned by the Pharaoh Thutmose III (r. 1549–1503 BC), was originally erected at Deir el Bahri, opposite Thebes in Upper Egypt. At that time it stood about 60 meters tall and weighed

Base of the Egyptian Obelisk in the Hippodrome. Relief showing the royal family of Theodosius I seated in the Kathisma, or royal lodge some 800 tons, but it broke apart during shipment to Constantinople in the mid-fourth century AD and only the upper two-thirds survived. This fragment lay on the seashore where it was unloaded until 390, when it was finally erected on its present site by Theodosius I. The base is a marble block, decorated on its four sides with reliefs, supporting a further four brazen blocks upon which rests the shaft. The reliefs show Theodosius and his family in the Kathisma, the royal loge of the Hippodrome, as they look down on various scenes in the Hippodrome, including chariot races and other events. Evliya ranked the Egyptian Obelisk sixteenth in his list of talismans, describing it as "an obelisk of red colored stone, covered with various sculptures which foretell the fortune of the city."

The Palace of Ibrahim Paşa was erected on the west side of the Hippodrome c. 1520. It takes its name from a Greek convert to Islam who became one of Süleyman the Magnificent's closest companions during the early part of his reign. After being appointed vezir in 1523, Ibrahim married the sultan's sister Hadice the following year and received this palace on the Hippodrome as a wedding present from

The Mosque of Ahmet I, viewed from the Sea of Marmara

Süleyman. But Ibrahim's wealth and power eventually led to his downfall by provoking Roxelana's jealousy, and in 1536 Süleyman had him executed. All of Ibrahim's wealth and possessions were subsequently confiscated, including his great palace on the Hippodrome.

When we first came to Istanbul in 1960, the Palace of Ibrahim Paşa was an abandoned ruin, which I managed to explore one day by making my way in from the roof of the adjacent law courts. But now the building has been superbly restored and houses the Museum of Turkish and Islamic Art. The most impressive room is the great hall where Ibrahim Paşa held court when he was grand vezir, and from which he reviewed parades and imperial celebrations in the Hippodrome.

The Mosque of Sultan Ahmet I, known to many tourists as the Blue Mosque, was erected on the east side of the Hippodrome, its *külliye* standing on a vast platform supported by massive retaining walls on the slope of the First Hill descending to the Marmara. Work on the mosque began in 1609 under the direction of the architect Mehmet Ağa and was completed in 1616. According to tradition, during the dedication ceremony Sultan Ahmet wore a hat shaped like the Prophet's foot as a token of his humility. Ahmet did not have long to enjoy his achievement, for he died a year later, to be buried in a *türbe* that was subsequently built for him at the northwest corner of the complex. Buried beside Ahmet are his wife Kösem and three of his sons: Murat IV, Osman II, and Prince Beyazit. Beyazit, the Bajazet of Racine's great tragedy, was killed by his brother Murat IV while imprisoned in the Cage in Topkapı Sarayı.

Together with Haghia Sophia, the mosque is one of the two great landmarks on the skyline of the city as seen from the Sea of Marmara, and I can remember gazing at it on the several occasions when we left Istanbul by ship, once wondering if we would ever return. It has a particularly beautiful gray stone exterior, augmented by the gilded ornamentation on the crowns of the escalation of domes and on the tips of the six minarets.

The interior of the mosque is equally impressive, though during the summer months it is so crowded with tourists that it loses the serenity that I remember experiencing here on my first visits, when the only sounds in the vast space under the dome were the repeated prayers of the faithful. I tried to picture the prayer hall as it would have been in Ottoman times, particularly when the sultan would come here for the Friday noon service, accompanied by all the dignitaries of the court and their entourages. The sultan would enter via the ramp at the northeast corner of the courtyard, and pass through *hünkar kasrı,* a suite of rooms that served as a royal *pied-à-terre*, now used as a carpet museum, and from there he would proceed to the *hünkar mahfili,* the royal loge to the left of the *mihrap.* All the rest of the imperial procession took their assigned places in the mosque, as one can see them in old engravings, each group identifiable by its distinctive costumes, those of the Janissaries standing out, with their curious folded headdress and the plumed turbans of their aghas.

At the southwest corner of the Hippodrome, Şehit Mehmet Paşa Yokuşu leads downhill toward the Marmara. After the second turning on the left it leads to Sokollu Mehmet Paşa Camii. The main gate is below, where a stairway leads up through a vaulted passageway into the courtyard of the mosque, surrounded by the domed cells of the *medrese,* one of the most entrancing cloisters in the city.

The mosque was built by Sinan in 1571–2 for Sokollu Mehmet Paşa, who was grand vezir under Süleyman the Magnificent and his two immediate successors, Selim II and Murat III. The interior of Sokollu Mehmet Camii is, in my opinion, the most beautiful of all of Sinan's grand vezirial mosques, surpassing even Rüstem Paşa Camii. Whenever I enter the mosque, I have the same feeling that I did at the time of my first visit, struck by the harmony of its lines, the enchanting marble decoration, and the delicate color of the stone. Most striking of all, however, are the tiles, which have been used with singularly charming effect.

Not far from the mosque's main gateway lies Kadirga Limanı Caddesi, which leads onto Kadirga Liman, a picturesque square and park surrounded by lively teahouses, cafés, and simple restaurants. Kadirga Limanı means "Galley Port," for in Byzantine and early Ottoman times this was a harbor, originally created by the emperor Julian the Apostate (r. 361–3). After subsequently being silted up, it was dredged by the empress Sophia, wife of Justin II (r. 565–80), after whom it was called the Port of Sophia. The port could still be seen in the mid-sixteenth century, by which time it was known as the Galley Port.

The street that leads off from the southeast corner of the square progresses towards Küçük Aya Sofya Camii, the former Byzantine church of Sts. Sergius and Bacchus. This is one of the most beautiful – and one of the most significant – of the surviving Byzantine churches in the city. It was begun by Justinian and his empress Theodora in 527, soon after he became emperor, and five years before he began work on the present Haghia Sophia and Haghia Eirene. The church was completed no later than 536, a year before Haghia Sophia and Haghia Eirene.

The interior plan is a roughly rectangular shape housing an octagon

left above
The *mimber*, or pulpit, in the Mosque of Ahmet I

left below
The vast prayer room in the Mosque of Ahmet I, showing three of the huge piers that support the great dome

overleaf
The Mosque of Ahmet I with its six minarets. The domed building on the far right is the tomb of Ahmet I, while the smaller domed structure to its left is the lecture room of the medrese, or theological school.

which is formed by eight octagonal piers interspersed with pairs of columns both in the nave and galleries. They are arranged straight on the sides but form a semicircular exedra at the corners. The capitals on the lower level are of the melon type, while those in the gallery are pseudo-Ionic, a few of them bearing the monogram of Justinian and Theodora, whose names also appear in the long inscription on the entablature.

Having served as a church for almost a thousand years, Sts. Sergius and Bacchus was converted into a mosque by Hüseyin Ağa, chief white eunuch under Beyazit II, in the first decade of the sixteenth century. Because of a purported resemblance to the Great Church, the building is now known as Küçük Ayasofya Camii, the Mosque of Little Haghia Sophia.

The shore highway and the Byzantine sea-walls lie to the east of the mosque. The highway was built on filled-in land along the shallows of the Marmara in 1959; before then the sea came right up to the defense walls. The Byzantine sea-walls along the Marmara were for the most part rebuilt in the mid-ninth century as a defense against the Arabs, who in the previous century had besieged Constantinople on a number of occasions. Consisting of a single line of walls 12–15 meters high, with 188 towers at set intervals, the Marmara defenses run a distance of 8 kilometers, penetrated by thirteen gates. A large part of the fortifications along the Marmara has been destroyed in modern times, particularly during the building of the railway in the 1870s. It is impossible not to be impressed by what remains, however, particularly the walls and towers below the First Hill.

Just before the first exit from the highway, there is an array of ancient column fragments that have been erected in the strip of grass beside the sidewalk. These are all from the Great Palace of Byzantium, whose fragmentary ruins continually come to light during construction projects on the Marmara slope of the First Hill. The Great Palace, begun by Constantine the Great, was laid out on terraces amidst gardens on the First Hill just to the east of the Hippodrome, extending from there down to the Marmara. This vast complex was extended, restored, and adorned by a number of Constantine's successors, and it was the principal imperial residence up until the late eleventh century.

The ruins of the Palace of the Boukoleon, with the eastern loggia of its seaside façade and the three marble-framed windows which provided light to a huge vaulted room, are a short way from the highway exit. Some corbels, jutting out underneath the windows, are evidence of a balcony running the length of the façade. An opening higher and to the right on the façade was up until the late 1960s framed by two columns, one of which has now disappeared. The curious-looking row

of large square marble slabs near the base of the façade attracted my notice when I first saw them, and when I put my hand into the crevice between two of them I found from their shape that they were Doric capitals, doubtless from some ancient temple that had stood near by.

The vaulted room behind the eastern loggia, which was reveted in porphyry, was the lying-in room for the royal ladies of Byzantium. It was this that gave rise to the term *porphyrogenitus,* "born in the purple," applied to those of truly noble blood who succeeded to the Byzantine throne.

When the Latins captured Constantinople in 1204, a French knight rode along the strand below the Palace of the Boukoleon, and he later wrote that he saw looking down from its windows some of the most beautiful women that he had ever seen. These women and others who were living in the Boukoleon were soon evicted to make room for King Baudoin, the first of the Latin rulers who reigned in Constantinople in the years 1204–61. After the Greeks recaptured Constantinople in 1261, Michael VIII Palaeologos found that the Boukoleon and the other pavilions of the Great Palace were unfit for habitation, and so he took up residence in the Palace of Blachernae on the Sixth Hill, just inside the city walls above the Golden Horn. Thenceforth the Great Palace by the Marmara was abandoned, and at the time of the Turkish Conquest it was in ruins, the sight of which led Fatih to recite a threnody by the Persian poet Saadi: "The spider is the curtain-holder in the Palace of the Caesars/The owl hoots its night call on the Towers of Aphrasiab."

The Mosque of Ahmet I above the Marmara sea-walls and the Palace of Boukoleon. Print by Flandin, early nineteenth century

When I first saw the Boukoleon, I noticed that there was a family of squatters living in the ruins. I could see a middle-aged man, who seemed to be the head of the family, taking his ease in the arcaded chamber on the right side of the façade, and I gave him the title of Last Emperor of Byzantium, on the grounds that he was in possession of the imperial palace. But the emperor before long was dispossessed, as other rulers were in Byzantine history, and since then the Boukoleon has been uninhabited, so far as I can see.

About 400 meters beyond the Boukoleon, there is an old seaside restaurant called *Karışma Sen,* which means "Mind Your Own Business." I encountered this restaurant in the autumn of 1960, when Dolores and I and our three small children were trying to walk entirely around the city walls. We gave out here and spent the next few hours in the restaurant, and so I did not finally complete my circumambulation of the walls until a later stroll that autumn, which I did by myself.

Since the shore highway along the Marmara was not completed until 1959, it would not have been possible to attempt a circumambulation of the walls until I did it in 1960, or so I thought. But Evliya tells us that in the year 1634, while Murat was off on his Erivan campaign, Bayram Paşa, who had been left as governor of Istanbul, filled in the shallows along the Marmara outside the sea-walls and built a shore road. Evliya goes on to enumerate the number of paces around the land and sea-walls, gate by gate, concluding that it amounted to "exactly 30,000 paces," which would be about 14 miles, agreeing with my own estimate. Evliya tells us that during the reign of Sultan Ibrahim the shore road along the Marmara was washed away by storms, so that the next time he paced out the circumference of the city he had to walk inside the Marmara sea-walls. The shore road along the Marmara was not rebuilt until 1959, and so it would appear that Evliya and I are the only ones ever to have walked entirely around the city outside its ancient walls, which increases my feeling of kinship for my invisible companion.

Ahır Kapısı, the Stable Gate which is the only surviving gateway in the Byzantine sea-walls along the Marmara, is just beyond the *Karışma Sen* restaurant. The gateway, whose Byzantine name is unknown, takes its Turkish name from the fact that it led to the sultan's mews near by.

Beyond Ahır Kapısı one can see the Incili Köşkü, the Kiosk of the Pearl, a marble seaside pavilion of Topkapı Sarayı built into and atop the Byzantine sea-walls. According to an inscription on a fountain, the kiosk was founded by Sinan Paşa, admiral of the Ottoman fleet under Murat III, in AH 986 (AD 1578). In January 1595, Murat, who particularly liked this kiosk, spent his final days here, listening mournfully to the dirges of his musicians while he awaited death. One afternoon the Ottoman fleet sailed by on its return from the Aegean and fired a twenty-one gun salute in his honor. However, the sound of the gunfire caused the kiosk's ceiling plaster to fall down like snowflakes on Murat and his musicians. The sultan is reported to have said, "And so is destroyed the kiosk of my life," and was moved back to finally die in the Saray.

When we first came to Istanbul, we sometimes in late spring had family picnics atop the kiosk, from where we had a superb view of the Marmara and the Asian suburbs of the city. After lunch we would make our way across the railway tracks into what were once the lower gardens of the Saray along the Marmara. This area is occupied by the Turkish military and is strictly off-limits to the public, but the situation was much more relaxed then, and no one ever objected to our visits, particularly the Anatolian peasants who had erected their *gecekondu,* or "houses built by night," under the imperial kitchens of the Saray. This was part of the area occupied by the Great Palace, of which we could see remnants here and there in the fields, most notably the substructures of the Byzantine church of St. George of the Mangana, founded in the mid-eleventh century by the emperor Constantine IX Monomachus.

Back inside the city walls, past Ahır Kapısı, the neighborhood was once one of the most picturesque in the city. Its narrow, winding streets were lined with old wooden houses of the late Ottoman era, many of which have now been restored as pensions or replaced by modern hotels, so that the quarter has now lost much of its charm, though some still remains. Nowhere else in town are there such marvelous street names as here, though few tourists are able to translate the street signs to tell them that they are walking along the Street of the Shame-Faced, the Street of the Bushy Beard, the Street of Ibrahim of Black Hell, the Street of the Sweating Whiskers, or the Avenue of the White Moustache, the latter giving its name to the whole neighborhood inside Ahır Kapısı.

Not far through the gate lies Akbıyık Meydanı, the Square of the White Moustache, off Keresteci Hakkı Sokağı. This is one of the few places in the quarter that still retains its old Ottoman charm, much of which comes from the beautiful *çeşme,* or street-fountain, that forms the focal point of the square. A calligraphic inscription records that the *çeşme* was founded in 1743 by "the mother of Ali Paşa, vezir in the reign of Sultan Mahmut I." The fountain is now dry, so that it no longer plays the same central role in the life of the square as it did three decades ago, when I wrote in my *Stamboul Sketches* about "the children who stop there to drink during their games in the square; the women who chat there while waiting for their water-buckets to fill; the exhausted peddler who cools himself under the water-tap and counts the pitiful handful of coins he has earned in his long day's labor."

Akbıyık Caddesi, the street opposite the fountain, runs under the railway line and uphill to the wide Mehmet Ağa Caddesi, which in turn-leads to Torun Sokaği, the Street of the Grandchild, where one can find the rear of the mosque of Sultan Ahmet I and the entrance to the Mosaic Museum. The mosaics in the museum were discovered in 1935 during excavations searching for remnants of the Great Palace of Byzantium. These revealed extensive mosaic pavements, dated to the early sixth century, as well as columns, capitals, and other architectural fragments. The ruins were identified as being the northeast portico of the Mosaic Peristyle, a colonnaded walkway that may have led from the imperial apartments to the palace of the Kathisma, the royal enclosure on the Hippodrome.

Kabal Sakal Sokağı, the aforementioned Street of the Bushy Beard, is near the museum. This is a seventeenth-century Turkish bazaar street which was in utter ruins when we first came to Istanbul, but it has since been restored and is now lined with shops catering to the tourist trade. At the northern end of the arcade Mimar Mehmet Ağa Caddesi emerges in the park between the mosque of Ahmet I and Haghia Sophia.

6

THE FIRST HILL TO THE THIRD

Today the first stretch of the main avenue leading from Aya Sofya Meydanı on the First Hill is known as Divan Yolu, the Road of the Divan, from the fact that it was the principal approach to Topkapı Sarayı for the thousands who, four days every week, attended meetings of the Divan, the Imperial Council. The avenue goes towards the Third Hill and the tramline, which follows the course of the ancient Mese, or Middle Way, and was formerly the principal thoroughfare of Byzantine Constantinople and continued as such in Ottoman Istanbul.

Yerebatansaray Caddesi, the street that leads off half-right from the northwest corner of Aya Sofya Meydanı, approaches the entrance to Yerebatansaray, the "Underground Palace," an enormous subterranean structure known in English as the Basilica Cistern.

The cistern was built, or at least rebuilt, by Justinian after the Nika Revolt of 532. It takes its English name from the fact that it was built

under the Stoa Basilica, or Imperial Portico, which was badly damaged in the Nika Revolt and subsequently repaired by Justinian.

No one seems to have been aware of the cistern's existence in the early Ottoman era, until it was rediscovered by Petrus Gyllius soon after he came to the city in 1544. Gyllius tells of how he discovered the cistern in his search for the Imperial Portico:

The whole area was built over, which made it less suspected there was a cistern there. The people had not the least suspicion of it, though they daily drew their water out of the cells that were sunk into it. By chance I went into a house where there was a way down to it and went aboard a little skiff. I discovered it after the master of the house lit some torches and rowed me here and there across through the pillars, which lay very deep in water. He was very intent on catching his fish, with which the Cistern abounds, and speared some of them by the light of the torches. There is also a small light that descends from the mouth of the well and reflects on the water, where the fish usually come for air.

When I first went down the cistern in 1960, the scene was much as Gyllius describes it, and all that one could see were the first few rows and columns of the colonnades that were visible from the landing below the entryway. But now walkways have been constructed so that visitors can make their way through the entire cistern and study its well-lit structure in detail, though this has dispelled some of the mystery that had made it such a romantic place, the scene of several suspense novels and films, the most notable being Ian Fleming's *From Russia with Love.*

A grand construction, Yerebatansaray is far and away the largest of Istanbul's numerous and ancient underground reservoirs. Seventy meters wide and 140 meters in length, it comprises 12 rows of 28 columns, making 336 columns in total, although 90 of those in the southwest corner were walled off in the nineteenth century. Standing to a height of about 8 meters with their centers some 4 meters apart, the columns are capped with Byzantine Corinthian capitals, with imposts above them supporting domical groin vaults.

The far left corner of the structure is designed somewhat differently from the rest, and there the walkway takes one down a few steps to what may have been a *nymphaeum,* or monumental Roman fountain. Two of the columns there are mounted on ancient classical bases supported by the colossal heads of a pair of Gorgons, one of them upside down and the other on its side.

At the beginning of Divan Yolu, at the intersection with Yerebatansaray

An itinerant seller of prayer beads

Caddesi, there is an Ottoman *suterazi,* or water-control tower. The marble shaft beside the *suterazi* was discovered during excavations by Turkish archaeologists in 1969. This was part of the Miliarium Aureum, the Golden Milestone, known more simply as the Milion. Like its prototype in Rome, which was the reference point for all roads in Italy, the one here was the zero marker for the Via Egnatia, the great Roman highway that extended from Constantinople to the Adriatic. According to the *Patria Constantinopoleos,* a guidebook compiled c. 995 AD, the Milion marked the site of one of the gateways of the ancient town of Byzantium, probably the Thracian Gate, mentioned c. 400 BC by Xenophon in his *Anabasis,* or the *March Up Country.* Thus this is one of the oldest monuments remaining from Byzantium, part of the Roman city that lies buried beneath the streets of modern Istanbul, and I remember the excitement I felt when I saw it being resurrected from the earth that had covered it for many centuries.

Further down Divan Yolu, there is an elegant little mosque named Firuz Ağa Camii, which appears in many of the old prints depicting imperial Ottoman processions along this avenue. The mosque, which was built in 1491 for Firuz Ağa, Chief Treasurer under Beyazit II, is near to a park bordering an archaeological site which was excavated in several stages in the years 1939–52. It is believed that the exposed ruins are of the two contiguous palaces of Antiochus and Lausus, dating from the first quarter of the fifth century AD. The Palace of Lausus was renowned for the ancient Greek statuary that it contained, including works by Praxiteles, Lysippos, and Phidias, the latter represented by his famous bronze statue of Zeus that stood in Olympia, one of the seven wonders of the ancient world.

The first side street to the left off Divan Yolu, just to the west of the two palaces, leads on its right to the entrance of Binbirdirek Sarnıc, the Cistern of 1001 Columns. This is the second largest of the city's ancient subterranean cisterns, surpassed in size only by Yerebatansaray. Petrus Gyllius identified this as the Cistern of Philoxenus, named for one of the senators brought from Rome by Constantine the Great after he founded Constantinople. Current scholarship dates the cistern from the mid-fifth century to the early sixth.

The Binbirdirek Cistern measures 64 by 56.4 meters, only about a third the area of Yerebatansaray. The domical groin vaults are supported by 224 double columns – 16 rows of 14 – though 12 of these have been walled in since ancient times. The columns consist of two shafts joined together by a drum, the lower shaft being sunk 4.8 meters in the dried mud which has accumulated in the cistern over the centuries. The total height of the double columns is 12.4 meters, and to the crown of the domes about 14.5 meters. The cistern has been dry for centuries, and in late Ottoman times it was used as a silk mill. When I first visited it in 1960, the remains of one of the silk looms could still be seen there, along with a large number of deflated footballs that had fallen in through the broken domes of the cistern from the playground above. Binbirdirek has since been restored and is now open as a shopping mall, which somewhat diminishes its Roman grandeur.

The route up Divan Yolu continues to reveal a succession of monuments, all but one of them Ottoman. Just beyond the intersection of Babali Caddesi and Divan Yolu lies the large *türbe* of Mahmut II (r. 1808–39) and its block-long garden courtyard. Mahmut's son Abdül Aziz (r. 1861–76), his grandson Abdül Hamit II (r. 1876–1909) and many imperial princes and consorts are also buried here.

The *türbe* is across from an Ottoman *kütüphane,* or library, of the mid-seventeenth century. This is one of the elegant buildings of the Köprülü *külliye,* whose other institutions are mentioned below. These were erected in 1659–60 by two members of the celebrated Köprülü family, Mehmet Paşa and his son Fazil Ahmet Paşa, both of whom served as grand vezir, as did three of their descendants. (The Köprülüs are one of the very few Ottoman families whose name has survived to the present, and one of the current generation is a good friend of mine.) The library is still in use as a research center, its collection containing many books and manuscripts belonging to its founders, also known as Mehmet the Cruel and Ahmet the Statist. Mehmet was given this name because of the many thousands he executed while serving as grand vezir.

Two other institutions of the Köprülü *külliye,* the mosque and the *türbe* of Mehmet the Cruel, are further down the avenue. Rather uncharacteristically, the *türbe* is roofed only by an ornate iron grille. Legend has it that the grave was intentionally left exposed to the elements, so that the shade of the cruel grand vezir, who was burning in hell, could be cooled by the falling rain. The Çemberlitaş Hamamı, one of the finest extant examples of a classical Turkish bath, is opposite the Köprülü mosque. The *hamam* was founded by the *valide sultan* Nur Banu, wife of Selim II and mother of Murat III, prior to 1583 when she died.

At the intersection of Vezirhanı Caddesi and Divan Yolu, just beyond the Çemberlitaş Hamamı, stands the Column of Constantine, the most august of Istanbul's ancient monuments. This column, dedicated by Constantine the Great on May 11, 330, marked the founding of Constantinople as the new capital of the Roman Empire. The column, surmounted by a statue of the emperor, stood in the center of the Forum of Constantine, bordered by columned porticoes.

Evliya considered the Column of Constantine to be one of the talismans of the ancient city, and described it thus:

In the Poultry Market there is a needle-like column formed of many pieces of red emery stone, a hundred royal cubits high ... Kostantin [Constantine the Great] *placed a talisman on top of it in the form of a starling, which once a year clapped its wings and brought all the birds in the air to the place, each with three olives in its beak and talons.*

It is interesting to note that the street that intersects Divan Yolu on the other side of the column is Tavukpazarı Sokağı, the Street of the Poultry Market, although there is no reference to such a market here other than in Evliya's description of the Column of Constantine and in other sections of the *Seyahatname*.

The Kapalı Çarşı, or Covered Bazaar. Print by William Bartlett, c. 1838

Evliya also mentions the Poultry Market in his description of the Slave Market: "The Slave Market is a great *han* on the Tavukpazari, with three hundred rooms on the upper and lower stories. At the bottom of the gate, which is closed with iron locks, dwells the Inspector, who takes a tithe of all slaves bought and sold here."

The *han* that Evliya mentions is the Vezir Hanı, the huge building on the right that gives its name to Vezirhanı Caddesi. This is another structure of the Köprülü *külliye*. These huge and solidly built *hans* were inner-city caravansarais where a traveling merchant could sell or store his goods as well as eat and sleep. Like the Vezir Hanı, they are made of stone and brick, with two or three stories overlooking a large open courtyard in the center. There are scores of Ottoman *hans* still in use in Istanbul. Along with the Vezir Hanı, many are in a ruinous state of deteriation but they remain rather grand, conjuring up an image of the former oriental atmosphere of the old city.

The large mosque to the west of the Vezir Hanı is Nuruosmaniye Camii, whose name means "the sacred light *(nur)* of Osman." This was initiated by Mahmut I in 1748 and completed seven years later by his brother Osman III, who succeeded him. It was the earliest, large-scale Ottoman building in the new baroque architectural style, which was imported from western Europe early in the eighteenth century.

The mosque courtyard of Nuruosmaniye Camii is one of the busiest in the city, since it is outside one of the entrances to the famous Kapalı Çarşı, or Covered Bazaar, the approach to which is always flanked by professional beggars and itinerant peddlers. Occasionally in the past I would also see here one of the travelling musicians called *aşık,* or "lover," here meaning "love" in the mystical sense of Persian poetry. The *aşık* pursue an ancient tradition, and they are among the few survivors of the wandering minstrels typical of the medieval world. Their folk songs and poems deal with every aspect of Turkish life, including politics, with the result that they often attract the attention of the police – so much so that I have not seen one in a mosque courtyard in many years. The *aşık* always also sing to their peasant audiences ballads of life and love in Anatolia, as in the beautiful song entitled "Kara Toprak" ("the Black Earth"), composed by the late Aşık Veysel, the blind bard, whom I heard singing it many years ago, accompanying himself on the *saz.* "My sweetheart is the black earth," he sang in the opening and closing lines, "I wounded her with my hoe and shovel, but she smiled and gave me roses."

At its northern end, Vezirhanı Caddesi leads to Mahmut Paşa Camii, the oldest of the grand vezirial mosques in the city. The mosque was built in 1462 by Mahmut Paşa, a converted Greek nobleman who served as grand vezir under Fatih, but its interest lies not just in its great age. It is also a very fine example of the "Bursa style" of mosque structure, created in the first Ottoman capital.

Atik Ali Paşa Camii, an attractive mosque built in 1496 by Hadım (Eunuch) Atik Ali Paşa, grand vezir of Beyazit II, can be found on Divan Yolu, past the Column of Constantine. The complex used to include a *tekke,* an *imaret,* or public kitchen, and a *medrese,* but most if it was destroyed when the avenue was widened, and now only a part of the *medrese* remains, across the avenue from the mosque.

Nearby, the *külliye* of Koca Sinan Paşa, encircled by a charming marble wall with iron grilles, comprises a *medrese,* a *sebil,* and the *türbe* of Koca Sinan Paşa (conqueror of the Yemen and grand vezir under Murat III and Mehmet III), who died in 1595. The complex was built by Davut Ağa, the successor to Sinan as Chief of the Imperial Architects, in 1593.

Across the avenue from the *sebil,* another marble wall with grilles surrounds the *külliye* of Ali Paşa of Çorlu, Mustafa II's son-in-law. He also became grand vezir under Ahmet III, but fell out of favour and was decapitated on the island of Mytilene in 1711.

One of the final points of interest on Divan Yolu is the octagonal mosque of Kara Mustafa Paşa of Merzifon, with a *sebil* and a *medrese.* A grand vezir who was in command of the failed second siege of Vienna in 1683, he was also beheaded. An Ottoman historian records that his head "rolled at the feet of the Sultan [Mehmet IV] at Belgrade." The building of the complex began in 1669 and was eventually completed by his son twenty-one years later. The *medrese* has been converted into a research institute devoted to the work of the celebrated Turkish poet Yahya Kemal, who died in 1958, and who has been described as the "Chesterton of Turkish letters."

Divan Yolu becomes Yeniçerliler Caddesi, the Avenue of the Janissaries, which passes on the south side of Beyazit Meydanı, a chaotic and irregularly shaped square. The Beyazidiye, comprising Beyazit II's mosque and associated religious institutions, stands on the summit of the Third Hill. Built in the years 1501–6, the Beyazidiye was the second imperial mosque complex to be erected in the city, after that of Fatih. It was founded by Beyazit II, son of and successor to Mehmet II, and consists of the great mosque itself, a *medrese,* a Kuran school, a primary school, a public kitchen, a hospice for travelers, a *hamam,* and several tombs, the most notable of which is the *türbe* of the founder.

The Beyazidiye is surrounded by a vast outer courtyard, which encompasses the mosque and its various pious foundations, attracting hordes of itinerant peddlers today just as it did in Evliya's time. As Evliya describes it:

Round the inner and outer courts of this mosque there are shops of all kinds of trades, with a public kitchen, a refectory, and hostel for travelers; a school for instructing the poor and rich in the Kuran; and a college for lectures on the art of reciting it. This court had six gates; and is adorned, externally, with lofty trees, most of them mulberries, under the shade of which some thousands of people gain a livelihood by selling various kinds of things.

The original Fatih Camii was destroyed by an earthquake in 1766, so the Beyazidiye is the oldest extant imperial mosque in Istanbul. Its building heralded the two-hundred year-long great classical period of Turkish architecture.

When I last visited the Beyazidiye, I had the feeling that the scene there had not changed since I first saw it. The faithful of every class, ragged beggars alongside well-dressed businessmen, still leave their shoes at the doorway and make their way to their favorite spot. Theology students still read aloud from the Kuran in the side aisles, and bearded clerics continue to debate theological issues at the rear of the mosque, while in the *müezzin's* gallery a young man begins chanting verses from the Kuran.

The outer courtyard of the Beyazidiye was once the site of the famous Bit Pazarı, or Flea Market, of which I have fond memories from

right above
The mosque of Beyazit I

right below
The Column of Constantine, with the Nuruosmaniye Camii in the background

overleaf
The Theodosius Cistern, a smaller Roman cistern to the west of Binbirdirek

my early days in Istanbul. This has now been banished to a warehouse elsewhere in Istanbul, though a number of itinerant flea merchants have been making there way back to the outer courtyard of the Beyazidiye. But they have a long way to go before they can recreate the atmosphere of the original Bit Pazarı, which I described in my *Stamboul Sketches* as "the maddest and most colorful of all the street markets in Istanbul."

The northeastern quarter of the outer courtyard of the Beyazidiye is occupied by an outdoor café known as *Çınaraltı,* or "Under the Plane Tree," although the venerable plane itself has now disappeared, though not from my memory. The clientele includes shoppers and merchants as well as students and faculty from Istanbul University, whose main campus borders the outer courtyard of the Beyazidiye. Among the itinerant peddlers who have set up their stalls in this part of the courtyard is the *aşık* Hüseyin Avni Dede, who works in collaboration with the well-known British poet Richard Kane. The thin volumes of their collaborative efforts have works by Hüseyin in Turkish and Kane in English on facing pages, both of the poems usually having the same subject. Their most popular book is entitled *Tekşekerli Çinaraltı,* or *Tea with One Sugar under the Plane Tree.*

The Gate of the Spoonmakers leads into the Sahaflar Çarşısı, or Secondhand Book Market. One of the oldest markets in the city, it is on the site of the Chartoprateia, the former book and paper market of Byzantine Constantinople. The guild of the booksellers in this market is one of the oldest in the city, and was represented in the procession of the guilds in the reign of Murat IV, where Evliya remarked that "the Booksellers are 200 men, with 60 shops."

The ancient stone portal of Hakkakler Kapısı, the Gate of the Engravers, is at the far end of the Sahaflar Çarşışı. An entrance to the Kapalı Çarşı, the famous Covered Bazaar, is to its right. Established on this site by Fatih soon after the Conquest, the Kapalı Çarşı occupied about the same area then as it does today. It has been destroyed several times, most recently by an earthquake in 1894 and a fire in 1954, but the Bazaar still has a similar appearance to when it was first built, although much of the fabled oriental atmosphere of the market has vanished since Ottoman times.

The Covered Bazaar is a small city in itself; according to a survey made in 1976, there are more than 3,000 shops of various kinds, along with storehouses, stalls, workshops, many of them in old Ottoman *hans*, as well as a restaurant, a teahouse, several lunch counters, a bank, and a public toilet, altogether employing more than 20,000 people.

Although it seems a veritable labyrinth, the Bazaar is laid out on a

fairly regular rectangular grid, at the center of which is the Old Bedesten, one of Fatih's original buildings, where the most expensive goods were securely kept. Shops selling the same kinds of goods tend to be concentrated in the same areas, and the streets are named after the various guilds that did business there in Ottoman times. Names such as the Street of the Turban Makers and the Street of the Sword Makers are reminders of the lost oriental atmosphere of the bazaar.

One particularly colorful part of the Kapalı Çarşı that has now vanished was the Armor Bazaar. Evliya tells us that in the imperial procession the Armor Bazaar was represented by seventeen different guilds, headed by that of the Sword Cutlers, whom he describes thus:

The Sword-cutlers are 1,008 men, with 205 shops ... The faith having been established by the sword, the sword cutlers gained the precedence over all the other handicraftsmen. All those who live in peace as well as in war stand in need of this profession; a sword being indispensable in each Muslim's house ... During the passage of the procession they polish swords and play a thousand tricks, as sticking naked swords into their ears, throats and stomachs, and some represent fighting, and pass on in files.

The Kapalı Çarşı is part of the old market quarter that extends down the north slope of the Third Hill to the Golden Horn. The main street of this quarter is Uzun Çarşı Caddesi, the Avenue of the Long Market, an apt name, for it is flanked by a continuous line of shops and by an army of hucksters hawking their wares to the passing crowds. This quarter has the oldest *hans* in the city, all of them still in commercial use, of which Evliya mentions by name more than twenty-five. The oldest is probably Kürkçü Hanı, the *Han* of the Furriers, founded by Mahmut Pasha c. 1474. Furriers still do business in the *han*, which means that their trade has been established there for more than five centuries. Evliya tells us that in the procession of the guilds the Fur Merchants marched in two contingents, the Greeks who did business in the Kürkçü Hanı forming a group separate from the other, putting on an extraordinarily lively show:

The Greek fur makers of the market-place of Mahmut Pasha form a separate procession, with caps of bear-skin and breeches of fur. Some are dressed from head to foot in the skins of lions, leopards, and wolves, with kalpaks of sable on their heads. Some dress again in skins, as wild men and savages, so that those who see them are afraid, each one being tied by six- or sevenfold strong chains, and led by six or seven people. These wild men assailing their leaders and keepers spread amongst the people a noise and confusion which is beyond all description. Some are dressed ... in strange figures,

with their feet turned to the sky, apparently, while they walk with their real feet on the ground. Others, clad in the skins of lions, leopards and bears, represent these animals walking on all fours and dragged with chains. Every time they grow mutinous they are beaten by their guards. Some representing swine, apes, and other animals that are not dangerous follow in crowds without chains. Others assail them with dogs and hounds, representing the show of a hunting party with halberds in their hands.

Binbirdirek Sarnıçı, the Cistern of 1001 Columns. Print by William Bartlett, c. 1838

The most interesting of all these old *hans* in the market quarter is the Büyük Valide Hani. This was founded by the *büyük valide sultan* Kösem, mother of Murat IV and Ibrahim, shortly before her death in 1651. This venerable *han* has changed very little since I first saw it, as I reassure myself by rereading what I wrote of it in *Stamboul Sketches*. The chief products still seem to be, as they were then, "noise, odor, and local color."

Strolling peddlers hawk their wares among the merchants, customers, workers, *hamals,* and drivers who enter and leave the main courtyard, some of the latter carrying goods on horse-drawn wagons that hold their own in encounters with large trucks. At a vine-shaded café in the outer courtyard an itinerant barber is shaving one of a group of merchants, whose hand gestures would be recognizable to Evliya Çelebi.

The rear gate of the Büyük Valide Hanı, which points the way back to the summit of the Third Hill, leads onto streets that have since Evliya's time been outdoor markets for cheap clothing and shoes. Evliya tells us that in his time there were 200 sellers of old shoes who did business in this area. They marched in the imperial procession with the Shoe Merchants and Shoemakers, the latter being one of the most powerful guilds in the city. Evliya describes them thus as they pass in the imperial procession:

The Shoemakers pass all armed, but barefoot and bareheaded, adorning their shops with all kinds of shoes and slippers, of all dimensions, including boots of an enormous size, big enough to hold two men. The Shoemakers hawk their wares according to an account which is known only among themselves, and the scheme of which is none other than to cheat the buyers, of which they boast. They are a merciless sort of men, but everyone stands in need of them. They are followed by the Old Shoe Merchants, who adorn their shops with ancient shoes.

These and other guilds that Evliya describes are still doing business in this old market quarter.

7

ISTANBUL: THE THIRD HILL

The north side of Beyazit Square is bordered by the main campus of the University of Istanbul. The principal building of the university is the former Seraskerat, or Ministry of War, built by the French architect Auguste Bourgeois in 1866. The Beyazit Tower, a prominent element in the Istanbul skyline, erected in 1828 by Mahmut II as a fire-watch station, rises up from the university's courtyard. When we first came to Istanbul, we climbed up to the observation deck, from which there is an unsurpassed view of the old city; but for security reasons, the tower is no longer open to the public.

At the northern end of the square is the *medrese* of the Beyazidiye *külliye*, now used to house the Museum of Calligraphic Art. Past the *medrese*, the wonderful ruins of Beyazit's *hamam* look upon Ordu Caddesi, the continuation of Yeniçeriler Caddesi. As it was probably the most opulent public bath in Istanbul and the building material appears to contin-

above
The interior of the
Süleymaniye

right
The Beyazit Tower,
with the Sea of
Marmara in the
background

ue to be in quite good condition, I keep hoping that it will be restored.

On both sides of the avenue between the *medrese* and the *hamam* there are massive architectural fragments of the ancient Forum of Theodosius, unearthed in roadworks on Ordu Caddesi at intervals in the years 1928–58. This forum was the largest of the public squares in Byzantine Constantinople, built by Theodosius I in the years 386–93 on the site of the ancient Forum Tauri, which dated back to the time of Constantine the Great. At the western end of the forum there was an enormous triumphal archway, and, at its center, a commemorative column surmounted by a silver statue of Theodosius I, its shaft decorated with a spiral band of reliefs showing the emperor's victories. Huge fragments of the archway can be seen on both sides of the avenue, their bases still *in situ*, along with other monumental remains of the forum. Two fragments from the reliefs on the Column of Theodosius are built into the *hamam* of Beyazit II. Both fragments show ranks of soldiers, with one of the reliefs set upside down, so that the troops appear to be marching on their own heads.

Evliya lists the Column of Theodosius among the talismans of the ancient city, and says that it was erected "as a talisman against the plague, which could never prevail in Istanbul as long as this column was standing. It was afterwards demolished by that sultan, who erected a heart-rejoicing *hamam* in its place; and since that time plague has prevailed in the city."

On the south side of Ordu Caddesi, there are the remains of two interesting Ottoman *hans* that have been restored in recent years. The one on the east, known as Şimkeşhane, was built by Fatih as a mint, but this was later moved to the First Court of Topkapı Sarayı, leaving the Şimkeşhane to be used by the spinners of silver thread. The *valide sultan* Rabia Gülnüş Ümmetullah, mother of Mustafa II and Ahmet III and wife of Mehmet IV, rebuilt the *han* in 1707 following a fire. The *han* to its west was built c. 1740 by Seyyit Hasan Pasha, grand vezir under Mahmut I.

The imperial mint was still housed in Şimkeşhane in Evliya's time, and he describes it thus in the *Seyahatname*: "When the mint is in good order, there is coined every day ten quintals of silver and one of gold ... There are no fewer than 1,000 men employed in the mint, 300 of whom are infidels, but righteous men."

The delightful little *külliye* of Ragıp Paşa, built by the architect Mehmet Tahir Ağa in 1762 for Ragıp Paşa, grand vezir under Mustafa III, is situated farther down the south side of Ordu Caddesi. The *külliye* is centered on a public library, which has been restored and once again serves its original purpose. Above the entrance from Ordu Caddesi is a primary

school, now converted to a children's library. These are among the finest of the public libraries from the Ottoman era that have survived in Istanbul, a tribute to Ragıp Paşa, one of the last great men to hold the office of grand vezir, also distinguished as one of the finest poets of his time.

The inner courtyard of the Süleymaniye, with its surrounding portico and the şadirvan in the center

Near the Laleli Cami, which I will come to later in this chapter, there is a flight of steps up to a large open terrace. At the far left corner of the terrace is the former Byzantine church of the Myrelaion, now a mosque known as Bodrum Camii.

When I first saw this building in 1960, it was a derelict ruin, abandoned after being destroyed by fire in 1912. The building remained in ruins until a program of restoration was undertaken by the Istanbul Archaeological Museum in 1964–5, when the site was excavated by Professor Cecil L. Striker of Pennsylvania State University, who has since clarified the architectural history of the church in his book on the Myrelaion.

The Myrelaion, dedicated to "the place of the holy myrrh," was founded by the emperor Romanus I Lecapenus (r. 919–44), apparently early in his reign. The Myrelaion was a double church, the lower one being a funerary chapel, where in 922 Romanus buried his wife, the empress Helena. Excavation revealed that the terrace on which the church stands was built on top of an immense subterranean structure of the fifth century AD, which the archaeologists call the Rotunda. Romanus also built a palace here, on the eastern side of the terrace, using the Rotunda as a cistern.

The church was converted into a mosque late in the fifteenth century, by which time the palace had disappeared and the Rotunda had been buried beneath its ruins. After the restorations of 1964–5, Bodrum Camii once again became a working mosque, while the Rotunda was converted into a very attractive subterranean shopping center.

During the excavations a fragmentary sculpture in porphyry was found in the Rotunda by the Turkish archaeologist Nezih Fıratlı. Professor Fıratlı established that this was part of the missing foot of one of the so-called Tetrarchs, the porphyry group set into the southeast corner of the basilica of San Marco in Venice. This sculpture was part of the loot taken by the Venetians when they and the Latin knights of the Fourth Crusade sacked Constantinople in 1204. It is believed that the statue group originally stood in Constantinople at the Philadelphaion, the point where the Mese split into two branches, which is believed to be at the present site of Laleli Cami.

Laleli Cami, the Tulip Mosque, is, in my opinion, the finest of all the baroque mosques in Istanbul. Constructed in the years 1759–63 by

Mehmet Tahir Ağa, perhaps the most creative and greatest Turkish baroque architect, the mosque was founded by Mustafa III. The *külliye* also includes a subterranean shopping mall, now well restored, as well as an *imaret,* a *sebil,* and a *türbe,* in which Mustafa III is buried along with his son Selim III, who was murdered by the Janissaries in 1808.

To the west of Laleli Cami, Gençtürk Caddesi leads to Şehzadebaşı Caddesi and the principal landmark on the western spur of the Third Hill, Şehzade Camii, the Mosque of the Prince. It was constructed by Süleyman the Magnificent in memory of his beloved son Mehmet, who died of smallpox in 1543, when he was only twenty-one. The architect was Sinan, who completed the Şehzade Camii *külliye* in 1548, making it his earliest grand scale imperial mosque complex. He referred to it as his "apprentice work," but as it is one of the most beautiful mosques in the city, it is clear that this apprentice was already a genius. As Evliya writes of Şehzade Camii, "Its dome is an elegant piece of workmanship, and though not as large as that of the Süleymaniye, it rears its head majestically into the sky."

Prince Ahmet's *türbe,* a surpassingly beautiful work of Sinan, is in the graveyard garden of the mosque, along with a number of other remarkable tombs, but unfortunately only one of these is open to the public, that of Destari Mustafa Paşa, dated by an inscription to 1611.

East along Şehzadebaşi Caddesi, beyond the precincts of Şehzade Camii, lies a charming *medrese* with a large *sebil* at a corner. This complex was built in 1720 by Nevşehirli Ibrahim Paşa, grand vezir and son-in-law of Ahmet III, the Tulip King. The *külliye* was designed just at the axis between the classical period of Ottoman architecture and the germination of the baroque era. It successfully combines aspects of both styles, making it a favorite subject for painters and engravers in times past. Behind the *sebil* is the *türbe* of Ibrahim Paşa, who was strangled by the Janissaries on September 20, 1730, when Ahmet III was deposed, ending the Age of Tulips.

The avenue leads towards a former Byzantine church known as Kalenderhane Camii, which stands next to the eastern end of the Roman aqueduct of Valens.

When I first visited Kalenderhane Camii in 1960, it was abandoned and in poor repair. The identity and date of this building were unknown until it was excavated and restored in the years 1966–78, after which it was rededicated as a mosque. The excavation project was under the co-sponsorship of Dumbarton Oaks and Istanbul Technical University, the co-directors being Professors Cecil L. Striker and Doğan

Kuban. Their work has established that the present edifice was originally a church erected c. 1200, built on the ruins of earlier structures dating back to c. 400. It was also shown that the church was dedicated to the Theotokos Kyriotissa, Our Lady Mother of God.

The church was taken over by the Latins soon after their conquest of Constantinople in 1204, and it reverted to the Greeks following their recapture of the city in 1261, after which it was restored and redecorated. The church appears to have been converted into a mosque during the reign of Fatih, when it was given over to the Kalender dervishes – hence the name.

During the restoration a number of frescoes were discovered, and when the first of these came to light, Lee Striker invited Hilary Sumner-Boyd and me to see them. We watched with excitement as the wall that had immured them for more than seven centuries was slowly removed. The paintings proved to be a fresco cycle of the life of St. Francis done c. 1250, predating the paintings in Assisi. Striker later uncovered a number of mosaics, the earliest of which, a depiction of the Presentation in the Temple, was dated to the seventh century, making it the single pre-iconoclastic figurative painting to be discovered in Istanbul. The uncertainty over the dedication of the church was finally dispelled when a late Byzantine mosaic of the Theotokos Kyriotissa was uncovered over the main door to the narthex. The most important of these mosaics and frescoes are now on exhibit in the "Istanbul through the Ages" pavilion at the Archaeological Museum.

The *imam* of Kalenderhane Camii never remembers me from one visit to the next, so whenever I appear he repeats the same story about the nocturnal visitors who come to see him from what he calls the "celestial regions." He is not on good terms with these visitors, he says, so when he goes off to the "other world" himself he will have to go in disguise, for otherwise he will be recognized and barred by these people.

Just to the east of Kalenderhane Camii a street passes through an archway in the aqueduct, giving a medieval aspect to the scene. At the far end of the street is the Süleymaniye, the great imperial mosque complex of Süleyman the Magnificent.

The Süleymaniye stands on a vast platform on the northern spur of the Third Hill, dominating the skyline of the old city when viewed from across the Golden Horn. The *külliye* was built for Süleyman by Sinan, who began work in 1550. Evliya, in his description of the Süleymaniye, says that "three whole years were employed in laying the foundations. The workmen penetrated so far into the ground, that the sound of their pickaxes was heard by the bull that bears up the world at the center of the earth."

The mosque is in the middle of a very large outer courtyard, around three sides of which the other buildings of the *külliye* are arrayed as symmetrically as possible. The complex includes the great mosque itself as well as four *medreses* and their preparatory school, a school for reading the Kuran, a school of sacred tradition, a primary school, a medical college, a hospital, an insane asylum, a public kitchen, a caravansarai, a market street, a public bath, and two tombs: one for Süleyman and the other for his wife Roxelana. The Süleymaniye was finally completed in 1557, and on the day of dedication, according to Evliya, Sinan said to Süleyman, "I have built for thee, O sultan, a mosque that will remain on the face of the earth till the day of judgment."

The tombs of Süleyman and Roxelana are in the walled garden behind the mosque. Besides Süleyman himself, those buried here include his daughter Mihrimah and two of his successors, Süleyman II and Ahmet II, both of whom came to the throne after many years in the Cage.

The *türbe* of Roxelana is smaller and simpler than Süleyman's, but it is decorated with even finer tiles. Her tomb is dated 1558, the year of her death, seven years before Süleyman passed away. Süleyman marked Roxelana's passing with a four-line threnody, more moving than the many love poems that he wrote to her during their years together, and I always recall these lines when I visit their tombs.

above
The tomb of Süleyman the Magnificent

right
The Süleymaniye, looking down on the Golden Horn

I languish on sorrow's mountain
Where night and day I sigh and moan:
Wondering what fate awaits me
With my beloved gone.

The various pious foundations of the Süleymaniye have been well restored, and several of them are once again serving the people of Istanbul as they did in the days of Süleyman. Two of the four *medreses,* those on the south side of the complex, now house the celebrated Süleymaniye research library, with over 32,000 manuscripts, one of the most important in the city. The little primary school beside the *medreses* now serves as a children's library. The medical college, once the foremost in the empire, has been converted to a maternity clinic. The *imaret,* or public kitchen, now houses the Darüzziyafe, a restaurant specializing in Ottoman cuisine.

The enormous *dar-üş şifa,* or hospital, is not presently open to the public. Evliya described the Süleymaniye hospital: "The hospital of the Süleymaniye is an establishment so excellent that the sick are generally

cured within three days of their admission, since it is provided with the most admirable physicians and surgeons." As was typical of the larger hospitals in Ottoman times, the Süleymaniye included an area for the treatment of insanity. Foreigners were struck by the charitable nature, size and management of these asylums. Evliya writes of the care provided in one of the institutions of his time: "They have excellent food twice a day; even pheasants, partridges, and other delicate birds are provided. There are musicians and singers who are employed to amuse the sick and insane and thus to cure their madness."

The caravansarai of the Süleymaniye is also not presently open to the public. This huge building featured lodging, stables and storage for travelers, as well as a kitchen, a bakery and an olive press. In accordance with Ottoman custom, free food and lodging at one of these caravansarais were offered to all accredited visitors to Istanbul. As Evliya writes: "The caravansarai is a most excellent establishment where all travelers receive twice a day a bowl of rice, a dish of barley soup and bread, every night a candle, and for each horse provender, but the gift to travelers is only for three days."

Opposite the northwest corner of the Süleymaniye's outer corner there is a little *külliye* founded by Sinan. The *külliye* is triangular in form, with a *sebil* at its apex and the three walls surrounding the graveyard, at the center of which is Sinan's open marble *türbe*. The south wall of the graveyard is covered with a calligraphic inscription by the poet Mustafa Sa'i listing the accomplishments of Sinan, who was chief of the imperial architects under Süleyman, and his two immediate successors, Selim II and Murat III. Mustafa Sa'i credits Sinan with a total of 321 structures, including 81 mosques, 42 of which were erected in Istanbul over a career that spanned half a century.

At the corner opposite Sinan's *türbe,* there is a huge block of marble scored with numerous cut marks. One day, when Godfrey Goodwin and I were looking at the stone, on which two old men were sitting, we asked the director of the Süleymaniye museum about this, and, speaking in Turkish, he said that this was one of the places where the sultan's chief executioner chopped off the heads of convicted criminals and rebels. At this the two old men got up in horror, one of them saying, "We have used this stone as a resting place since our childhood, but now we will never sit here again," whereupon they walked away shaking their heads.

Şifahane Sokağı leads past the hospital of the *külliye* and out of the Süleymaniye complex. Away to the right of this street is the former Byzantine church known as Kilise Cami, which literally means "Church Mosque."

overleaf
Şehzade Camii, the
Mosque of the Prince;
the main dome and
supporting arches

This was identified by Gyllius as the church of St. Theodore, based on what the local Greeks told him, but current opinion has abandoned this identification. Nothing is known of the history of the church other than the fact that it was converted into a mosque soon after the Turkish Conquest. The church and its narthex have been dated to c. 1100 or slightly later, while the exonarthex and its attractive portico are believed to have been added c. 1320, when the structure may have been rebuilt around its original core. When I first visited Kilise Cami, in the spring of 1961, there were still mosaic portraits in the three domes of the exonarthex, dated c. 1320, but these have now almost entirely vanished.

Situated nearby is another Ottoman library of the eighteenth century, that of Atıf Efendi. Of all the Ottoman public libraries in the city, this is the most charming and original. Built in 1741–2, of stone and brick, it is in the baroque style and comprises two elements: a block of houses and the library itself, which is entered from an interior garden court.

The Vefa Caddesi leads to the famous Vefa Bozahanesi, the oldest establishment of its kind in Istanbul. *Boza* is a drink made of millet, a particular favorite of the Janissaries, and still very popular in Turkey, sold in cafés such as this or by itinerant vendors. There is a silver cup in a glass case on the wall, displayed there because Atatürk once drank from it.

Evliya describes the sellers of *boza* as they pass in the procession of the guilds, in which they marched in the forty-sixth and last section, along with the tavern keepers.

The Sellers of boza are 1,005 men, with 300 shops ... The boza makers are a very necessary occupation in a military camp; though fermented, it is not prohibited like wine, for it gives heat and strength to the bodies of Muslim warriors, and serves to allay hunger. Drinking it to excess brings on the gout and dropsy, and the proverb says "That dogs are no friends to boza drinkers." The reason is that boza drinkers, being liable to the above-mentioned diseases, always carry a stick in their hand, which is no way of recommending themselves to the favour of dogs. The boza sellers are for the most part Tartar gypsies ... They pass on wagons crying "Boza!" and distributing it among the spectators.

Katip Çelebi Caddesi goes down the northern slope of the Third Hill toward the Golden Horn and ends at Atatürk Bulvarı, the broad and extremely busy highway that extends from the Atatürk Bridge up the deep valley between the Third and Fourth Hills.

At this point there is a rather striking brick and stone baroque mosque, Şebsafa Camii which was built by Fatma Şebsafa Kadın, from

the harem of Abdül Hamit I, in 1787. Its distinctive features include a porch with a cradle vaulted upper story , and a two-story narthex, surmounted by three small domes. The latter creates an attractive gallery that looks over the middle of the mosque, which is covered by a tall dome. The *külliye* also includes a long *mektep,* or primary school, to the north of the mosque, distinguished by its pretty cradle-vaulted roof. I always stop to admire this charming little *külliye* at the end of a stroll around the Third Hill, for it is the only thing of beauty in a neighborhood that has become a wasteland of modern commercial buildings, standing beside the highway as a monument to the more human Ottoman city that it represents, at least in my mind.

8

AROUND THE FOURTH HILL

Şebsafa Kadın Camii is halfway down the valley that leads up from the Golden Horn between the Third and Fourth Hills. The west side of the same boulevard is bordered by huge Roman vaults which are the retaining walls for the terrace that supports Zeyrek Camii, the multi-domed structure on the heights of the Fourth Hill, which has given its name to the surrounding neighborhood.

Excavations have recently revealed a huge substructure that can be entered through one of the portals in these retaining walls. Evliya considered this substructure to be one of the ancient talismans of the city, as he writes in the *Seyahatname*: "On the skirt of the place called Zeyrekbashi [the heights of Zeyrek] there is a cavern dedicated to St. John, and every year, when the piercing cold of winter has set in, several black demons hide themselves there."

At the south end of the retaining wall a steep street called Zeyrek

Mehmet Paşa Sokağı leads up to Zeyrek Camii, the former Byzantine church of the Pantocrator.

The Pantocrator was founded by the emperor John II Comnenos and his wife, Eirene, whose mosaic portraits are in Haghia Sophia. The complex, erected within the period 1118–36, included a composite building that used to comprise a monastery with two churches and a funerary chapel between them. The monastery and the south church were built by the empress Eirene and dedicated to Christ Pantocrator. After Eirene's death in 1134 the emperor John erected a second church, dedicated to the Virgin Elousa (the Merciful or Charitable), a short distance to the north. When this was finished, John decided to join the two churches with a third church, dedicated to the Archangel Michael. This was designed to serve as a mortuary chapel for the imperial Comnenos dynasty, beginning with the empress Eirene, who was reburied there after its completion. John II was interred there after his death in 1143, and his son and successor Manuel I was buried there in 1180. During the first half of the fifteenth century the chapel also served as a mortuary for the Palaeologos family, the last dynasty to rule Byzantium, including two of the last three emperors: Manuel II, who died in 1425, and John VIII, who died in 1448. Buried alongside John was his wife, Maria of Trebizond, the last empress of Byzantium, who had died a few years before her husband.

Shortly after the Conquest, the Pantocrator was converted into a mosque by Molla Mustafa Zeyrek, and so it came to be called Zeyrek Camii. The conversion greatly altered the internal divisions of the building. At present the mosque is situated in what had been the south church.

A program of restoration and study of the Pantocrator has now been begun by Professor Robert Ousterhaut of the University of Illinois, together with Professors Metin and Zeynep Ahunbey of Istanbul Technical University. The roof and domes have been repaired, while a start has been made on a restoration and archaeological study of the building.

Despite the partial restoration, the Pantocrator is still as desolate as when I first saw it in the fall of 1960. The *imam,* then as now, was living in a wooden house inside the outer narthex, and his wife and children were staring at me curiously from the latticed windows, probably wondering why a foreigner would have come to see this ruinous old mosque. The previous evening I had read the travel memoir of the Burgundian pilgrim Bertrandon de la Broquière, who visited the church of the Pantocrator in the early 1430s in the company of John VIII Palaeologos and Maria of Trebizond. Bertrandon says that Maria was the most beautiful woman he

Panoramic view from the Third Hill west to the Fourth Hill, with the Aqueduct of Valens spanning the valley between them and the Mosque of the Conqueror on the horizon

had ever seen, but thought it a pity that she wore so much make-up. The emperor and empress were very interested in learning the fate of Joan of Arc, who had just been burnt at Rouen, and Bertrandon told them "the whole truth" about the "Maid of Orleans." And this was the scene in my mind's eye as I entered the Pantocrator at the time of my first visit.

Rahmi Koç has restored a ruined Ottoman building behind the Pantocrator to create an elegant restaurant–café called the Zeyrekhan, a good place to stop and rest while strolling around the Fourth Hill. There is an ambitious plan to restore the whole Zeyrek quarter, which is made up largely of old wooden Ottoman houses that are now in an advanced state of decay, one of the worst slums in the city. The quarter is inhabited principally by Arabic-speaking Turks from the region around Siirt in eastern Anatolia, who are living as squatters in the old houses, and the plans to restore Zeyrek run into the question of what to do with these people, for their rough Anatolian ways do not fit in with the gentrified neighborhood that the planners have in mind.

On my strolls around the city, I have observed that, the poorer and more run-down the neighborhood, the more children there are playing in the streets. At the time of my most recent visit to Zeyrek the streets were full of very lively children, and I was pleased to see that they were

above left
A street in the old city, with a venerable wooden house in the background on the left

above right
An Ottoman street-fountain in the baroque style, with its dedicatory inscription above

playing the same games I had observed when I first passed this way in 1960. These games are much the same as those I can remember playing as a child myself in New York – only the names are different, as I observed in the chapter on "Street Games" in my *Stamboul Sketches:* Blind Man's Buff is known here as *Korebe*, Tag is *Kovalamaca*, and Hopscotch is *Ayna Oynu,* "although the names of some of the games here seem more colorful than ours, such as 'The Prostitute's Bundle,' 'The Fish Fled,' 'The Velvet-Maker's Beauty,' and 'The Golden Cradle'."

Westward from the Pantocrator is the picturesque main square of the Zeyrek neighborhood and the former Byzantine church now known as Eski Imaret Camii. This has been identified as St. Savior Pantepoptes, Christ the All-Seeing, one of the most important Byzantine churches in the city. The church was founded before 1087 by the empress Anna Dalassena, the mother of Alexius I Comnenos. She established the Comneni dynasty which was to rule Byzantium with excellent authority throughout the eleventh and twelfth centuries. Anna was the power behind the throne for the first two decades of her son's reign. She retired in 1100 to the convent of the Pantepoptes, where she died and was buried five years later. The church was converted into a mosque almost immediately after the Conquest. It served for a time as the *imaret* of Fatih Cami, and hence the name Eski Imaret Camii. Up until recently it was a Kuran school for boys, who slept in the gallery above, but now it is once again serving as a mosque. The very intelligent *imam*, who is a dead ringer for the actor Robert Duval, has made the mosque a community center, receiving members of the congregation in his office in the narthex, his motor scooter parked in the outer narthex. On the walls of his office he has displayed an engraving of the building done in 1875 by Alexander Paspates, as well as a plan of the church, both of which I gave him in the early 1990s, pleased to see that this beautiful and historic structure was in good hands.

From Atatürk Bulvarı the view of the crest of the hill is framed by the Aqueduct of Valens. The aqueduct was completed in 368 by the emperor Valens, who a decade later was killed in battle by the Goths near Adrianople (Edirne). This impressive structure was kept in good repair by both Byzantine emperors and Ottoman sultans, and continued in use until the late nineteenth century. It was most recently restored in 1990. The arcade of the aqueduct, which carried water across the deep valley between the Fourth and Third Hills, was originally about a kilometer in length, of which some 625 meters remains standing. Its maximum height, where it spans the avenue, is 28–29 meters;

its maximum elevation above sea-level 63.5 meters. It consists of a single line of arches at the two ends and in the middle two superimposed sets of arches, whose procession across the valley gives a Roman aspect to the skyline of the city when viewed across the Golden Horn.

On the right of the avenue, before it reaches the aqueduct, there is a small classical *külliye*. This was founded by Gazanfer Ağa, who, as I noted earlier, succeeded his brother Cafer Ağa as chief of the white eunuchs under Süleyman the Magnificent. The *külliye* includes a small *medrese*, a charming *sebil* with grilled windows, and the *türbe* of the founder, in the form of a marble sarcophagus. The *medrese* now serves as the Caricature Museum, which had the distinction of being closed down briefly a decade ago when one of the cartoons on exhibit was considered by the then mayor of Istanbul as being an affront to his dignity.

After passing through the aqueduct, Atatürk Bulvarı crosses Şehzadebaşı Caddesi at Saraçhane, the old Ottoman Saddlers' Market. When the present traffic interchange was being built in the early 1960s, ancient architectural fragments came to light at the southwestern quadrant of the intersection, as I noticed one day as I was passing by in a taxi. An excavation was begun by Dumbarton Oaks under the supervision of Martin Harrison, who identified the remains as those of the famous church of St. Polyeuktos.

The church was built in the years 524–7 by the princess Anicia Juliana, a great-great-granddaughter of Theodosius I and daughter of Olybrius, emperor of the West. When completed, St. Polyeuktos rivaled and perhaps even surpassed in its magnificence the Theodosian church of Haghia Sophia, which was destroyed in the Nika Revolt of 532. Coin finds on the site indicate that the church was destroyed shortly after the reign of Isaac II Angelos (r. 1185–95, 1203–4), probably during the sack of Constantinople by the Latins in 1204, as evidenced by architectural members from St. Polyeuktos found in western Europe, particularly in Venice. At present only a single column remains standing on the archaeological site, and there is not even a sign to tell the passer-by that this is the great church of Anicia Juliana praised in the dedicatory inscription found here and now preserved outside the Archaeological Museum, who in her dedication proudly stated that her edifice surpassed Solomon's temple in its grandeur. When Justinian erected the new church of Haghia Sophia in the years 532–7, he took pains to make it even larger and grander than St. Polyeuktos, leading him to exclaim that he too had surpassed Solomon.

To the west of the archaeological site is the picturesque *külliye* of

The prayer hall of
Şehzade Camii

Amcazade Hüseyin Pasha, an ornate example of the smaller classical complexes, which was founded of the illustrious Köprülü family. Hüseyin Pasha, the founder, was a cousin (in Turkish, *amcazade*) of Fazil Ahmet Pasha, and was the fourth member of the family to serve as grand vezir. He held that post under Mustafa II in the years 1697–1702, when he founded this somewhat romantically chaotic *külliye,* which includes a small octagonal mosque, a large school above a row of shops, a library, a *medrese,* two small graveyards with open *türbes,* a *sebil,* a *şadırvan,* and a *çeşme.* The *külliye* has been restored in recent years and now serves as the Museum of Turkish Architectural and Constructional Elements. However, it never seems to be open. Early in the 1990s I came here with a large class from the University of the Bosphorus, and my students noisily demonstrated outside until the curator, with great reluctance, finally allowed us to enter. Then the curator, an otherwise pleasant woman of middle years, looked at me with curiosity as I pointed out the most interesting exhibit in the museum, the two-meter high pinnacle of one of the minarets of Fatih Camii, toppled but otherwise undamaged in the great earthquake of 1894.

An ancient mosque called Dülgerzade Camii, built some time before 1482 by Şemsettin Habib Efendi, one of Fatih's officials, is located further along the avenue. The side street to the left beyond the mosque leads to an ancient monument known locally as Kız Taşı, the Maiden's Stone. Kız Taşı is actually a Roman honorific column, some 17 meters high, commemorating the emperor Marcian (r. 450–57), who was represented by an equestrian statue surmounting the monument. On the base fragments of sculpture remain, including two Nikes, or Winged Victories, in high relief, which led to the column being called the Maiden's Stone. Evliya listed the Maiden's Stone as the third of the ancient city's talismans, giving this brief but characteristically fabulous description of its magic powers, where the Puzantin whom he mentions is an obvious corruption of "Byzantine": "At the head of the Saddlers' Market, on the summit of a column stretching to the skies, there is a chest of white marble in which the unlucky daughter of King Puzantin lies buried; and to preserve her remains from ants and serpents was this column made a talisman."

Another little *külliye* is situated farther along the avenue. This is the *medrese* founded in 1700 by the Şeyh-ül Islam Feyzullah Efendi, a great scholar and one of the most enlightened men of his time. The *medrese* now houses the People's Library of Istanbul, one of the most important centers of Ottoman historical research in the city.

Two old men in the
courtyard of the Mosque
of the Conqueror
Fatih Camii, the imperial mosque complex of Mehmet the Conqueror, is across the avenue. The massive walls along the right side of the street are the backs of the *medreses* attached to the mosque complex. It can be approached by a right turn off the avenue on to Aslanhane Sokağı, the Street of the Lion House, which borders the eastern end of the *külliye*.

Fatih's grand mosque complex was the the largest and most extravagant *külliye* in the entire Ottoman Empire. An inscription records that the complex was built in the years 1461–5 and that the architect was Atik Sinan, who was probably a Greek named Christodoulos. Besides the great mosque itself, the *külliye* consisted of eight *medreses* and their annexes, together with a hospital, public kitchen, caravansarai, primary school, public bath, and a graveyard with two *türbes*.

The original mosque built by Fatih was devastated by an earthquake on May 22, 1766. Work immediately began on its reconstruction, and the present mosque, designed on a completely different plan, was finished in 1772. The courtyard, the graveyard's southern wall and adjoining gate, the main entrance portal of the mosque, the minarets up to the first balcony, and the *mihrap*, are probably the only residue of the Fatih's original complex. The other buildings in the *külliye* were probably restored to their original design by Mustafa III after they were badly damaged in the earthquake.

The graveyard behind the mosque contains the *türbes* of Fatih and his wife Gülbahar, mother of Beyazit II, both tombs having been reconstructed after the 1776 earthquake, on the original foundations. The baroque *türbe* of Fatih has an opulent "Empire style" interior. It was customary for a new sultan to come to this *türbe* straight after being girded with the sword of Osman Gazi in Eyüp, a ceremony equivalent to coronation. The interior walls of Fatih's *türbe* were hung with swords and other weapons captured in victorious Ottoman campaigns, the sight of which was meant to inspire the new sultan to emulate his great ancestor. Fatih's *türbe* also became a popular shrine, and a cult of emperor worship grew up around his tomb and those of several other warrior sultans, most notably Süleyman. Whenever I visit Fatih's *türbe* I always see worshipers there, praying directly to the large turban affixed to the head of his catafalque.

Gülbahar's *türbe* is striking for its classical simplicity, and thus probably resembles the original more closely than that of Fatih. According to one apocryphal legend, Gülbahar was the King of France's daughter who had been sent as a bride for Constantine XI Dragases, the last emperor of Byzantium. She was then taken prisoner by the Turks when they besieged the city, after which she was placed in Fatih's harem. Despite being the wife of Fatih and Beyazit's mother, it is alleged that Gülbahar rejected Islam and died a Christian. Evliya recounts a version of this legend in his description of Gülbahar's *türbe*.

The Mosque of the Conqueror, with some of its *medreses* in the foreground

I myself have often observed, at morning prayer, that the readers appointed to chant lessons from the Kuran all turned their backs upon the coffin of this lady, of whom it was so doubtful whether she departed in the faith of Islam. I have often seen Franks [Europeans] come by stealth and give a few aspers to the tomb-keeper to open her türbe for them, as its gate is always kept locked.

This story is also told by the Italian traveler Cornelio Magni, writing at about the same time. He says the tomb-keeper persuaded him that Gülbahar was a Christian princess who lived and died in her faith. According to Magni: "The tomb remains always shut, even the windows. I asked the reason for this and was told: 'The sepulcher of her whose soul lives among the shades deserves not a ray of light.'" After much entreaty and the intervention of an emir who passed by, the tombkeeper let him in. "I entered with veneration and awe," he says, "and silently recited a *De profundis* for the soul of this unfortunate Princess."

The neighborhood around Fatih Camii has always been the most Muslim quarter of Istanbul, and one almost has the feeling of being in Iran rather than Turkey, particularly with the resurgence of Islam in recent years.

During our first year in Istanbul, we visited Fatih Camii one evening on *Kadır Gecesi,* the Night of Power, which commemorates the *Miraç,* the ascension of the Prophet Mohammed into heaven. *Kadır Gecesi* is considered to be the most sacred and mysterious night in the year. All the elements in nature – humans, animals, plants, and even inanimate objects – are said to feel the mystical forces generated on that night, and to give token of their subservience to the omnipotent creator. It is believed, too, that on this night there are written down in the Book of Fate the names of those who are to die during the coming year. As the Kuran says of *Kadir Gecesi:*

Verily we sent down the Kuran in the night of al'Kadir. And what shall make thee understand how excellent is the night of al'Kadir? The night of al'Kadir is better than a thousand months. Therein do the angels descend and the spirit of Gabriel, also, by the permission of their Lord, with his decrees concerning every matter. It is peace till the rising of the morn.

9

THE FIFTH AND SIXTH HILLS

The neighborhood to the west of Fatih Camii, the Mosque of the Conqueror, is called Çarşamba, or Wednesday. This takes its name from the street market that has thronged the streets of this quarter every Wednesday for centuries past. There are neighborhoods elsewhere in Istanbul named for other days of the week where such traveling markets set up there stalls, but none of them can be compared to the Çarşamba Pazarı, which does business in this part of the Fatih district for many blocks in all directions.

At the end of Yavuz Selim Caddesi the imperial mosque of Selim I stands in its walled garden at the far side of an enormous Roman reservoir. The reservoir has been identified as the Cistern of Aspar, constructed by a Gothic general executed by the emperor Leo I in 471. This is the second largest of the three great Roman reservoirs in the city, all of them built in the fifth century to store water in the event of a siege by the bar-

barians who were invading the Balkans. The reservoir, which has been dry for many centuries, is square in plan, 152 meters on each side, and was formerly 10 meters deep.

Until the late 1970s the reservoir was the site of a very picturesque village of old wooden houses, whose roofs and the tops of the trees that embowered them barely reached the level of Yavuz Selim Caddesi. The first time I passed this way, in the spring of 1961, there was a stork nesting atop the minaret of the village mosque, perched at the same level as the street on which I was walking. I looked down and saw an old man surrounded by peacocks, several of whom were flaring their gorgeous tails in a rainbow-like display of colors. Later, when I descended into the reservoir, I learned that he was the *imam* of the mosque and that he raised peacocks for sale, and I wondered, but did not ask, who would buy such exotic creatures, which I imagined would be a suitable present for a princess. He told me that the name of the village was Çukur Bostan, the Sunken Garden, which Evliya mentions in his description of the mosque of Selim I. But this little paradise was demolished in the late 1970s to make way for a huge parking lot, as I discovered when I returned to Istanbul after a long absence, looking in vain for the peacocks that once adorned the Sunken Garden.

Beyond the reservoir is the Selimiye, the mosque of Selim I, which crowns a spur of the Fifth Hill overlooking the Golden Horn. The *külliye* was built by an unknown architect for Süleyman the Magnificent, who dedicated it to the memory of his father, Selim I. It was completed in 1522, the first imperial mosque of Süleyman's reign. With its wide, shallow dome and gathering of smaller domes to the sides, the mosque is one of the principal adornments on the skyline of the old city when viewed from across the Golden Horn.

Selim I is buried in the graveyard garden behind it, in an octagonal *türbe*. Evliya knew this *türbe* well, as he notes in his *Seyahatname:* "There is no royal sepulcher which fills the visitor with so much awe as Selim's. There he lies with the turban called Selimiye on his coffin like a seven-headed dragon. I, the humble Evliya, was for three years the reader of hymns at his *türbe*."

Abdül Mecit died in 1861 having chosen to have his *türbe* close to that of Selim as a mark of admiration for his great ancestor. Abdül Mecit's conquests – unlike those of Selim – were restricted to the Harem, fathering forty-two children with twenty-one wives and concubines. His sons included the last four sultans: Murat V, Abdül Hamit II, Mehmet V, and Mehmet VI, who presided over the final destruction of the Ottoman Empire.

Manyasizade Caddesi leads to Ismail Ağa Camıı. Built by the Şeyh-ül Islam Ismail Efendi in 1724, this delightful building is a fine example of a work in a traditional style between the classical and the baroque. Further long the same avenue and to the right lies another fine Ottoman library, founded in 1775 by Damatzade Murat Molla, a distin-guished judge and man of letters. This is an attractive and characteristi-cally eighteenth-century Ottoman library, comparable to those of Atıf Efendi and Ragıp Paşa.

The area also boasts a little Byzantine church down a side street off Manyasizade Caddesi. This is known as Ahmet Paşa Mescidi, which has been identified tentatively as the former Byzantine church of St. John the Baptist in Trullo. The church's Byzantine history continues to be unknown, but from its architecture it probably dates to the twelfth or thirteenth century. The church remained in the hands of the Greeks until 1586, when Hirami Ahmet Paşa (from whom it derives its name) converted it into a mosque. During my early years in Istanbul, it was abandoned and ruinous, but now it has been well restored and is once again serving as a mosque. It is a charming little building, set in the cen-ter of what must have been a little *plateia* on the Fifth Hill. Looking like the Byzantine chapels one sees on the Greek islands, here it is in the middle of a sprawling Turkish city, a veritable miracle of survival, still serving as a house of God.

A much larger and grander Byzantine building lies further along and to the right of Manyasizade Caddesi. This is Fethiye Camii, the for-mer church of the Theotokos Pammakaristos, Mother of God the All Blessed, standing on an artificial terrace on the ridge linking the Fifth and Sixth Hills.

This complicated building comprises the main church together with a later *parekklesion,* or side chapel, to the south, both of which were altered in the late Byzantine period and then radically changed when the building was converted into a mosque. The *parekklesion* was convert-ed into a museum after restoration by the Byzantine Institute of America, while the rest of the building serves as a mosque.

The main church was built in the reign of Alexius I Comnenos (r. 1081–1118) by the emperor's brother-in-law and his wife, Anna Doukaina. Toward the end of the thirteenth century, the church was rebuilt by a general named Michael Doukas Glabas Tarchaniotes. Then, c. 1310, a *parekklesion* was added on the south side of the church by Michael's widow, Maria Doukina Comnena Palaeologina Blachena, who erected it as a funerary chapel for her departed husband.

Mosaic of St. Gregory the Theologian, in the conch of the side chapel to the right of the apse of the parekklesion of Fethiye Camii

Ο ΑΓ[ΙΟ]C ΓΡΗΓΟΡΙΟC

After the Conquest the church remained in Greek hands, becoming, in 1456, the site of the Greek Orthodox Patriarchate after the Church of the Holy Apostles had been abandoned by Gennadius, the first Ecumenical Patriarch under the Ottomans. It remained the site of the Patriarchate until 1568. In 1573, Murat III converted the church into a house of Islamic worship and named it Fethiye Camii (the Mosque of the Conquest) in honor of his conquest of Georgia and Azerbaijan.

During the conversion, most of the interior walls were demolished to increase the available space, and the *parekklesion* became part of the prayer room. After restoration by the Byzantine Institute, the main building was divided off from the side chapel and reconstituted as a mosque, while the *parekklesion* was converted into a museum to exhibit the surviving mosaics. The mosaics, which dated to c. 1310, are, in my opinion, among the finest works of the Byzantine Renaissance.

This section of the main avenue takes the name Fethiye Caddesi and leads to the small mosque of Draman Camii, situated on a high terrace which is accessible by a double staircase. This is the center of a little *külliye*

The prayer hall of the Selimiye, the mosque of Selim I

overleaf
Fresco of the
Anastasis, or
Resurrection, in the
conch of the parekkle-
sion of Kariye Camii,
the former church of
Christ in Chora

founded (as inscriptions show) in 1541 by Yunus Bey. He was Süleyman the Magnificent's well-known interpreter, which translates as *drağman,* or dragoman, in Turkish. The complex also includes a *medrese* and a *mektep* built by Sinan.

The main avenue changes its name again, this time to Draman Caddesi and stretches towards a Byzantine building now known as Kefevi Camii, formerly called Kefeli Camii. This interesting building is in good condition and is still used as a mosque. The entrance to the long and narrow structure, which has two rows of windows and a wooden roof, is in the center of the western wall. Its identification is uncertain; it could have been the property of the Monastery of the Prodromos (St. John the Baptist) in Petra, which is known to have been located in this area, but the building was probably a refectory rather than a church. Current estimates of its date range from the ninth century to the Palaeologan era.

When Armenians from Kaffa in the Crimea were moved to Istanbul in 1475, they were given this building as a church, which was dedicated to St. Nicholas and used by both Roman Catholic and Gregorian Armenians. Then in 1629–30 it was converted to a mosque, whose name, Kefeli, is a corruption of Kaffali, meaning "from Kaffa."

To the left of Kefevi Camii, Selma Tomruk Caddei goes up the northern slope of the Sixth Hill to Fevzi Paşa Caddesi. On the left there is another of the three enormous Roman reservoirs that still survive in the city. This is the Cistern of Aetios, named for the Prefect of Constantinople who built it in 421. Even though it seems large, it is actually the smallest of the three reservoirs, at 224 meters long, 85 meters wide, and originally 15 meters deep. All three cisterns fell out of use in the late Byzantine era. This one was used as a kitchen garden before, in the late 1960s, it was converted into a football stadium, the Vefa Stadium. I can remember seeing the last of its Roman vaults being covered up when the spectators' seats were installed.

Away to the right, Kariye Camii, the former church of Christ in Chora, stands on the Sixth Hill about 150 meters inside the Theodosian walls. The name of the church, "in Chora," means "in the country," because the original church and monastery were outside the city limits, beyond the walls of Constantine. The name also had a symbolic sense: inscriptions on mosaics in the church refer to Christ as the "country" or "land" of the living, and to the Virgin Mary as the "dwelling-place of the Uncontainable."

The building in its original form was founded in the years 1077–81 by Maria Doukina, mother-in-law of Alexius I Comnenos, and is likely to

have been built in the contemporary four-column style. However, the original church was short-lived as the eastern foundations seem to have slipped, causing the apses to fall in. The opportunity to elaborately redesign the building was probably taken early in the twelfth century by the *sebastocrator* Isaac Comnenos, third son of Alexius I and grandson of Maria Doukina.

The present church was constructed during a further period of activity some two centuries later. The nave area remained virtually unchanged, but new additions included an outer narthex and the *parekklesion* while the inner narthex was rebuilt, to name only the major changes. Along with these structural alterations, the church was completely redecorated, its interior adorned with the superb marble revetment, mosaics, and frescoes that are here today. All of this rebuilding and redecoration was carried out in the years 1315–21 by Theodore Metochites, a leading figure in the Byzantine renaissance who served as both Prime Minister and First Lord of the Treasury during the reign of Andronicus II Palaeologos. As his friend the historian Nicephorus Gregoras wrote of Metochites:

From morning to evening he was most wholly and eagerly devoted to public affairs as if scholarship was absolutely indifferent to him, but later in the evening, having left the palace, he became absorbed in science to such a degree as if he were a scholar with absolutely no connection with any other affairs.

The peak of Metochites' career came in 1321, when he was appointed Grand Logothete, or Prime Minister, just weeks before he presided at the dedication of the newly rebuilt and rededicated church of Christ in Chora. But his career ended abruptly seven years later, when Andronicus III usurped the throne, after which Metochites was sent into exile, along with most other officials of the old regime. He was allowed to return to the capital in 1330, on condition that he retired as a monk to the monastery of the Chora, where he died on March 13, 1332. Toward the end of his life Metochites wrote of his hope that the church of Christ in Chora would secure for him "a glorious memory among posterity till the end of the world."

Early in the sixteenth century the Chora was converted into a mosque called Kariye Camii by the eunuch Atik Ali Pasha, grand vezir under Beyazit II. The mosaics and frescoes were never completely covered, but over time most were obscured by plaster and paint, or didn't survive the earthquakes. The church and its works of art were generally unknown to the scholarly world until 1860, when the Greek architect

Pelopidda Kouppas brought them to the attention of Byzantinists in the West. In 1948 the Byzantine Institute of America, under the direction of Paul A. Underwood, began a project to uncover the surviving mosaics and frescoes and to restore them and the fabric of the church to their original condition. After a series of eleven annual campaigns the project was carried through to completion in 1958, and since then Kariye Camii, the former church of Christ in Chora, has been open to the public as a museum.

The mosaics fall into seven quite distinct groups, four of which are cycles of the Life of Christ and the Blessed Virgin, the others being individual mosaics, including dedicatory and devotional panels. One of the most notable of the latter shows the Enthroned Christ with Donor, in the inner narthex in the lunette over the door to the nave, in which Metochites, wearing a huge turban, offers a model of his church to Christ.

The final part of Metochites' decoration, probably carried out in 1320–22, was on the wonderful frescoes of the *parekklesion*. The chapel's decoration reveals its purpose as a burial place. The paintings above the level of the cornice illustrate the Resurrection and the Life, Heaven and Hell, the Last Judgment, and the Mother of God.

The *parekklesion* houses four tombs set in deep niches that originally held sarcophagi. Some fragments of the mosaics and frescoes still survive. The easternmost of the two tombs in the north wall is very probably that of Theodore Metochites, distinguished by its ornately carved and decorated archivolt above. The tomb directly opposite this is that of Michael Tornikes, a general who was a close friend of Metochites, identified by a lengthy inscription over the archivolt.

There are three tombs in arcosolia, or funerary recesses, in the north wall of the outer narthex, two of them preserving part of their fresco decoration. There is also one tomb in an arcosolium in the inner narthex. This is the grave of the despot Demetrius Doukas Angelos Palaeologos, youngest son of Andronicus II Palaeologos, who died c. 1340. Only a small part of the fresco decoration has survived, and the only intact figure is that of the Virgin. Beneath her a fragmentary inscription reads: "Thou art the Fount of Life, Mother of God the Word, and I, Demetrius, am thy slave in love."

When I look back upon my many visits to Kariye Camii, one in particular stands out. One day, in the mid-1990s, I led a group of Greek Orthodox seminarians on a tour of the Byzantine monuments of the city. They had been carefully instructed by the Greek Orthodox Patriarchate not to make any display of their religious feelings, particularly in Haghia Sophia. The seminarians behaved circumspectly in Haghia Sophia, and all went well on the rest of the tour until we entered

left
The dome of the parekklesion of Fethiye Camii, showing the mosaic of Christ Pantocrator surrounded by twelve Prophets

the *parekklesion* of the Chora and saw the fresco of the Resurrection. There they finally lost control of their pent-up feelings, and when one of them began chanting the Easter Hymn of Resurrection the others joined in at top volume. The Turkish watchman rushed into the side chapel to stop the demonstration, shouting that this was a museum and not a church, and the seminarians ceased their singing with a final exclamation of *"Christos Anestis!"* or "Christ is Risen!"

As we left Kariye Camii, one of the seminarians turned to me and said "But the Chora is still a church, and so is Haghia Sophia, aren't they, sir?" I couldn't answer him, such was the weight of history in that simple question.

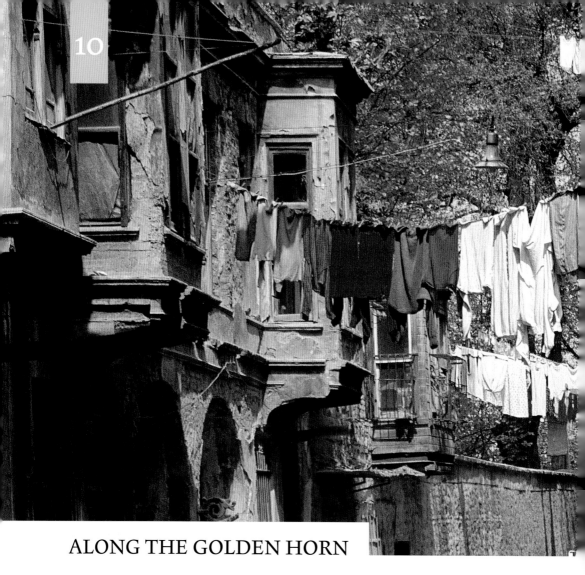

10

ALONG THE GOLDEN HORN

I first strolled along the Golden Horn, starting at the Atatürk Bridge and going all the way to Eyüp, the most important Muslim shrine in Istanbul, in the early fall of 1960. The buildings of the old city came right down to the water, which was fringed by boatyards and the shacks of artisans, interspersed with wooden *iskeles,* where boatmen would row passengers across to the other side for a single copper coin, as had their predecessors for centuries past. But then in the early 1970s Mayor Bedrettin Dalan demolished all the structures along the shore to make way for a park, which was much praised by people who knew nothing about Istanbul. The park is hardly used by the people who live in the old neighborhoods along the shore, and no one walks along the seaside "promenade" because of the sometimes overpowering stench from the Golden Horn, which is still an open sewer despite wildly expensive and highly publicized projects to clean it up. The old boatmen can still be

Street scene in one of the old neighborhoods along the Golden Horn

found around the *iskeles* of the Golden Horn ferries, though these days they have very few customers since the neighborhoods on both sides are now slums. On my strolls I sometimes ask one of the boatmen to take me across, just for old times' sake, and we chat about places along the shore now gone for ever, such as the Sea Museum of Yaşar Artiste, or the moored caique-taverns where the boatmen and their passengers could pause for a raki at the end of a crossing.

There are numerous fragments of the Byzantine sea-walls up the shore road past the Atatürk Bridge. The sea-walls along the Golden Horn began at Saray Burnu, below the acropolis on the First Hill, where they met the maritime defense-walls along the Marmara, both of them extending along the shore to join the two ends of the land-walls. The walls along the Golden Horn were repaired or reconstructed on a number of occasions during the Byzantine era, most notably in the second quarter of the ninth century by the emperor Theophilus. Comprising a solitary line of walls about 7 kilometers long and 10 meters high, the Golden Horn fortifications were dotted at consistent intervals with 110 defense towers. The solid line of the sea-walls was also broken by about twenty gates and posterns. The remnants of one, the Porta Hebraica, are near the mosque where Evliya had his fabulous dream. Aside from that, only two ancient gateways remain and fragments of a third, although the locations of the others can easily be determined, since the streets that lead into the old neighborhoods along the Golden Horn converge on the sites of these ancient portals, whose Turkish names are still used and appear on street signs.

The huge building of the new Kadir Has University, a private institution founded at the beginning of the new millennium, is a short way beyond the Atatürk Bridge. The university is housed in the former Cıbalı Tobacco Factory, one of the first modern industrial establishments in the Ottoman Empire, built in 1884. The factory took its name from that of the Cıbalı quarter, the first of the old neighborhoods that along the Golden Horn. Excavations made during the conversion to a university revealed Byzantine substructures, which are now exposed to view for the benefit of visitors.

One of the surviving gates in the sea-walls, the ancient Porta Puteae, known in Turkish as Cıbalı Kapı, is nearby. A modern plaque beside the gate commemorates the breaching of the walls here by the Ottomans on May 29, 1453, the day that the city was taken by Mehmet II. On April 12, 1204, this gate also faced the positioning of the far left flank of the Venetian fleet when the Latin knights of the Fourth Crusade captured and sacked the city.

The Greek Orthodox church of Haghios Nikolaos (St. Nicholas) is about 250 meters past Cıbalı Kapı. The church is housed in one of the so-called "meta-Byzantine" houses that are shown in late Ottoman engravings, a continuous line of them standing on the shore of the Golden Horn with their backs to the sea-walls. The name comes from the supposition that these houses were built in the early Ottoman era in the Byzantine style, that is, brick and stone structures whose upper stories projected out on corbels. Only a very few of these buildings now stand along the Golden Horn, most of them abandoned and falling into ruins.

Initially, the church of St. Nicholas was a *metochion,* or dependency, of the Vathopedi Monastery on Mount Athos, the semi-autonomous peninsular theocracy on the Aegean coast of northern Greece. When I visited the monastery in the early 1970s, the abbot showed me the *typikon,* or charter, of this church on the Golden Horn. The earliest recorded mention of St. Nicholas is by the German traveler Stefan Gerlach in 1573, although the present church dates from a rebuilding in 1837.

In the exonarthex of the church there is an *ayazma,* or holy well, dedicated to St. Charalambos, which also has a separate entrance from the street outside. There are many hundreds of these holy wells and springs

left
The dome and supporting arches of Gül Camii

below
Gül Camii, the former church of St. Theodosia, overlooking the Golden Horn

in and around the city, a few of them datable back to early Byzantine times. The waters of these *ayazma* are considered to have miraculous curative properties, and are still popular among the people of Istanbul, Muslims as well as Christians, as I have learned in talking to those I meet at these subterranean wells and springs.

A left turn off the shore road, just beyond the church, passes through Aya Kapı, the Holy Gate, a small postern in the Byzantine sea-walls. Known in Byzantine times as the Gate of St. Theodosia, it led to a church of that name. The building that has been identified as that famous church, now known as Gül Camii, is a short way inside the gateway.

Petrus Gyllius was the first to identify Gül Camii as the former church of St. Theodosia, and, although recent scholarship has led to some doubt about this, most scholars still agree with Gyllius. There has also been considerable discussion about the date of the church, current opinion placing it in the twelfth century.

The church figured prominently in the final hours of Byzantine history, for the emperor Constantine XI Dragases stopped to pray here after his final visit to Haghia Sophia in the evening of May 28, 1453, since the following day was the feast day of St. Theodosia. After the city fell on the morning of May 29, the first Turkish soldiers who made their way into the church found that it was adorned with roses because of Theodosia's feast day. After the church was converted to a house of Islamic worship, it was called Gül Camii, the Mosque of the Rose, perpetuating one of the enduring traditions of the Turkish Conquest.

This is in my opinion one of the most beautiful of the extant Byzantine churches of the city, preserved in almost perfect condition, a domed basilica with side aisles and a western ambulatory surmounted by galleries. The dome is supported by four piers, of which the two on the east each contain a small chamber above the floor. These may have tombs of saints whose relics were venerated in the church, one of whom would have been St. Theodosia, martyred in 726 because of the iconoclastic policy of Leo III.

When I first visited Gül Camii in 1960, one could still gain entrance to the chamber in the southeast pier, but this has now been closed off. The chamber is approached by a helical stairway of thirteen steps, which I ascended by the light of a candle in a niche halfway up, accompanied by the old *imam*. When we stopped by the niche I saw that it contained a perfectly preserved skull, which glowed in the flickering light of the candle. I looked at the *imam,* but he simply raised his eyes to heaven and led me on to the chamber at the top of the stairway. There I saw a catafalque covered with a green embroidered cloth, identified by an inscription in Ottoman Turkish, which van Millingen has translated as: "Tomb of the Apostles, disciples of Christ, peace be to him."

A Greek tradition, first mentioned in 1852, in a letter from the Patriarch Constantius to the scholar Scarlatos Byzantios, has it that the chamber in the southeast pier of Gül Camii was the tomb of Constantine XI Dragases. According to the patriarch, this tradition had long been current among the Greeks of the city, who believed that Constantine was secretly buried here after his remains were identified at the Fifth Military Gate, where he died in battle against the Turks when they broke into the city. Many of my older Greek friends still believe in this tradition, and in times past they visited the supposed tomb of Constantine in Gül Camii, but the younger generation is more skeptical. The old *imam* who first led me to this chamber had a different opinion, saying that it was the tomb of Gül Baba, a Turkish saint who was the eponymous founder of Gül Camii.

Further up the Golden Horn, a short distance beyond Aya Kapı, there is another portal in the sea-walls, called Yeni (New) Aya Kapı. This was built in 1582 by Sinan, rather than being one of the original gateways in the Byzantine sea-walls. A bath, the Havuzlu Hamam, probably also by Sinan, was founded outside the walls at this point by the *valide sultan* Nur Banu, wife of Selim II and mother of Murat III. Local residents petitioned the Divan to create a gate here for easy access to it. I came upon this bath on my very first stroll along the Golden Horn, in September 1960, when it was already in an advanced state of ruin, and I keep hoping that some day it will be restored.

Beyond Yeni Aya Kapı a street named Sadrazam (Grand Vezir) Ali Paşa Caddesi veers off at a slight angle to the left from the shore road. The Gate of the Petrion, an opening in the Byzantine sea-walls, is sited here. A type of walled enclave, dating from the reign of Justinian, the Petrion comprised the lower slope of the Fifth Hill down to the Golden Horn, and the gate formed the eastern entryway to the enclosure through the sea-walls.

The naval assaults upon the sea-walls by both the Crusaders and the Turks give the Petrion an important place in the history of Istanbul. Doge Dandolo's Venetian galleys sailed right up against the sea-walls of the Petrion in their first assault upon the city on July 13, 1203, capturing twenty-five defense towers. The assault was described by the French knight Villehardouin, in his chronicle of the Fourth Crusade:

The Doge of Venice, though an old man [he was nearly ninety] and totally blind, stood at the prow of his galley with the banner of St. Mark unfurled before him. He cried out to his men to put him on shore or he would deal with them as they deserved. They obeyed him instantly, for the galley touched ground and the men in it leaped ashore, carrying the banner of St. Mark to land before the Doge.

On April 12, 1204, during the Crusader's last assault, the Petrion was again in the thick of things when two knights jumped from the flying-bridge of the galley *Pelerine* onto a defense tower. They then began the attack that was to breach the walls and result in the capture and sack of the city.

The Ottoman fleet attacked the Petrion early in the morning of May 29, 1453. It withstood the assault but the defenders subsequently surrendered, having learned that the city had been taken after the land-walls were breached. Since the Petrion was surrendered, rather than captured, Fatih allowed the area to be exempt from the sacking endured by the rest of the city. Evliya writes that because of this the fishermen of the Petrion "are even now free from all kinds of duties and give no tithe to the Inspector of the Fisheries."

Away from the shore road, Sadrazam Ali Paşa Caddesi leads to the entrance of the Ecumenical Patriarchate, the spiritual center of the Greek Orthodox church and of Orthodox Christianity in general. The Greek Orthodox Patriarchate has been established on its present site since 1599, after having been housed temporarily in two other churches after it was forced to leave the Pammakaristos in 1568. The patriarchal church of Haghios Georgios (St. George), first mentioned by Stefan Gerlach in 1573, has been rebuilt and expanded several times, taking on its present basilical form in the mid-nineteenth century. The church and the other buildings of the patriarchate house a rich collection of Byzantine and post-Byzantine paintings and other works of art, the most notable, in my opinion, being a beautiful portative mosaic icon of the Virgin dating from the eleventh century. The church also has a number of sacred relics, most notably the porphyry column to which Christ was supposedly tied when he was scourged during his Passion.

The first service I attended at this church was on the eve of Orthodox Easter in 1961, when the Patriarch Athenagoras presided, looking like an Old Testament prophet with his towering stature and long white beard. I had met Athenagoras a few weeks before, quite by chance, in a Greek grocery store in the village of Bebek on the European shore of the Bosphorus. He heard me speaking American English to a friend and came over to introduce himself, asking me where I was from, beginning a very pleasant chat without any pretension whatsoever, while the Greek staff of the store stood by in awe as if they were in the presence of God Almighty.

Soon after I returned to Istanbul in 1993, I was introduced to the present Ecumenical Patriarch, Bartholomeus, who told me that he had read *Strolling Through Istanbul*. Bartholomeus told me of his project to restore some of the old Greek Orthodox churches in Istanbul, many of which are now seldom, if ever, used because of the decline in the Greek population of the city. He also makes a point of going to services at these churches as often as possible, so as to bring them back into the life of the Greek community.

Sadrazam Ali Paşa Caddesi comes to an end a short distance beyond the Patriarchate. The short street that leads out to the shore road at this point ends at the site of the ancient Porta Phanari, the Gate of the Lighthouse, known in Turkish, though it has long since disappeared, as Fener Kapısı, which gave its name to this famous quarter.

The Feneriotes, the Greeks of this quarter, began to find great commercial success in the early sixteenth century, and a number of them rose to high office under the sultan, most notably as *hospodars* of Moldavia and Wallachia, client principalities of the Ottoman Empire. Much of this wealth was brought back to the Fener, where the *hospodars* erected a palace and other notables built mansions, a few of which survive as the "meta-Byzantine" houses along the Golden Horn.

Beyond Fener Kapısı and to the left, a stepped lane goes up the slope of the Fifth Hill, passing the eastern gateway to an enormous walled enclosure. This was one of the entrances to the palace known in Turkish as Vlach Saray, the residence of the Greek *hospodars* of Moldavia and Wallachia, which has long since disappeared. Beside the gate there is a plaque with a portrait relief of Demetrius Cantemir, a Feneriote Greek who in 1710 became *hospodar* of Wallachia, residing here in Vlach Saray whenever he was in Istanbul.

Within the walls that once enclosed Vlach Saray there are two Greek Orthodox churches, one of them in ruins. The ruined church, which burnt down in 1976, was dedicated to the Panaghia Paramithias, St. Mary the Consoler, which was the site of the Greek Orthodox Patriarchate in the years 1586–96. It also served as the chapel for the palace of the *hospodars* of Moldavia and Wallachia. One can catch a glimpse of the ruins from the street that passes the western side of the enclosure, where there is a gap in the walls. One day in 1976, I made my way through that gap to look at the ruins of the church, which had

burnt down the night before, its walls still smoldering, and I tried to help as some priests from the Patriarchate attempted to rescue what remained of the sacred icons and other treasures.

An old boatman waiting to ferry passengers across the Golden Horn

The other church, which can be visited via a gate in the enclosure wall on Vodina Caddesi, is Haghios Georgios Metochi. The first mention of this church is in 1583, by Tryphon Karabeinikov, who had been sent by the czar Ivan the Terrible to distribute funds to the Orthodox churches in Istanbul. It has been the Metochion of the Jerusalem Patriarchate since the seventeenth century, hence the last part of its name. A careful study of the manuscripts of the church was made in 1906 by the Danish scholar J. L. Heiberg, who discovered in palimpsest a perfect and complete copy made in the tenth century of Archimedes' *Method of Treating Mechanical Problems, Dedicated to Eratosthenes,* written in Alexandria c. 250 BC. Every year, when I teach my course in the History of Science at the University of the Bosphorus, I have one of my best physics or mathematics students do a paper on this manuscript, which is per-

haps the most important extant work of Archimedes, in which he laid the foundations for the integral calculus, nineteen centuries before Newton and Leibniz.

At the top of the steps and to the left stands a rust-red Byzantine church with a high drum supporting its dome. Even though the church is dedicated to the Theotokos he Panaghiotissa, the All-Holy Mother of God, it is usually referred to as the Panaghia Mouchliotissa, or St. Mary of the Mongols. The building has little architectural interest, but it is important historically as the only Byzantine church in the city to have remained continuously in the hands of the Greeks since before the Turkish Conquest.

Princess Maria Palaeologina, illegitimate daughter of Michael VIII Palaeologos, either founded or rebuilt the church c. 1282. Her father sent her to marry Hulagu, the Great Khan of the Mongols, in 1265, but he died before she reached him. Instead, she married his son, the new Khan Abagu, and lived at the Mongol court in Persia. The Khan and many of his court converted to Christianity due to Maria's influence. However, when Abagu was murdered by his brother Ahmet in 1282, she had to return to Constantinople, where the emperor Michael offered her hand to Charabanda, another Khan. She refused, having decided to retire as a nun and founded this church, together with a convent, dedicated to the Mouchliotissa, Our Lady of the Mongols. The Princess Maria, now known as the Despoina (Lady) of the Mongols, spent the rest of her days in the convent of the Mouchliotissa.

A decade or so after the Turkish Conquest, Mehmet II was persuaded by his Greek architect Christodoulos (who is probably Atik Sinan, architect of Fatih Camii) to issue a *firman,* or royal decree, confirming the right of the local Greeks to retain possession of the Mouchliotissa, whereas all of the other Byzantine churches in the city were eventually converted into mosques except for Haghia Eirene, which was taken over by the Janissaries. The Greeks remain in possession of the Mouchliotissa to the present day, and Fatih's *firman* is displayed on the rear wall of the nave, together with the decrees of later sultans reiterating the permission for the Greeks to retain this church.

When I first attended services in the Mouchliotissa, in the spring of 1961, there were only a handful of parishioners present, most of them old widows, as evidenced by their black clothing. I spoke afterwards to the old priest, who said mournfully that it was only a matter of time before he and the last of his parishioners passed on, and he feared that the Mouchliotissa would be abandoned. But the next time I went to

Mass there, in the second year of the new millennium, I was pleasantly surprised to find that the little church, which had recently been restored by the patriarch Bartholomeus, was almost full. And so I found a pew at the rear and watched as the Orthodox liturgy unfolded, the nave filling with the sound of the priest's deep, nasal voice and the chanted response of the cantor. Clouds of pungent incense rose up to the dome, and the light from a dozen candelabras gave a lambent glow to the ancient paintings on the iconostasis, a scene that had been perpetuated for more than seven centuries in the Mouchliotissa, a living survival of the otherwise vanished world of Byzantine Constantinople.

Near Fener Kapısı, across the park bordering the Golden Horn, there is a restored meta-Byzantine mansion that now houses the Women's Library and Research Center. The center, which opened in 1990, was the first institution of its kind in Turkey, and is still, for all I know, the only one. In the mid-1990s the institute hosted an international congress on women's studies here, and I was asked to lead them on a tour of the city. After consulting with Aslı Mardin, one of the directors, we decided that the tour would include only monuments founded by women, the wives and mothers of the Byzantine emperors and Ottoman sultans. But even a preliminary listing showed that there were far too many such monuments to be visited on a one-day tour. This fact surprised everyone when I mentioned it in my opening remarks at the congress, for Istanbul has never been known as a woman's city, but I reminded them that women had always been the power behind the throne here, both in Byzantine Constantinople and Ottoman Istanbul.

The church of St. Stephen of the Bulgars was erected further along the shore of the Golden Horn in 1896, when the Bulgarian national church was seeking to assert its independence from the Greek Orthodox Patriarchate.

The astonishing thing about St. Stephen's is that it is constructed entirely of cast iron – not only the structure of the church itself, but also its interior furnishings and decorations, all in a neo-Gothic style. Each section was made in Vienna and carried to Istanbul to be assembled here on the shore of the Golden Horn. Both the outside and inside of St. Stephen's is actually quite striking, and it is aided by the small community of Bulgarian Christians who worship here and keep it in good condition. The congregation also includes Bulgarian gypsies, as I discovered one Sunday morning when I came upon a Romany wedding here, another one of the surprises that Istanbul always has in store for those who think that they know everything there is to know about the city.

The oldest and grandest of the extant meta-Byzantine mansions in the city, though it is now in an appalling state of decay, lies a few hundred meters along the shore. The mansion is known as the Metochion of Mount Sinai, since it belongs to the monastery of St. Catherine founded by Justinian on the Sinai peninsula. St. Catherine's, like other monasteries, was represented in Constantinople by one of its archimandrites, who are mentioned as living in this mansion on the Golden Horn as early as 1686. The Metochion of Mount Sinai was badly damaged in the anti-Greek riots in 1955, and then in the mid-1970s it was closed by the Turkish government, since which time it has been abandoned and subject to further ruination.

When I first came upon the Metochion, in the spring of 1961, it appeared to be abandoned, but when I rang the bell the door was opened by a gray-bearded gentleman in informal clerical costume. I asked him if I could see the Metochion, and he said that he would be glad to show me around, introducing himself as the Archimandrite Damian. He first took me to the great hall that had been the library and reception room of the mansion. This was still a shambles after the 1955 riots, in which he explained, the mob had destroyed all of the books and manuscript in the Metochion's collection, a few scraps of which were still lying on the floor amidst the wreckage and fallen plaster that remained. He then invited me to have tea with him and his mother, who had come to live with him in the Metochion after his father died. Damian and I became good friends, and we exchanged visits several times a year until the Metochion was closed, after which he retired to the Metochion of Mount Sinai in Athens, his mother having died in the interim. I visited him there once, but when I returned the following summer I was told that he had passed away. I still think of Damian, for he was a very special friend, and I am particularly reminded of him whenever I passed the ruined Metochion of Mount Sinai on the Golden Horn.

The next significant find along the Golden Horn is the ruin of Balat Kapısı, another of the Byzantine sea-gates, sometimes identified as the Gate of Haghios Ioannis Kynegos, St. John the Hunter. Balat, the name of the neighborhood inside the gate, the next quarter up the Golden Horn beyond Fener, is a corruption of the Greek *palation*, or "palace," stemming from the proximity of the Byzantine Palace of Blachernae, whose ruins stand just inside the land walls of the city above the Golden Horn.

Balat was one of the principal Jewish quarters of the city until recent times, and there are still half a dozen synagogues there, the oldest one dating back to the late Byzantine period. This is the Akhrida

Synagogue, which is a couple of hundred meters to the left inside Balat Kapısı. The synagogue, which dates to the first half of the fifteenth century, has recently been restored to its original appearance. My one and only visit there was at the beginning of the new millennium, when I attended the Sabbath prayer in the company of an Israeli filmmaker, who was interested in doing a documentary concerning a book that I was writing. The book, which was published on September 12, 2001, was about Sabbatai Sevi, the self-styled messiah who in 1666 converted to Islam with many of his followers, giving rise to the crypto-Jewish sect known in Turkish as the Dönme. Sabbatai is known to have preached in the Akhrida Synagogue in the years immediately after his apostasy, though I did not mention this to the rabbi and others whom I met there

Young boys visiting Eyüp Camii prior to their circumcision

that day, for the name of the man they call the "False Messiah" is still anathema among the orthodox Jewish community in Istanbul.

Just inside Balat Kapı to the right there is a small mosque, one of Sinan's minor works. A long and superbly carved Arabic inscription over the magnificent entrance portal records that the mosque was constructed by Ferruh Ağa, Kethuda (Steward) of Semiz Ali Paşa, grand vezir of Süleyman the Magnificent, in 1562-3. This is, in my opinion, the handsomest and most interesting of Sinan's many mosques of this simple type.

Along the street, which leads to the Greek Orthodox church of Haghios Demetrius Kanabou, stretches of the Byzantine sea-walls can still be seen between the houses beside the shore road. The first mention of this church after the Conquest is by Tryphon in 1583, the present structure dating from a rebuilding in 1730. St. Demetrius must have originated in the Byzantine era as it known that a church of that name has been on this site in 1334. The church may have been founded by the family of Nicholas Kanabou, who had been emperor for just a few days when, in April 1204, the city was sacked by the knights of the Fourth Crusade, and he was killed. St. Demetrius was the patriarchal church in the years 1597–9, just before the Patriarchate was shifted to its current abode.

The church is built up against a well-preserved stretch of the Byzantine sea-walls, which serves as a retaining wall for the very pretty garden that borders the building on its west side. At the outer edge of the garden one has a clear view across the Golden Horn, which at this point is spanned by the old Galata Köprüsü, moved here after the present bridge between Karaköy and Eminönü was completed in the early 1990s. The district on the other side of the bridge is Hasköy, once a delightful village but now a slum, though still very interesting. Rahmi Koç has brought some life back to Hasköy by opening his new Industrial Museum on the shore of the Golden Horn just above the bridge.

The former Byzantine church known as Atık Mustafa Paşa Camii lies beyond the church of Haghios Demetrius Kanabou, towards the shore road.

The church was in times past thought to be that of Sts. Peter and Mark. The theory has now been dismissed, although no other one seems acceptable. It has been dated to the ninth century on the basis of its architectural style, but nothing whatsoever is known of its history in the Byzantine era.

The church was converted to a mosque in the first decade of the sixteenth century by Koca Mustafa Paşa, also known as Atik Mustafa Paşa, grand vezir under Beyazit II. The apsidal chamber to the right of the bema is now a shrine dedicated to Cabir ibn Abdullah, a Muslim warrior who is believed to have been killed in one of the Arab sieges of the city. There are a number of shrines to these Muslim *şehitler,* or martyrs, in this part of the city, just inside the land-walls, where during the Arab sieges the Byzantine defenders dispatched many Islamic warriors to paradise. When I first came to the city, these shrines were neglected and almost forgotten, but now with the resurgence of Islam in Turkey they have all been restored and are the object of pilgrimage. When I last visited Atik Mustafa Paşa Camii, at the beginning of the new millennium, I purchased from the *imam* a newly published guidebook in Turkish to the places of Islamic pilgrimage in Istanbul, many of which were the burial places of these Arab martyrs. The *imam* told me that he was from the town of Of, on the Black Sea coast of Anatolia, which intrigued me, for I knew that everyone there and in the valley above it were Greek-speaking Muslims, whose ancestors had converted to Islam after the Turkish Conquest.

The people of Of are fervent fundamentalists and are not to be trifled with, for the men are usually armed and prefer to settle disputes with their guns when words fail. And so, although I had serious doubts about the historicity of these Arab martyrs and their shrines, I refrained from disagreeing with the *imam* when he praised them as great heroes. I excused myself in my own mind by thinking that I would have done the same in the Patriarchate, if one of the priests there had asked me my opinion concerning the historicity of the porphyry column at which Christ was supposedly scourged during his Passion.

Ayvansaray Kapı is further left along the coast. This is probably the site of the ancient Porta Kiliomene, the last gate in the sea-walls along the Golden Horn before they are joined by the northern end of the land walls. As Alexander van Millingen writes in making this identification: "Here, probably, was the Porta Kiliomene, at which the emperors – as late, at least, as the beginning of the thirteenth century – landed and were received by the Senate, when proceeding by water to visit the Church or the Palace of Blachernae. Nowhere else could one disembark so near that sanctuary and that palace."

I had read this description on the evening before my first stroll along the Golden Horn in 1960, and I felt great excitement when I reached Ayvansaray Kapı and walked to the end of the short street that leads in from the shore road, approaching the entrance to the famous shrine of the Blachernitissa, Our Lady of Blachernae. I still feel this excitement when I visit the shrine, passing through the pretty garden in front of the church and its sacred spring.

The first church at the shrine of Blachernae was built in 451 by the empress Pulcheria, sister of Theodosius II and wife of the emperor Marcian. Soon afterwards, the church came to enshrine the revered robe and mantle of the Virgin, brought from Jerusalem by two pilgrims who had reportedly stolen them from a Jewess. The church also contained a sacred icon of the Blachernitissa, which was credited with driving back the barbarian Avars when they very nearly broke into the city at this point in 626.

Destroyed by fire in 1434, the church of Blachernae was subsequently rebuilt several times, most recently in the early 1960s. The shrine is as popular today as it ever was, and the pilgrims who come to drink of its curative waters are of all faiths, for the reputation of the Blachernitissa is universal. But only the Greeks can read the inscription over the font, a copy of the famous palindrome from the Holy Well of Haghia Sophia: "Do not just cleanse your body with this water; cleanse your soul as well."

The Greeks of the city still congregate here on the feast day of the Blachernitissa, when they sing the beautiful hymn known as the *Akathistos,* a thanksgiving to the Virgin for having saved Constantinople from the Avars in 626, a very moving testimony to a faith that has survived even the ultimate fall of Byzantium in 1453.

The caretaker at the shrine is one of my oldest friends in the city. He is an Arabic-speaking Christian from Antioch, as are the janitors at all of the Orthodox churches in the city, for there are no longer enough Greeks to go around. He came to Istanbul with his wife and children in 1960, the same year as I did, and at the same age. He immediately went to work at the shrine, for though the salary was pitifully low, and still is, he at least had free housing for his family. His children have now all grown and moved away – one to Greece, three to Germany, and one to Australia – and whenever I see him we take count of our grandchildren, in which he is now far ahead of me, fifteen to my six. When I was in the hospital this past autumn for a hip replacement he sent me a bottle of holy water from the sacred well, and when I see him again I can tell him with some truth that it speeded my recovery. Our meetings are very important to me, for he and I have grown old apace, and though we have lived very different lives, fate decreed that we should spend the greatest part of our existence in Istanbul, where both of us are still exiles.

Beyond Ayvansaray Kapı comes the point where the sea-walls are joined by the land-walls. To the left, there is the long line of the land-walls as their towers march down from the summit of the Sixth Hill to the Golden Horn, with the ruins of the Palace of Blachernae visible a few hundred meters away, all of which I will return to in a later chapter.

Along the right side of the shore road, a walkway goes under the bridge, which carries the circumferential highway over the Golden Horn, and leads towards the outlying monuments of Eyüp, the great Muslim shrine on the upper reaches of the Golden Horn. The monuments along the shore road include five mosques, the most remarkable being Zal Mahmut Paşa Camii, built by Sinan in the 1570s. The approach towards the heart of Eyüp goes through a veritable suburb of the dead, whose cobbled lanes are lined with Ottoman tombstones and tombs. The most notable of the funerary monuments is that of Sokollu Mehmet Pasha, another work by the great Sinan, built c.1572.

Eyüp Camii, standing in the center of its vast outer courtyard, is always crowded with pilgrims who have come to visit the *türbe* of Eba Eyüp Ensari, friend and standard-bearer of the Prophet Mohammed. Many years after the death of the Prophet, Eba Eyüp Ensari is believed to have been killed as he helped lead the first Arab siege of Constantinople,

The prayer hall of Eyüp Camii

overleaf
Sunset on the Golden
Horn, with the
silhouette of the Fatih
Camii, the Mosque of
the Conqueror, on the
Stamboul skyline

in the years 674–8. Eyüp's grave lay outside the city walls and was miraculously discovered by Fatih and his spiritual adviser Akşemsettin during the Ottoman siege of Constantinople, a story told by Evliya in his
characteristic apocryphal style:

*Mehmet II having laid siege to Constantinople was, with his seventy saintly atten-
dants, seven whole days searching for Eyüp's tomb. At last Akshemsettin exclaimed,
"Good news, my Prince, of Eyüp's tomb"; thus saying he began to pray and then fell
asleep. Some interpreted this sleep as a veil cast by shame over his ignorance of the
tomb; but after some time he raised his head, his eyes became bloodshot, the sweat
ran from his forehead, and he said to the Sultan, "Eyüp's tomb is on the very spot
where I spread the carpet for prayer." Upon this, three of his attendants together
with the Sheikh and Sultan began to dig up the ground, when at the depth of three
yards they found a square stone of verd-antique on which was written in Cufic letters: "This is the tomb of Eba Eyüp." They lifted up the stone, and below it found the
body of Eyüp wrapped up in a saffron-covered shroud, with a brazen play-ball in his
hand fresh and well preserved.*

Outside the north gate of the mosque, a pathway leads to the great Muslim
cemetery of Eyüp, the last resting-place of many notables from Ottoman
times as well as of countless generations of the ordinary people of Istanbul.
The older tombstones often have amusing epitaphs, such as those translated for me thirty-five years ago by the late Cevat Şakir Kabaağaç, the great
Turkish writer known more familiarly as the Fisherman of Halicarnassus.

*A pity to good-hearted Ismail Efendi, whose death caused great sadness among his
friends. Having caught the illness of love at the age of seventy, he took the bits
between his teeth and dashed full gallop to paradise.*

*Stopping his ears with his fingers, Judge Mehmet hied off from this beautiful world,
leaving his wife's cackling and his mother-in-law's gabbling.*

*(On a wayside tomb): Oh, passer-by, spare me your prayers, but please don't steal my
tombstone!*

I could have died as well without a doctor than with the quack that friends set upon me.

*I have swerved away from you for a long time. But in soil, air, cloud, rain, plant,
flower, butterfly, or bird, I am always with you.*

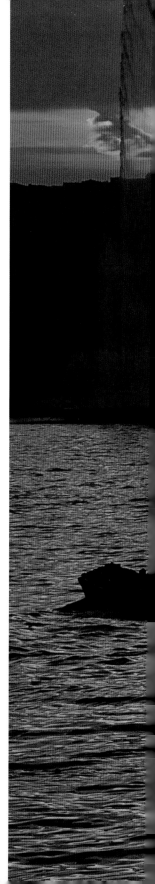

(On a tombstone with the relief of three trees, an almond, a cypress and a peach-tree, the fruit of the latter being the symbol of a woman's breasts):

I've planted these trees so that people may know my fate. I loved an almond-eyed, cypress-tall maiden, and bade farewell to this beautiful world without savoring her peaches.

At the top of the hill above the cemetery, there is a famous café known as the Teahouse of Pierre Loti, named after the French novelist, who frequented it during his stay in Istanbul in the last years of the Ottoman era. The café commands a superb view of the Golden Horn, a scene particularly beautiful at sunset and twilight. Clearly visible are the upper reaches of the Golden Horn and the two streams that flow into it at its northern extremity. These are the Alibey Suyu on the west and Kağithane on the east, the ancient Barbyzes and Cydaris, respectively, together known in English as the Sweet Waters of Europe.

During Ottoman times the shores of the Sweet Waters of Europe were the site of royal palaces, seaside mansions, pavilions, and gardens, particularly during the reign of Ahmet III (r. 1703–30), the Tulip King, whose grand vezir and son-in-law Nevşehirli Ibrahim Paşa ran the empire while the sultan devoted himself entirely to pleasure. The sultan's favorite residence on the Sweet Waters was called Sa'adabad, "The Palace of Eternal Happiness." The spirit of the Tulip King's reign was expressed in a couplet by his court poet Nedim, who, writing of the fêtes at Sa'adabad, sang "Let us laugh, let us play/ Let us enjoy the delights of the world to the full." But this long party finally came to an end in 1730, when rebels deposed Sultan Ahmet, killing both Ibrahim Paşa and Nedim. The Tulip King spent the rest of his days confined to the Cage in Topkapı Sarayı, while Sa'adabad and the other palaces and mansions on the Sweet Waters of Europe were abandoned and fell into ruins. Today they have disappeared completely, leaving only a memory, perhaps recalled by those having a twilight drink in Pierre Loti's café in Eyüp above the Golden Horn, as we so often did in the past.

11

THE SEVENTH HILL

The Seventh Hill slopes down to the Sea of Marmara in the southwestern sector of the old city. The crossroads in Aksaray, along with Beyazit Meydanı, is one of the two great squares in old Istanbul, though neither looks even remotely like the main square of a European city. Both squares are located on the site of an ancient Roman forum, in Aksaray's case the Forum Bovis. A short distance to the west of the Forum Bovis the main thoroughfare of Byzantine Constantinople, the Mese, divides into two branches, one heading northwest along the course of the modern Adnan Menderes Caddesi to the Edirne (Adrianople) Gate, while the second leads to the southwest, roughly along the route of the present Cerrahpaşa Caddesi and Samatya Caddesi to the famous Golden Gate. Until the early 1970s Aksaray was a vivacious market square, lined with pleasant cafés and restaurants, but the construction of a horrific elevated traffic interchange has utterly ruined it for human use.

The *mihrap* and *mimber* of a small but elegant mosque in the old city

At the northwest corner of the interchange, the elevated highway passes over the last of Istanbul's imperial mosques, Valide Sultan Camii. The mosque was constructed for the *valide sultan* Pertevniyal, wife of Mahmut II and mother of Abdül Aziz, in 1871. Erected by the Armenian architects Hagop and Sarkis Balyan, it contains elements from Turkish, Moorish, neo-Gothic, neo-Renaissance, and Empire styles; in times past it was much admired, but modern architectural historians dismiss it as "a garish rococo hodgepodge," to quote the late Hilary Sumner-Boyd.

Beyond the west end of the overpass Ordu Caddesi branches into three avenues, with Adnan Menderes Caddesi heading northwest, Turgut Ozal Caddesi west, and Cerrah Paşa Caddesi southwest. The old, elegant Murat Paşa Camii can be seen in the space between the first two of these avenues. It is one of only two "Bursa-style" mosques that survive in Istanbul, the other being the somewhat larger and more ornate Mahmut Paşa Camii on the Second Hill. The mosque was built in 1469 for Murat Paşa, a member of the imperial family of the Palaeologues who converted and rose to the rank of vezir under Fatih.

Late in the spring of 1972, when *Strolling Through Istanbul* was about to be published, I heard from an archaeologist friend that an early Christian catacomb had just been discovered just north of Murat Paşa Camii. I took a taxi there immediately, but when I arrived I found that the police had closed off the excavation and would not permit me or anyone else to enter. I learned why when I picked up a Turkish newspaper the following morning, for on the front page there was an interview with the director of the Bureau of Antiquities, who said that thieves had plundered the catacomb the night after its discovery. The Turkish archaeologist Nezih Fırati has published a plan of that part of the catacomb unearthed in the excavation, which comprised a series of eight vaulted chambers in a row, which he dated to the early Byzantine period. Whenever I pass the site of the excavation, which is now completely covered over, I regret not having had the chance to explore it.

Cerrah Paşa Camii is situated on Cerrah Paşa Caddesi up the eastern slope of the Seventh Hill. The mosque was built in 1592 by Cerrah Mehmet Paşa, a barber and circumciser who in 1598 briefly served as grand vezir under Mehmet III. Davut Ağa, Sinan's successor as chief of the imperial architects, designed Cerrah Paşa Camii which is, in my opinion, among the half-dozen most successful of the grand vezirial mosques in the city and well worth a visit.

A huge mass of marble is wedged between two old houses on Haseki Kadın Sokağı, a right turn off Cerrah Paşa Caddesi. A gateway beside the house to the right leads into the yard of an automobile repair shop, from where one can examine the battered marble structure.

This is the base of an honorific column erected in 402 by the emperor Arcadius, whose equestrian statue surmounted the monument. It stood in the center of the Forum of Arcadius, through which the Mese passed on its way to the Golden Gate. The column, which was some 50 meters high, remained standing until 1714, when what remained of it was deliberately demolished because of fears that it might collapse and destroy the surrounding houses.

When I first saw the monument, in the spring of 1961, the owner of the house to its left invited me in so that I could make my way through into the base of the column. Once inside the base, I climbed a winding stone stairway to the top, where I could examine the single band of reliefs on the small section of the column shaft that remains in place. These represent the triumphs of Arcadius, as do other fragments of the reliefs that are exhibited in the Archaeological Museum. Evliya saw the column when it was still standing, at least in part, and he numbers it first in his list of the talismans of the city.

At the end of Haseki Kadın Sokağı is the *külliye* of Bayram Paşa, who served as grand vezir under Murat IV. The complex, which was completed in 1634, is split by the street. The *mescit, türbe, tekke,* and *sebil* are on the left with the *medrese* and *mektep,* or primary school, to the right.

Nearby, the *külliye* of Haseki Hürrem was founded by Süleyman for his wife Haseki Hürrem. The *külliye* was built by Sinan and finished in 1539, his earliest mosque complex in the city. Besides the mosque, the complex includes a *medrese,* primary school, hospital, and *imaret,* or public kitchen.

When I first visited the complex, in the early 1960s, the public kitchen was open, one of only three Ottoman *imarets* in the city that were still performing their original function. Around 500 impoverished people from all over Istanbul used to come here to be fed daily at about eleven o'clock in the morning. I happened to arrive here at that time, and the director of the *imaret* graciously invited me to dine with them, and I had a delicious lunch of lentil soup and pilaf. Several years passed before I visited the complex again, and when I did so I learned that the *imaret* was no longer functioning, for the entire *külliye* was being restored. The restoration has since been completed and the hospital is now open as a clinic, but the *imaret* is no longer serving food to the poor, despite the fact that the economic plight of so many people in Istanbul is worse than it has been for many years.

Recessed from the street and somewhat hidden by the houses and trees, Daud Paşa Camii is about quarter of a mile from Haseki Hürrem Camii. An inscription over the entrance records that the mosque was built in 1485 by Daud Paşa, grand vezir under Beyazit II. This is one of the oldest and most distinguished mosques in the city, but it is sadly neglected. Every time I come this way I hope to see signs of a restoration, but so far I have been disappointed.

A few hundred meters further along the street lies the large and intriguing complex of Hekimoğlu Ali Paşa, grand vezir under Mahmut I, which was built by the architect Ömer Ağa in 1735. Some think of this *külliye* as the final great classical mosque complex, while others see it as the first in the new baroque style; the truth is, it has elements of both. When I first saw this complex it was nearly as dilapidated as Daud Paşa Camii, but since then it has been well restored.

The street that leads north from the main entrance to the mosque goes to the summit of the Seventh Hill, known to the Greeks in times past as Xerolophos, or the Dry Hill, where, according to ancient tradition, the populace congregated to pray for rain in times of drought.

The summit of the hill is occupied by the third and largest of the extant Roman reservoirs in the city. This is the Cistern of St. Mochius, from a famous church of that name which stood in the vicinity, said to have been founded by Constantine the Great. The cistern was built in the late fifth or early sixth century; like the other two surviving Roman reservoirs, it became redundant in the later Byzantine era. It is a vast rectangle, measuring 170 by 147 meters on the inside, with walls 6 meters thick, and the present depth ranging from 10 to 15 meters. The reservoir has now been converted into a playground and sports area known as the Fatih Educational Park.

When I first saw the reservoir, it served as a kitchen garden and orchard, with a few wooden houses at its eastern end forming a picturesque sunken hamlet. The Turkish name for the reservoir is Altımermer, or the Six Marbles, a name stemming from a number of ancient marble column fragments there, some of which could still be seen when I first passed this way.

The eponymous marble columns of Altımermer were included by Evliya among the talismans of the ancient city, although in reading the *Seyahatname* we find that he lists seven rather than six. According to Evliya, this extra talisman was a brazen rooster placed there by Socrates, who in Islamic tradition is considered one of the sages of antiquity. As Evliya describes it:

This cock clapped its wings and crowed once in every twenty-four hours, and on hearing it all the cocks in Istanbul started to crow. And it is a fact that all the cocks there crow earlier than those of other places, setting up their ku-kirri-ku at midnight, and thus warning the sleepy and forgetful of the approach of dawn and the hour of prayer.

Hekimoğlu Ali Paşa Camii

But cocks no longer crow in Altımermer, for the little farm village in the Cistern of St. Mocius has vanished, and so the locals must now rely on their alarm clocks or the calls of the surrounding *müezzins*.

South of Hekimoğlu Ali Paşa Camii, within the grounds of the government law courts, there are the remains of an interesting complex known as Isa Kapı Mescidi, which is partly Byzantine and partly Ottoman.

The ruins of a Byzantine church and an Ottoman *medrese* make up the complex. The south and east walls of the church are all that remains, along with fragments of its three apses, one of which still had traces of frescoes when I first saw it, but these have now disappeared. The church is thought to date from the fourteenth century, but its history remains unknown and even the name of the saint to whom it was dedicated is a mystery. In around 1560, Hadım (the Eunuch) Ibrahim Paşa, who at the time was grand vezir under Süleyman, converted the church into a mosque and added to it an elegant *medrese* by Sinan. 1894's great earthquake destroyed both mosque and *medrese*, after which they were abandoned, even their identity forgotten until they were rediscovered by Russian scholars in 1925.

Isa Kapı translates as the "Gate of Christ," and it has been suggested that this monument relates to one of the gates in Constantine the Great's city walls which may have stood in the vicinity. The evidence is inconclusive, but, nevertheless, some of us romantics would like to believe that this ruin is associated with the Gate of Christ, thus linking modern Istanbul with the city of Constantine, who inferred that he was guided by Christ when he traced the course to be followed by the walls of his new capital.

Sancaktar Tekkesi Sokağı leads towards an octagonal Byzantine building known as Sancaktar Mescidi. It was unconvincingly attributed by Paspates to be part of the famous Monastery of Gastria. It is suggested that the monastery was established soon after 330 by St. Helena, mother of Constantine the Great, deriving its name of "Gastria", or "Vases," from the pots of flowers and herbs she had brought back from Jerusalem together with the fragment of the True Cross she had discovered there. The church has been dated variously from the eleventh century to the fourteenth, although two authorities have in recent years stated that the apse goes back to the fourth century, to Helena's time. Here again, a romantic might be allowed to think that this is another survival of the city of Constantine, particularly because in his time this

area, then in the countryside outside the Constantinian walls, was known in honor of the emperor's mother as Helenaia.

When I first visited Sancaktar Mescidi in 1961, it was an abandoned shell, but now it has been well restored and is once again serving as a mosque, as I saw when I visited it a year ago for the first time in four decades. The old men who were sitting in the little covered courtyard of the mosque welcomed me warmly, and the young *imam* complimented me on having found this very out-of-the-way place, saying that I was the first tourist to come for a visit. I thanked the *imam*, saying that I been to Sancaktar Mescidi some years earlier, although I refrained from telling him that my first visit was probably before he was born.

Marmara Caddesi leads back to Koca Mustafa Paşa Caddesi, which in turn leads on to Ramazan Efendi Caddesi with its charming little mosque preceded by a pretty garden courtyard. This is Ramazan Efendi Camii, a minor but exceptional work of Sinan.

The mosque was founded by an official in the Ottoman court named Hoca Husref, but it soon took the name Ramazan Efendi Camii, after the first *şeyh* of the *külliye*'s dervish *tekke*. A lengthy inscription over the inner door by the poet Mustafa Sa'i, Sinan's friend, establishes the year of construction as 1586. Therefore, this is the final mosque erected by the great man and must have been completed when he was well into his nineties.

The mosque is simple, comprising nothing more than a small rectangular room with a flat roof, a replacement for the original wooden dome, destroyed in an earthquake. It is renowned for the magnificent panels of Iznik tiles with which it is adorned. The old men who see me admiring these tiles sometimes talk to me about them, expressing pride that their little mosque is so beautifully decorated.

Koca Mustafa Paşa Caddesi bends towards a tree-shaded square lined with teahouses, non-alcoholic cafés, and simple eating places. On the left side of the square is the main entrance to the courtyard of Koca Mustafa Paşa Camii, after which the avenue and the entire district on the Marmara shore of the Seventh Hill are named. This is one of the most popular Muslim shrines in Istanbul, as one can tell from the number of professional beggars and sellers of religious trinkets and tracts who flank the entrance to the courtyard, catering to the pilgrim trade.

The complex consists of the mosque itself, a large *medrese*, a *hamam*, and seven tombs, the largest of which is the *türbe* of the founder, Koca Mustafa Paşa, grand vezir of Beyazit II. He is also known as Atik Mustafa Paşa, as in the name of the converted Byzantine church on the Golden Horn.

Mustafa Paşa's mosque here on the Seventh Hill is also a converted

Byzantine church, identified as that of St. Andrew in Krisei. The church was founded and dedicated to St. Andrew of Crete c. 1284 by the princess Theodora Raoulina, a niece of Michael VIII Palaeologos. Because of the district in which the church was located, it came to be called St. Andrew in Krisei. The structure was rebuilt after its conversion to a mosque, and its exterior is entirely Ottoman, including the dome.

When the church was converted into a mosque, the interior arrangements were reoriented by 90 degrees because of the bearing of the building. Thus the *mihrap* and *mimber* are under the semidome against the south wall and the entrance is in the north wall, in front of which a wooden porch was added in the Ottoman period. The columns in the central bay of the narthex have beautiful sixth-century capitals of the pseudo-Ionic type, resembling those in the galleries of Sts. Sergius and Bacchus.

I was admiring these capitals on a recent visit, when the young *imam* came over to introduce himself and I congratulated him on the exceptionally fine condition of the mosque interior, which was quite spotless. He appreciated the compliment and said that he was proud to be in charge of such an ancient mosque, though he knew nothing of its history and thanked me when I told him what I knew of its Byzantine past. Then he excused himself, saying that the time for the mid-afternoon prayer was approaching, and I left as the mosque began to fill up with the faithful, the oldest of whom greeted me gravely as we passed at the doorway.

The pilgrims who come to Koca Mustafa Paşa Camii are there principally to visit the six tombs in the courtyard. The most interesting of those buried there is Sümbül Efendi, whose *türbe* is the second from the right, directly in front of Mustafa Paşa's tomb. Sümbül Efendi was the first *şeyh* of the Bektaşi dervish *tekke* that was founded here in the sixteenth century, and such was his saintly reputation that his *türbe* became one of the most popular Muslim shrines in the city. Buried next to Sümbül in the *türbe* is his daughter Rahine, to whom young women often pray if they are in search of a husband.

There are literally hundreds of such shrines in Istanbul, many of which I learned of from Evliya, as I write in a chapter of my *Stamboul Sketches* entitled "The Saints in Our Alleyways." Although there are no official saints in Islam, Istanbul is full of humble monuments to those informally canonized only by the veneration they receive from the pious poor of the city. "The evidences of veneration are very simple: some scraps of cloth tied to the grilled window of a *türbe,* the stumps of guttered candles atop a graveyard wall, a pile of stones beside a turbaned tombstone."

One group of folk saints mentioned by Evliya have no tombs or shrines, and we know of them only from the *Seyahatname*. These are the harmless and amusing characters that Evliya refers to as "saint-fools, holy idiots, and ecstatic or inspired men." The greatest of saint-fools in Evliya's time was Boynuzlu Divanesi, the Lunatic with the Horns, otherwise known as Ahmet Dede. Evliya explains how this merry madman came by his name.

The interior of Hekimoğlu Ali Paşa Camii

In the long days he used to sit upon the bridge at Kasim Pasha and say to all who passed "Shallah," (instead of "Inshallah," if God pleases) "you'll go to the Kaaba [i. e., Mecca]." The wonder was that he knew men by their names, whom he had never seen before, and saluted them as old acquaintances, and instantly remembered those he had not seen for twenty or thirty years, as well as all their relations. His bosom was filled with horns of goats, gazelles, and sheep. Merry fellows frequently went to try him, by saying, "Ahmet, show me my horn!" If they happened to be married he would answer with some anecdote concerning their wives, and would give to some a small, to others a great horn from his collection. If the man who asked was not married he used to answer, "Thy horn is not yet grown." If someone said, "Ahmet Dede, I'll give thee a horn, dance a little," he would get up instantly, knock with the fingers of his right hand like a stork, and begin to dance like Venus in the sky, during which people brought him all kinds of horns. If you went to him afterwards and asked him where your horn was, he would put his hand into his bosom and show you the very same which you had given him. In brief, he was a light-hearted fool. Since he undertook the journey into Abyssinia and the country of the negroes, we have not heard of him.

Koca Mustafa Paşa Caddes contiues on towards a steep slope of the Seventh Hill and the Marmara shore. Down the slope, the Armenian Gregorian church of Surp Kevork (St. George) is on Marmara Caddesi.

The present church is a large nineteenth-century basilica erected on the site of the famous Byzantine church of the Theotokos Peribleptos, the "Celebrated Mother of God", built in 1031 by the emperor Romanos III Argyros. Five years after the Conquest the Peribleptos was given by Fatih to the Armenians as their patriarchal church. The Armenians rededicated the church to St. George, and it served as the seat of their patriarchate until 1643, when it was supplanted by the church of Surp Asdvadsadzin in the Kumkapı quarter. The church was destroyed by fire in 1872, after which the present basilica of Surp Kevork was built on its ruins. It is known to the Turks as Sulu Manastir, the "Watery Monastery," because of the subterranean holy well in the courtyard of the church.

The substructures of the Peribleptos were excavated and surveyed in 1997–8 under the auspices of the Istanbul Rescue Archeological Survey, directed by Ken Dark and Ferudun Özgümüş. Ferudun gave me a personally conducted tour of the substructures shortly after they were excavated. Then by the light of an electric torch he showed me that the plan of the building he and Ken Dark had drawn, a cross-in-square church with five apses, agreed with the description of the Peribleptos by Ruy González de Clavijo, who in 1403 passed through Constantinople on an embassy from Henry III of Castile to Tamerlane.

Afterwards Ferudun and I sat in the courtyard of Surp Kevork, where all of the elderly Armenians who still live in this quarter while away their

The minaret of Hekimoğlu Ali Paşa Camii

afternoons. One of them whom I spoke to, a white-haired gentleman of about seventy with the clearest blue eyes, told me in perfect English that he had been born in a village in southeastern Anatolia, and that in his youth he had spoken Armenian at home and in church and Kurdish in the market-place, just as he now spoke Turkish in the streets of Istanbul. "We have our church," he said, "and that is how we retain our identity."

Canbaziye Sokağı, which leads steeply downhill from the church towards the Marmara, provides a view of the domes of a large Turkish bath known as Ağa Hamamı, a work of Sinan now used for commercial purposes.

The street turns right on to Orgeneral Abdurrahman Nafiz Gürman Caddesi, formerly Samatya Caddesi. The latter name comes from the old name of this quarter on the Marmara shore of the Seventh Hill – Samatya – a corruption of the Greek Psamathion. There are references to the name Psamathion dating back to antiquity, when this was a Greek fishing village on the Marmara, at a time when Byzantium was still confined to the acropolis on the First Hill. Samatya Caddesi, as I still call it, follows the course of the southern branch of the Mese, leading to the Golden Gate.

After the first intersection, one can see the courtyard wall of a Greek church, that of Haghios Georgios Kyparissas, St. George of the Cypresses. The original church on this site is believed to have been founded in the medieval Byzantine period. The first reference to it after the Conquest is by Stefan Gerlach in 1583, while the present church dates from a rebuilding in 1834.

The campanile of another Greek church, that of Haghios Menas (St. Menas), stands on the heights above the avenue. This too was first mentioned by Stefan Gerlach in 1583, and the present structure dates from a rebuilding in 1833. These rebuildings of Greek churches in the 1830s stem from the reform movement that began under Mahmut II, when the Christian minorities in the Ottoman Empire were given greater human rights, which, among other privileges, allowed them to replace their old churches with new basilicas.

Beneath the church, but in no way connected with it, there is a very interesting ancient substructure, entered from the main avenue and presently used as a carpentry shop. Unearthed in 1835 by the German archaeologist Alfons Maria Schneider, the substructure is the crypt of the Martyrium of Sts. Karpos and Papylos, dedicated to two martyrs who perished in the persecution of Christians under the Roman emperor Decius in 250–51. The crypt consists of a circular domed chamber reminiscent of the tholos tombs at Mycenae. However, as it is constructed of brick, using the late Roman technique, rather than stone, the structure can be dated accordingly. At the east end there is a side chapel that opens into an ambulatory corridor extending around the periphery of the central chamber, its outer diameter measuring some 25 meters.

One of the most enduring urban myths of Istanbul concerns the ancient tunnels that are found all over the city, all of them supposedly leading to Haghia Sophia. After my first visit to the martyrium, in the spring of 1961, I went next door to the carpentry shop to sit in a teahouse, where I was shown a door that led to such a tunnel. I examined the tunnel, using a torch I had with me, and found that it led after a few steps to a locked wooden door. I looked through the cracks in the door and saw that it led into the ambulatory corridor of the martyrium, but when I returned to the teahouse I refrained from reporting this to the owner and his patrons, for I didn't want to shatter their romantic myth that the tunnel led to Haghia Sophia.

Further along the avenue there is a large Greek church, dedicated to Constantine the Great and his mother, Helena. The earliest recorded reference to the church is by Petrus Gyllius in 1547, while the present structure is due to a rebuilding in 1833, another product of the reforms of Mahmut II.

The second turning to the left beyond Sts. Constantine and Helena leads to the walled enclosure of Imrahor Camii, the former church of St. John of Studios, whose noble ruins are one of the great sights in the city, a basilica older than Haghia Sophia, part of what was once the most important monastery in Byzantine Constantinople.

I have always had great difficulty in gaining entrance to this site. Officially one must obtain permission from the director of Haghia Sophia, but even then the custodian is not at home, or, more likely, just doesn't respond when you ring the bell at the entryway to the courtyard. The neighborhood children usually rise to the challenge, climbing over the wall to alert the custodian, or, in his absence, opening the courtyard door anyway. And now, even when you get into the courtyard, you find that the basilica and its narthex are closed off by barbed wire, though you can at least look through into the nave.

The courtyard, once the atrium of the church, is extremely picturesque, what with the old wooden house of the custodian and its kitchen garden, watered from the ablution fountain of the mosque, laundry drying among the turbaned tombstones in what was once a dervish graveyard in front of the narthex and its beautiful colonnade, opening up into the nave and its flanking colonnade.

During our early years in Istanbul we sometimes came here of a Saturday to have a picnic in the courtyard, sitting in the pergola beside the fountain,

and while the children played in the garden we would read whatever material I had brought along about the Studion, talking about its history while
we sipped the last of the wine. According to the chronicler Theophanes,
the basilica and its associated monastery, the Studion, were erected in 463
by the patrician Studios, who dedicated the church to St. John the Baptist.
But a new study of the church by Urs Peshlow has led him to date the basilica to 449–50, making it the oldest extant church in the city.

The Studion continued to function for nearly half a century after
the Turkish Conquest. At the end of the fifteenth century the church
was converted into a mosque by Ilyas Bey, who served as *imrahor*, or
Chief Equerry, under Beyazit II. Imrahor Camii, as it came to be called,
was badly damaged in the great earthquake of 1894, after which it was
abandoned, the monastery having by then vanished. The Russian
Archaeological Institute made a study of the church in the period
1907–13, and in the years since then a number of other studies have been
made, most recently by Turkish archaeologists in the 1970s. I had hoped
that the latter study would lead to a restoration of the basilica, but it did
not, for this historic and beautiful church seems to have been forgotten
by the powers that be in archaeology, abandoning it to further ruination.

Whenever I come here I recall the words of a misogynist monk of the
Studion, an encomium in praise of his beloved monastery, written in
the mid-fifteenth century during the last twilight of Byzantium, apparently in a moment of transcendent happiness.

*No barbarian looks upon my face, no woman hears my voice. For a thousand years
no useless man has entered the monastery, none of the female sex has trodden its
court. I dwell in a cell that is like a palace; a garden, an olive grove, and a vineyard
surround me. On one hand is the great city with its market-places and on the other
the mother of churches and the empire of the world.*

The route back to the Marmara shore passes under the railway line and
then through an ancient portal in the Byzantine sea-walls. This is Narlı
Kapı, the Pomegranate Gate, which has given its name to the surrounding neighborhood here on the Marmara shore of the Seventh Hill. This
portal is mentioned in the *Book of Ceremonies,* which says that on the feast
day of the Decapitation of St. John the Baptist the emperor would land
here after coming by sea from the Great Palace, and the abbot of the
Studion would conduct him to the church of St. John.

Due south along the shore, the Theodosian walls meet the Marmara,
about a kilometer from Narlı Kapı.

12

AROUND THE LAND WALLS

During our early years in the city, several of our families at the old Robert College would organize a walk along the land-walls, which extend from Marmara to the Golden Horn. Every year in late spring, children included, we brought along a picnic lunch that we would have on one of the defense towers along the way, flowering judas trees scattering their blossoms upon us. In those days the area just inside the walls was quite rural, mostly old wooden houses with kitchen gardens, while outside the walls were vast cemeteries – mostly Turkish, with several Greek and Armenian graveyards as well – and beyond them the downs of Thrace. Now the area inside the walls is still surprisingly rural, though much of it has degenerated into a series of slums, while outside, except for the ancient moat, the new circumferential highway has cut a wide scar across the landscape, though beyond it the spectral cypresses of the various burial grounds screen out some of the ugly industrial developments that have ravaged the Thracian countryside.

The enclosed area of Byzantine Constantinople reached its geographical limit with Theodosius II (r. 408–50), who early in his reign decided to built a new line of land-walls between the Marmara and the Golden Horn. The prefect Anthemius completed the first phase of these fortifications in 413, erecting a single line of walls between the Marmara and the Golden Horn. The circuit extended a mile and a half farther out into Thrace than the Constantinian walls, which were thereupon abandoned and allowed to fall into ruins. However, the severe earthquakes of 447 damaged the fortifications and destroyed fifty-seven defense towers. The new prefect of the East, Constantine, immediately began reconstructing the walls, aided by the circus factions of the Hippodrome who collaborated on the work. In less than two months, the fortifications had been rebuilt; in fact, they were stronger than before, since they now consisted of a double line of walls, with both the inner and outer walls guarded by ninety-six defense towers, of which the inner ones were higher and stouter.

The Theodosian walls were pierced by ten gates and a few small posterns. Five of the ten gates were for public use, and five were generally used only by the military. The difference lay not so much in the structure of the gates as in the fact that the public gates had bridges over the moat leading to roads heading off into Thrace, while four of the five military gates gave access only to the fortifications. Both types were double gates, since they passed through both the inner and outer walls. The public and military gates alternated with one another in position along the wall, the first identified by proper names, the second merely by numbers.

Some of the enormous towers of the inner defense wall are comparatively intact but many more are cleaved, smashed or in ruins. The greater part of the inner wall is still standing but, likewise, earthquakes, armed assaults, and the elements have taken their toll. The outer walls have largely disappeared and one can find fragments of only half its towers.

Thirty inscriptions on the towers, gates, and curtain walls record repairs to the fortifications ranging over a period of a thousand years, the last dated shortly before the fall of the city to the Ottoman Turks under Fatih on May 29, 1453. A government program during the early 1990s restored long sections of the Theodosian walls, but the work was poorly done, using cement that will cause damage to the original building materials. In any event, in places one can now at least see the whole cross-section of the defense works, the inner and outer walls, the inner and outer terraces, known in Greek as the *peribolos* and *parateichion,* and the moat and its counterscarp, the fortifications that for a thousand years protected Byzantium.

A reconstructed stretch of the Theodosian walls, showing the inner and outer walls with their towers, and beyond them the outer terrace and the moat, now used as a kitchen garden

A stretch of the Theodosian walls on the Sixth Hill

The Theodosian walls and the Byzantine sea-walls along the Marmara are linked by the Marble Tower, the fine structure standing on a little promontory on the seaward side of the shore highway. 13 meters wide and 30 meters high, with marble cladding at the base, it is dissimilar to any other construction in the entire circuit of the Byzantine fortifications. It is thought that it may have been designed as an imperial pavilion, a *pied-à-terre* for the emperor when he came by barge from the Great Palace for excursions in the Thracian countryside.

Immediately to the north of the first tower, there is an ancient portal called the Gate of Christ. The name comes from the laureated monogram "XP" inscribed above the arched entrance, the first two letters of Christ's name. This probably perpetuates the name of the original Gate of Christ in the Constantinian wall, the "Isa Kapı" that I mentioned in the last chapter, another example of the extraordinary survival of antiquities in the modern city, right out in the open and not just in museums.

Across the railway line, which cuts through the Theodosian walls between the seventh and eight towers of the inner wall, the eighth tower of the inner wall forms the southwest corner of Yedikule, the Castle of the Seven Towers. This fortress, partly Byzantine and partly Turkish, was built soon after 1453 by Fatih. The seven towers include four built into the Theodosian walls, with three further towers placed inside the walls by Fatih, who connected them with curtain walls to form a five-sided enclosure. There are two central towers on either side of the famous Golden Gate in the Theodosian walls. These marble pylons are apparently part of the original gateway. The two outer gates and their curtain wall were added in the second half of the fourteenth century.

One theory is that Theodosius I erected the Golden Gate c. 390, and that Theodosius II incorporated the gateway into his fortifications when he built the Theodosian walls. Another view, which is now the majority opinion, is that the Golden Gate was erected by Theodosius II when he built the Theodosian walls.

The Golden Gate was designed as a triumphal archway. According to the *Book of Ceremonies,* when a new ruler was acclaimed as Augustus, he entered the city in procession through the Golden Gate, where the patriarch and the populace waited to welcome him, and the same procedure was followed when an emperor returned to the capital after a triumphal campaign. The last such occasion was on August 15, 1261, when Michael VIII Palaeologos passed through the Golden Gate to make his triumphal entry into the city after fifty-seven years of Latin rule.

A small gateway named Yedikule Kapısı leads into the city just to the north of the fortress. Above the arch on the inside there is a relief of Byzantine eagle. This must always have been the public entryway into the city in this vicinity, as indeed it is today, for the Golden Gate itself was reserved for ceremonial occasions.

Yedikule is now open to the public as a museum, its main entrance beside the easternmost tower. This is known in English as the Tower of the Ambassadors, as during the Ottoman era foreign envoys were frequently incarcerated there. Names, dates and the stories of their tribulations are carved on the walls of the tower in a variety of languages, as I discovered when I first visited Yedikule in the spring of 1961. A French inscription advises in verse: "Prisoners, who in your misery groan in this sad place, offer your sorrows with a good heart in God and you will find them lightened."

The pylon to the north of the Golden Gate was also used as a prison in Ottoman times, and it was one of the principal places of execution in the city. When I first visited Yedikule, there were on exhibit the instruments of torture and execution that were used here in Ottoman times, and the guard took pleasure in pointing out the infamous "well of blood" down which the heads of those executed in the tower were supposed to have been flushed into the sea. Sultan Osman II was executed here after he was deposed on May 22, 1622, a tale told by Evliya, who writes that "he was put to death in the Castle of the Seven Towers, by the compression of his testicles, a mode of execution reserved for the Ottoman emperors."

The quarter outside Yedikule is known as Kazlı Çeşme, the Goose Fountain, which takes its name from an ancient street-fountain decorated with the charming relief of a long-necked goose, dating back to Byzantine times. Until the late 1960s, this quarter was the site of a tannery, established there in Fatih's time. Evliya mentions the Goose Fountain in his description of the tannery quarter and its inhabitants.

The offensive smell prevents great people from taking up their abode here, but the inhabitants are so accustomed to it, that if any person perfumed with musk approaches them they feel annoyed. Outside this suburb is a fountain, where on a square piece of marble, is engraved a goose, of admirable workmanship. This fountain goes by the name of Kazli Cheshmeh, the fountain of the goose.

The Goose Fountain is still there, as I observed at the beginning of the new millennium, after not having seen it for forty years. But the tanneries are gone, including their smell, which is not even remembered by those who now live in Kazlı Çeşme.

The next entryway is Belgrad Kapı, known to the Greeks as the Second Military Gate. The Turkish name of the gate stems from the artisans of Belgrade who were brought here after Süleyman captured their city on his first campaign in 1521.

Then comes Silivri Kapı which, like all of the larger gates, is double, featuring gateways in both the outer and inner walls. Situated about 300 meters outside Silivri Kapı, it was known in Greek as the Gate of the Pege as it was the entranceway to the shrine of the Zoodochos Pege, the Life-Giving Spring. In Turkish it is Balıklı Kilise, or the Fishy Church, taking its name from the fish (in Turkish, *balik*) that swim in a pool fed by the sacred spring.

According to the Byzantine chronicler, the spring was first enclosed within a Christian cloister by the emperor Leo I (r. 457–74). Tradition has it that Justinian, while hunting on the Thracian downs one day, came upon a crowd of women at the sacred spring, who told him that its sacred waters had been given therapeutic powers by the Blessed Virgin. Soon thereafter Justinian built a large church to enclose the spring, using surplus materials from Haghia Sophia. Justinian's church was destroyed and subsequently rebuilt on several occasions, the present structure dating from 1833.

Old tombstones inscribed in the Karamanlı script – Turkish written in the Greek alphabet – pave the outer courtyard. The tombstones of the men are carved with representations of their profession or trade: the

An old neighborhood
just inside the
Theodosian walls

scissors of the tailor, the quilled pen of the scribe, the open book of the scholar or teacher, the hammer of the mason, the wine barrel of the tavern owner. Ornate tombs of bishops and patriarchs of the Greek Orthodox Church fill the inner courtyard. When I was last there I visited the tomb of the Patriarch Athenagoras, and I was reminded of the last time I saw him, when he was presiding over the Easter Eve service at the patriarchal church of St. George, looking like one of the biblical prophets in Byzantine icons.

Immediately inside the Silivri Gate there is a sizeable and charming mosque. Sinan built this for Hadım (the Eunuch) Ibrahim Paşa in 1551 when he was Süleyman's grand vezir.

The next gateway is Yeni Mevlevihane Kapi. This was known in Greek as the Gate of Rhegium, since it led to the Palace of Rhegium, 12 miles outside the city on the great Marmara inlet now known as Küçük Çekmece. It was also known as the Gate of the Red Faction, since that part of the walls had been built by the Reds, one of the four groups into which the mobs of the Hippodrome were divided. The Turkish name of the gate come from a *tekke* of Mevlevi dervishes founded by Merkez Efendi, the son-in-law of Sümbül Efendi. The *türbe* of Merkez Efendi is

155

in the large cemetery named for him outside the gateway. His tomb is still a very popular shrine, because he is buried beside an *ayazma* whose waters are reputed to have the power of curing fevers. Evliya writes of how Merkez miraculously discovered this healing spring.

Merkez once said to his fakirs [dervishes], "*I heard underneath the ground a voice saying: 'O Sheikh, I am a spring of reddish water imprisoned in this place for seven thousand years, and am destined to come to the surface of the earth by thy endeavor as a remedy against fever, Endeavor then to release me from my subterranean prison.'" Upon this speech all of his fakirs began to dig a well with him, and forth rushed a sweet spring of a reddish color, which if drunk in the morning with coffee is a proven remedy against fever, and known all over the world by the name of the ayazma of Merkez Efendi.*

Topkapı, the Cannon Gate, is known in Greek as the Gate of St. Romanus, because of its proximity to a church of that name. Its Turkish name comes from the enormous cannon balls that are preserved there, dating from the siege in 1453, when the gate faced the largest cannon in the Ottoman arsenal, the famous Urban. This enormous weapon, named for the Hungarian military engineer who made it for Fatih, was 8 meters long and 20 centimeters in diameter, and could fire a 1,200 pound cannon ball a distance of one mile. Urban caused considerable damage during the final days of the siege, when its bombardment was directed against the length of walls between the Sixth and Seventh Hills.

Just inside the walls north of Topkapı is Kara Ahmet Paşa Camii, one of the most accomplished and beautiful of Sinan's works. Sinan built this *külliye* in 1554 for Kara Ahmet Paşa, who at the time was Süleyman's grand vezir.

A short distance outside Topkapı there is an unusual and interesting mosque that is worth visiting. It can be approached by taking Topkapı Dautpaşa Caddesi, the road that leads off from the gate; the mosque stands about 500 meters off on the left. This is Takkeci Ibrahim Ağa, recognizable immediately by its unique wooden porch and dome. The mosque was founded in 1592 by Ibrahim Ağa who made the felt hats called *takke,* the most distinctive of which were the tall conical headdresses worn by the dervishes. (In Turkish, a maker of such hats would be called a *takkeci.*) Takkeci Ibrahim Ağa Camii is the only ancient wooden mosque in the city to have retained its porch and dome, spared by its remote position outside the walls from the many fires that destroyed or badly damaged all of the other structures of its type that once stood in the city.

When I first visited this mosque, it was in the open countryside, surrounded by the cypresses of an old Turkish cemetery, whereas now it is hemmed in by the three highways that intersect at the Topkapı gate of the city. The walled garden gives some protection from the noise and distraction of the traffic. On my last visit there, in the late 1990s, I sat on a bench in the garden with our son Brendan, who had come from Boston to live once again in Istanbul, after an absence of more than twenty years. The *imam* come over to greet us, asking us where we were from. I said that I was a professor at the University of the Bosphorus, and the *imam* smiled approvingly. He then turned to Brendan, who, summoning up his Turkish, said that he was a student and had come from Boston for a visit. The *imam* was very pleased at this, and passed on the information to the old men who had crowded round us, saying, "The young man has come all the way from Boston to pray with us in our mosque!" Brendan said later that this incident revealed to him that he had truly returned to Istanbul, his boyhood home.

The stretch of walls between Topkapı and Edirne Kapı, the next of the Byzantine public entryways, used to be called the Mesoteichion. Because the walls slope into the valley of the Lycus river, it was the weakest point in the whole defense system, and the Turkish attackers on either side could fire down on the defenders. Consequently, many of the defense towers along the Mesoteichion are just piles of stone and chunks of masonry. The Ottomans finally breached the city walls at this point on May 29, 1453.

Today, Adnan Menderes Caddesi splits the walls 300 meters north of Topkapı and indicates the course of the Lycus river. Stretching from inside the walls here to the Fifth Military Gate, about 400 meters to the north, is Sulukule, the quarter housing the oldest gypsy settlement in Istanbul. The gypsies have been here since the late thirteenth century, when an edict of Andronicus II Palaeologos gave them permission to live inside the walls, since they were employed by the emperor as gamekeepers. But other edicts issued by the church and state authorities warned the townspeople to beware of gypsy fortune-tellers, magicians, musicians, and bear-leaders. The gypsies of Istanbul are still engaged in these activities, although animal rights activists have now persuaded the authorities to ban their performing bears and so those talented animals and their masters are now unemployed, as an old gypsy friend told me recently when I met him in Sulukule.

The civic authorities periodically demolish the gypsy settlement in Sulukule, a row of brightly painted ramshackle structures built up against the Theodosian walls, and when the houses are torn down the bright paint remains on the courses of Byzantine brick and stone, part of the palimpsest of history that is Istanbul. But no matter how many times the gypsies are evicted from Sulukule they always return; there is no getting rid of them, for they are, after all, Istanbul's longest-established community by far.

The section of walls around the Fifth Military Gate was known as the Murus Bacchatureus, which was the emperor Constantine XI Dragases's command post during the final siege and where he was last seen before the walls were breached on the morning of May 29, 1453.

Edirne Kapı, on top of the Sixth Hill, is at 77 meters above sea-level the highest point in the old city. The gate's name is the Turkish equivalent of its Byzantine title, Porta Adrianople, so-called because it was the beginning of the road to Adrianople (modern Edirne). It was also variously called the Gate of Charisius or the Porta Polyandreum, the Gate of the Cemetery (from the large necropolis outside the walls which is now occupied by Turkish, Greek, and Armenian cemeteries). Funerary stelae from the necropolis are set into the courtyard wall of the Greek church of St. George, just inside the walls to the south.

Sultan Mehmet II made his triumphal entrance through Edirne Kapı on May 29, 1453, as commemorated by a modern plaque by the gate. Evliya, whose ancestor Yavuz Ersinan was there as Fatih's standard-bearer, gives a spirited description of this historic event:

The Sultan then having the pontifical turban on his head and sky-blue boots on his feet, mounted on a mule and bearing the sword of Mohammed in his hand, marched in at the head of seventy or eighty thousand Muslim heroes, crying out "Halt not conquerors! God be praised! Ye are the conquerors of Constantinople!"

The great mosque of Mihrimah Sultan, which commands the skyline of the Sixth Hill, is just inside Edirne Kapı. Regarded as one of Sinan's highest architectural achievements, it was built for the princess Mihrimah, the only daughter of Süleyman and Roxelana, in 1565.

From Edirne Kapı, the Theodosian walls stretch for a further 600 meters when they give way to walls constructed in later times, from about the seventh century to the twelfth. The exceptionally well-preserved remains of a Byzantine palace of great grandeur stand at the north end of the existing Theodosian walls. Its Turkish name is Tekfursarayı, the Palace of the Sovereign, while in English it used to be known as the Palace of the Porphyrogenitos. The English name of the

top
The prayer hall of
Mihrimah Sultan Camii

above
Mihrimah Sultan
Camii, on the summit
of the Sixth Hill, the
highest point in the
old city

palace stems from the belief, held by van Millingen and other scholars of his era, that it was erected by Constantine VII Porphyrogenitos (r. 913–59), thus dating it to the tenth century. This identification has since been abandoned, and the palace is now dated to the late thirteenth or early fourteenth century, when it was probably built as an annex to the nearby Palace of Blachernae. Its close proximity to the walls caused the palace to be damaged badly during the last siege in 1453.

Tekfursarayı has been restored in recent years, but since then it has become almost inaccessible. The caretaker, who lives on the premises, never answers the bell and so these days I have to satisfy myself by looking through the gate that closes off the interior of the palace, or examining the exterior from the end of the Theodosian walls. It is a romantic sight indeed, and when I look at the balconied windows on the west façade, I imagine the lords and ladies of the imperial family looking out across the downs of Thrace, where one day early in April 1453 they would have seen banners with the star and crescent unfurled as the Ottoman army under Mehmet II approached, beginning the siege that would bring the world of Byzantium to an end.

The wall leading north from Tekfursarayı is noticeably different from the Theodosian section. To compensate for its design as a single, moatless bulwark, it is thicker than the Theodosian walls and its huge towers are taller and nearer to each other. One can get close to the section that encloses the protrusion between Tekfursarayı and the Blachernae terrace by following the street nearest the wall and walking through the gardens of the houses. This is a picturesque quarter that has not changed since I first explored it forty-two years ago, except that the children who were playing there then may in some cases be the grandparents of the ones I see now.

Manuel I Comnenos (r. 1143–80) constructed the first part of this stretch of the walls, which begins just after Tekfursarayı. It heads westward at a sharp angle to the Theodosian wall and then veers north from the third tower. Well built, it is made up of tall arches, blocked in on the outer side, with nine towers and an entrance known as Eğri Kapı, the Crooked Gate.

Eğri Kapı gets its name from the narrow lane that has to swerve around a *türbe* situated in front of the gate. In the mid-eighteenth century, the chief black eunuch Beşir Ağa, inspired by the belief that the Prophet's companion Hazret Hafız was killed here during the first Arab siege, "discovered" his burial place and built a *türbe* on the spot.

Eğri Kapı has been identified as the Byzantine Gate of the Kaligaria.

It was here, on the evening of May 28, 1453, that the emperor Constantine XI Dragases said farewell to his friend George Sphrantzes, who would later write a history of the fall of Byzantium. After they parted, Sphrantzes watched as the emperor rode off to his post on the Murus Bacchatureus, where he met his death the next morning just as the city fell to the Turks.

The Wall of Manuel Comnenos ends at the third tower beyond Eğri Kapı. The remainder of the stretch from the third tower to the retaining wall of the Blachernae terrace, is of poorer crafsmanship and appears to have been constructed at a later date. A filled-in postern in this section may be the former Gyrolimne Gate, which was an entrance to the Palace of Blachernae, the retaining wall of which becomes part of the fortifications.

The picturesque back lanes lead to Dervişzade Sokaği, the Street of the Dervish's Son, which follows the line of the ancient city walls on their last stretch from the Sixth Hill down to the Golden Horn. As the street reaches the last ridge above the Golden Horn, it comes to the terrace that once supported the Palace of Blachernae, now vanished except for its massive substructures.

The present approach to these substructures is via a modern concrete stairway behind Ivaz Efendi Camii, founded in the years 1581–6 by the then chief judge of Istanbul. Emperor Anastasius I built the original palace here in the late fifth century, using it as a *pied-à-terre* when he visited the nearby shrine of the Virgin at Blachernae. Later rulers expanded and adorned the Palace of Blachernae, as it came to be called, particularly the emperors of the Comnenos dynasty, who made it the principal imperial residence at the end of the eleventh century. The superstructure of the palace vanished after the Turkish Conquest, and all that remains are its vast substructures. These are actually completely above the level of the ground outside the Byzantine fortifications, which here serve as the retaining wall of the Blachernae terrace. The only part of the superstructure that has survived is a ruined tower at the edge of the terrace. The tower is named for the emperor Isaac II Angelos (r. 1185–95, 1203–4), who was imprisoned there in the years between his two reigns.

The surviving elements of the substructure comprise two nearly parallel walls some 60 meters long, the distance between them varying from 2 to 12 meters in width, divided by arched cross-walls into three stories of lofty chambers. The large dungeons appear to be immensely tall because the wooden floors between the stories have not survived.

The owner of the café just beyond Ivaz Efendi Camii has the keys to the Blachernae substructures, and he accompanies visitors with a pow-

The Late Byzantine palace known as Tekfurasarayı, just inside the Theodosian walls on the Sixth Hill

erful fluorescent lamp. At the time of my first visit here, in the spring of 1961, this service was not available and I had brought along my own flashlight. But when I made my way down the stairway, I found that the substructures were brilliantly illuminated, for a Turkish cinema company was shooting a film there. They were taking a break for lunch, and after I introduced myself the director invited me to join them. He explained that the film was about the Turkish capture of Constantinople in 1453, and he introduced me to the actors who were playing sultan Mehmet II and the emperor Constantine XI Dragases. Unfortunately, I never saw the film after it came out, but there would have been no suspense for me, for I knew how it would end.

Dervişzade Sokaği goes down from the Blachernae terrace toward the Golden Horn. A turning on to a cobbled lane called Toklu Dede Sokağı leads to a little cluster of old ramshackle houses built under the northernmost towers of the ancient city walls.

Two parallel walls of different dates, joined at both ends to create a sort of citadel, form the fortifications from the north corner of the Blachernae terrace to the Golden Horn. The emperor Heraclius had the inner wall built in 627, after an attack by the Avars the previous year had revealed a serious weakness in the original fortifications in this area. The three hexagonal towers built to strengthen this part of the wall have been described as the finest of the entire defenses. In 813 an outer wall, studded with four small towers, was added by the emperor Leo V as he thought that the Wall of Heraclius was too ineffective.

A gateway from Toklu Dede Sokaği leads into the citadel, which since the Conquest has been the site of a Turkish graveyard. A *türbe* inside the gateway contains the graves of Ebu Şeybet ül Hudri and Hamd ül Ensari, two companions of the Prophet Mohammed who are believed to have met their death here during the first Arab siege of Constantinople.

When I first explored the citadel, in the spring of 1961, I found the very prominent tombstone of Toklu Dede, another companion of the Prophet, for whom the only street of this little lost village was named. After leaving the citadel, on my way back along this street to the Golden Horn, I came to an abandoned and ruined mosque, called Toklu Dede Camii, which the locals believed had been founded by the saint whose grave I had just seen in the citadel. But I knew that this identification was questionable, from what I had read the night before in Alexander van Millingen's book on the Byzantine churches of the city.

According to van Millingen, Toklu Dede Camii was originally a church founded in the eighth century and dedicated to St. Thecla, the famous companion of St. Paul; it was then rebuilt in the second quarter of the twelfth century by John II Comnenos. After the Conquest it was converted to a mosque and dedicated to Toklu Dede. Van Millingen suggested that Toklu Dede is apocryphal and that his name is a corruption of Thecla.

When I first saw Toklu Dede Camii, I could tell immediately that it had been a church, for at its eastern end there was a central apse flanked by a pair of smaller side apses, with the rest of the structure in ruins. When I saw it again a few years later, it had been rebuilt as a house, although the three apses at the eastern end were still there. The last time I saw it, in the first year of the new millennium, the house had been completely rebuilt and there was no sign of the apses, although Ferudun Özgümüş tells me that, according to his observations, part of the original structure of the church can still be discerned.

And so here we have another example of how history operates in Istanbul: a female Christian saint becomes a Muslim holy man, while her church becomes his mosque and then the house of a local family. I think of this whenever I walk down Toklu Dede Sokaği and pass the house. The entrance to the shrine of Blachernae is at the end of the street, where a left turn leads through Ayvansaray Kapı, the ancient Porta Kiliomene.

13

ÜSKÜDAR AND THE PRINCES' ISLANDS

Other annual excursions we enjoyed at the old Robert College were to Üsküdar, the great suburb on the Asian side of the Bosphorus, and to the Princes' Islands, the little suburban archipelago off the Asian shore of the Marmara.

Üsküdar is ancient Chrysopolis, the City of Gold, founded by the Athenians under Alcibiades in 409 BC. During Byzantine times it was a suburb of Chalcedon, the Greek city founded c. 680 BC on the Asian shore beyond the mouth of the Bosphorus. After the Turkish Conquest, Chrysopolis came to be called Üsküdar, a corruption of the Byzantine Scutari, and Chalcedon became Kadıköy.

The focal point of Üsküdar is Iskele Meydanı, the great seaside square, always filled with crowds swirling between the ferry landings and the bus stops and taxi ranks, those who daily commute between Europe and Asia and the peddlers who hawk their wares to them *en route.* This is where Asia begins, I thought, when I first stepped ashore from a Bosphorus ferry in Iskele Meydanı in the fall of 1960. I still have that feeling today, for in Üsküdar you have the impression that you have left Europe behind and have set foot in boundless Asia.

The Bosphorus ferries land just below Iskele Camii, the stately imperial mosque on the high terrace at the northern end of the square. It was constructed in 1547–8 for Princess Mihrimah, daughter of Süleyman and Roxelana. The architect was the great Sinan, who later built another mosque for Mihrimah on the Sixth Hill, which I described in the last chapter. At the foot of the steps below the mosque there is a very fine baroque fountain, built by Ahmet III in 1726.

The large imperial complex known as Yeni Valide Camii stands on the right side of the main avenue of Üsküdar. Ahmet III built this in 1708–10, dedicating it to his mother, the *valide sultan* Rabia Gülnüş Ümmetullah. The mosque was built in the very last phase of the classical period, and just before the baroque style had come to enliven Ottoman architecture.

On the seafront in recent years a very pleasant promenade has been built along the Asian shore of the Bosphorus as it flows into the Sea of Marmara. There are simple eating-places on caiques moored along the quay, where the poorer people of Üsküdar can eat the same fish as are served to the rich at posh restaurants farther up the Bosphorus, but at only a fraction of the price and, in my humble opinion, in better company.

Heybeliada, known to the Greeks as Halki, the second largest of the Princes' Islands

Şemsi Paşa Camii is near the beginning of the promenade. This is one of the more beautiful of the smaller mosque complexes in the city, built of glittering white stone and standing in a very pretty location right at the water's edge. It was built in 1580 by Sinan for the vezir Şemsi Paşa, and it is simply constructed of a square room with conch-shaped squinches supporting a dome. An unusual but attractive green grille divides the mosque from Şemsi Paşa's *türbe.* The triangular courtyard is created by the walls of the beautifully proportioned *medrese* on two sides and completed by a wall whose grilled windows overlook the Bosphorus.

Beyond the mosque there are park benches along the promenade, where the ordinary people of Üsküdar come in good weather to enjoy the magnificent view, with the old city of Istanbul surrounded by what Procopius called the city's "garland of waters," the Bosphorus joining the Golden Horn to flow together into the Sea of Marmara. One summer evening at the beginning of the new millennium, Dolores and I sat here with our friend Derek Johns, who had just arrived from London. Derek had been wondering where we might go for a drink before dinner, when Dolores took from her bag three glasses and a thermos, from

which she poured out martinis, perhaps the first ever mixed in Europe and drunk in Asia, a truly intercontinental cocktail.

Farther along the promenade there is a picturesque little fortress known as Kız Kule, the Maiden's Tower, standing on a little isle off the shore near the *iskele* at Salacak, one of the iconic images of Istanbul. According to Nicetas Choniates, Manuel I Comnenos built a small fortress on the islet in the mid-twelfth century, which he used to control the entrance to the Bosphorus. The fortress has recently been rebuilt, and now houses an expensive restaurant and café.

The ancient mosque on the brow of the hill, above the highway near Şemsi Paşa Camii, is Rum (meaning "the Greek") Mehmet Paşa Camii, which was built in 1471 and is the oldest extant mosque in Üsküdar. The founder was a Greek who converted to Islam and became one of Fatih's vezirs.

The back gate of the mosque leads onto the winding streets outside, and eventually, on the right, to an imposing baroque mosque known as Ayazma Camii. The mosque was built in 1760–61 by Mustafa III and dedicated to his mother, the *valide sultan* Mihrişah, widow of Ahmet III. The design of the exterior, in particular, makes this one of the more successful of the city's baroque mosques.

At the back of the mosque there is a picturesque graveyard with some interesting old tombstones. On a visit here in the mid-1990s I finally found the two Janissary tombstones that I had been told were somewhere in this graveyard. There was no mistaking them, distinguished by the long fold in the back of the headdress represented on the tombstones, the famous "sleeve of Haci Bektaş," patron saint of the Janissaries. When Mahmut annihilated the Janissaries in 1826, he obliterated every sign of their existence, so deep was his hatred of them, and he even had their tombstones uprooted and smashed; only these two in the graveyard of Ayazma Camii survived because

of their remote location. Now I check them whenever I visit Ayazma Camii, because they are still endangered by collectors and vandals.

Doğancılar Caddesi, the Avenue of the Falconers, with two pretty *çeşmes* at the intersection, can be found to the east of the mosque's south gate. A right turn towards the intersection with Salacak Iskelesi Caddesi leads to an austere tomb. Built by Sinan for Hacı Mehmet Paşa, who died in 1559, it sits on an octagonal terrace covered with tombstones.

Nearby, the Ahmediye *külliye* is an ornate and engaging complex, comprising a mosque, *medrese,* and library, built in 1722 by Eminzade Hacı Ahmet Paşa, Ahmet III's comptroller of the Arsenal. Although some elements lean towards the baroque, it can be seen as the last major building complex in the classical Ottoman style. The complex vies with those of Amcazade Hüseyin Paşa and Bayram Paşa to be the most attractive and original in Istanbul.

When I first saw this complex in the early 1960s, it was in a dilapidated condition and, having been abandoned, it was inhabited by squatters. By the time I saw it again, in the mid-1990s, it had been very well restored and was serving as a Kuran school, in which the students were housed and fed. The man in charge was not an *imam,* as is customary, but a retired air force officer in his early sixties, very well educated and articulate, an idealist who believed that the young boys in his school should learn science and history in addition to their usual religious studies, as he told me in a long conversation. Unfortunately I have not been back to the Ahmediye since then, but I hope to do so soon, though I expect that my friend will no longer be there, since the Kuran school has probably been closed by the new education law.

A stairway under the *dershane* at the southeast corner of the Ahmediye's courtyard goes down to the street below. Nearby, Toptaşı Caddesi, the Avenue of the Cannon Ball, leads uphill to the eponymous stone cannon ball, preserved on the median strip, and on towards Atik Valide Camii, the imperial mosque that dominates views of Üsküdar.

With the exception of the Süleymaniye, the *külliye* of Atik Valide Camii is both the largest and greatest of all of Sinan's architectural designs, even though he didn't complete it until 1583, when he was over ninety years of age. It was built for the *valide sultan* Nur Banu and includes a mosque, a *medrese,* an *imaret,* a *dar-ül kura,* or school for reading the Kuran, a hospital, a *hamam*, and a caravansarai. When I first visited Atik Valide Camii, in the spring of 1961, part of the *külliye* was being used as a prison, but this has been closed and the entire complex restored, so that it is now in excellent condition. On one of my visits I was invited up on to the roof of the *medrese* by the foreman of the restoration project, a barrel-chested man of about sixty, who explained the finer details of the masonry work that was being done by his crew, a group of half a dozen younger men, all of whom turned out to be his sons.

Behind the mosque, an alley beside the graveyard leads to a courtyard featuring a large cloister with domed porticoes resting on marble columns. In the center of what is one of the most beautiful mosque courtyards, the *şadırvan* sits amongst some venerable cypresses and plane trees. The mosque interior is equally beautiful, its carved marble *mihrap* set in a square projecting apse, entirely revetted in magnificent Iznik tiles.

Çinili Camii, the Tiled Mosque, is about one kilometer to the east of Atik Valide Camii. This is a small *külliye* founded c. 1640 by the *valide sultan* Kösem, wife of Ahmet I and mother of sultans Murat IV and Ibrahim. The little mosque, set in a delightful and abundant garden, is uncomplicated, consisting of a square room and a dome, revetted both on the façade and in the interior with Iznik tiles, from which it derives its name.

A ferry boat headed up the Bosphorus

The courtyard of Çinili Camii is always filled with old men, who after a life of hard work now take their ease here in benches shaded by the trees around the mosque. They always welcome me graciously, making room for me on one of the benches, which I accept gratefully, for it is a long and arduous climb up to Çinili Camii, the highest mosque in Üsküdar.

Evliya tells us that "Üsküdar is surrounded on all sides with delightful walks." He goes on to say that "the most celebrated walk of all is that of Büyük [Great] Çamlıca, where a kiosk was built by the present monarch [Murat IV], the chronograph of which was composed by me, poor Evliya." Büyük Çamlıca is about four kilometers east of Iskele Meydanı, recognizable by the many antennae that now rise from its summit. The highest of the two peaks of Mount Bulgurlu, the other summit being Küçük Çamlıca, it rises to 267 meters above sea-level, the highest point around the city. On the summit there is an immense teahouse in the midst of the pine grove that gives the peak its name (*cam* in Turkish means "pine"). The view is most wonderful. While the morning sun is in the east, it provides a panorama of the entire city and the Bosphorus, with the Princes' Islands floating in the Marmara. To the east, one can make out the snow-capped and cloud-plumed summit of Ulu Dağ, the Bithynian Olympos. In the evening, the sun sets behind the old city of Istanbul, silhouetting its minarets and domes against the fiery heavens while the Golden Horn glows like molten gold.

The suburbs along the Asian shore of the Bosphorus are now so built up that one can no longer hike down from Büyük Çamlıca to the strait as

in times past. But when I read Hilary Sumner-Boyd's description of these walks in the 1972 edition of our *Strolling Through Istanbul* I am reminded that "Especially in the spring are these hills and valleys most beautiful, for everywhere is a profusion of the most varied wild flowers and the most unusual birds, as for example the blue-green roller and the hoopoe, king of birds."

High-speed modern ferries go out to the Princes' Islands from Kabataş on the lower European shore of the Bosphorus. But I prefer to travel by the older ferries which leave from the iskele at Eminönü, as I have since I first came to Istanbul, and as others before me have done since the mid-nineteenth century. And even before the ferry service was inaugurated, a trip to the Princes' Islands was a favorite excursion for those seeking to escape from Istanbul for the day. Evliya writes of an excursion that he and his companions made one day, his first journey outside the city.

All the passengers were in high spirits, and some of them implored the Lord's assistance by singing spiritual songs. Some musicians encouraged me to sing along with them, and several of the boatmen accompanied us on their instruments, with such effect that the eyes of the listeners watered with delight. Amidst these amusements we came to the Princes' Islands.

The group includes nine islands, all but four of them tiny. The nearest one is 15 kilometers from Eminönü, the furthest about 30 kilometers, though they can seem far more remote than that, so different are they from the atmosphere and appearance of the rest of the city. Ferries stop at the four largest and most populous of the islands, the closest of which is Kınalı, followed by Burgaz, then Heybeliada, and finally Büyükada, the largest and most populous in the archipelago. During the summer months there are occasional ferries to Kaşık and Sedef. Tavşan and Sivri are uninhabited, while the only residents on Yassı Ada are the staff at the military installation there.

During the medieval Byzantine period the archipelago was known as Papadonissia, the Isles of the Monks, from the several monasteries that had been founded there. These monasteries became famous because of the emperors who were exiled there after losing their thrones, along with ecumenical patriarchs deposed in the frequent theological controversies that divided the Greek Orthodox Church.

According to the Byzantine chronicler Cedrinus, Justin II (r. 565–78) had in 569 built himself a palace and monastery on the largest of the isles, Megale, or the Great, which has the same meaning as the Turkish

Büyükada. Because of the presence of this palace the island was called Prinkipo, the Island of the Prince, and in time the entire archipelago came to be known as the Princes' Islands.

Ayazma Camii, Üsküdar

The islands were sparsely inhabited before the first regularly scheduled ferry service began in 1846. This brought a large influx of visitors who built summer houses on the four largest islands, and many of them eventually settled in as year-round visitors. These were largely well-off Greeks, but included substantial numbers of Armenians, Jews, resident foreigners, and a few prosperous Turkish families. The ferries also brought crowds of day trippers in the summer months, particularly to Büyükada, resulting in the construction of hotels, restaurants, cafés, and bathing establishments. This has to a certain extent marred the natural beauty of the islands, but in their hilly and heavily wooded interiors they remain unspoiled. Automobiles are not permitted on the islands, and so one must travel by the horse-drawn carts known as *phaetons*, which can be hired at the ferry stations. And as the *phaeton* jingles along, it takes you back in time and out of the modern world, which is why we all go out to the Princes' Islands whenever Istanbul becomes too much for us.

The first of the islands at which the ferry calls is Kınalı, now disfigured by the many antennae that rise from its summit. Kınalı means "henna-red", from the color of the sandstone cliffs that plunge into the sea near the eastern end of the island. The island is known in Greek as Proti, or "the First", because it is the closest of the isles to the city. The island has always been inhabited principally by Armenians, though others are now taking up residence. There were three monasteries on the island in Byzantine times, all of which at one time or another housed imperial exiles. The only one of these establishments that has survived is the Monastery of the Transfiguration, which stands on a hilltop overlooking the town and the port. The monastery was founded in the early Byzantine period, but the present church dates from a complete rebuilding in the mid-nineteenth century, as do the other monastic buildings.

The ferry's next stop is at Burgaz, known to the Greeks as Antigone. When we first came out to Burgaz, in the spring of 1961, everyone was speaking Greek, but now only a few Greeks are left, replaced by Turkish and Armenian families. The most prominent landmark in the town is the Greek Orthodox church of St. John the Baptist. This is a modern structure built on the site of a medieval Byzantine monastery of the same dedication. The famous St, Methodius, Patriarch of Constantinople, was imprisoned here in the years 829–42, in a subterranean cell that has been dedicated to his memory.

The third island is Heybeliada, known in Greek as Halki. The hill-top above the town is crowned with the Monastery of Haghia Triada, the Holy Trinity, which houses the famous Greek Orthodox Theological School. According to tradition, the school was founded in the second half of the ninth century by the Patriarch Photius, the prime mover of the medieval Byzantine renaissance. It continued to function until 1971, when it was closed by an act of the Turkish Parliament, though there are hopes that it may be reopened.

One day in the mid-1990s I visited the monastery in the company of Alkis Kourkoulas, a Greek journalist long resident in Istanbul. At that time the only resident of the monastery was a young British monk named Isaias, a convert to Greek Orthodoxy who had only recently come to the island after living for years in a monastery on Mount Athos. Isaias had invited Alkis some weeks before, telling him to bring me along. When we arrived at the monastery, Isaiah greeted us warmly but in something of a fluster, for which he apologized, saying that a dozen other guests had arrived unexpectedly, but that he had managed to arrange lunch for all of us. The other guests turned out to be the Archbishop of Crete and his entourage, who included a newly appointed bishop and other high-ranking clerics, all of whom were in a high-spirited mood and welcomed us to join them.

After lunch Isaias hired half-a-dozen *phaetons* and gave us all a tour of the island, which ended at the island's other monastery, that of St. George, on the seashore just outside town. We continued the party there, drinking Metaxa brandy and eating *meze,* with the Archbishop occasionally pelting one of his companions with an olive pit or pistachio shell and then winking playfully at me and Alkis. The party finally ended when we all had to leave to catch the last ferry back to Constantinople, which is what the Greeks still call the imperial city on the Bosphorus.

The ferry finally stops at Büyükada, the Greek Prinkipo, the largest and most populous of the Princes' Islands. It is also the most beautiful, according to Turks and Greeks of an older generation, although they all bemoan how much it and the other islands have been spoiled by new-comers who do not appreciate the unique spirit of this maritime suburb of Istanbul.

The town of Büyükada is famous for its beautiful old mansions, some of the finest of which can be seen along Çankaya Caddesi. One house of historic interest is the Izzet Paşa Köşkü at 55 Çankaya Caddesi, built in the latter half of the nineteenth century by the Greek banker Constantinos Ilyaso. Toward the end of the nineteenth century the

above
Yeni Valide Camii,
Üsküdar

right
Şemsi Paşa Camii,
Üsküdar

house passed to Izzet Paşa, head of the secret police during the reign of Abdül Hamit II. Leon Trotsky lived here during his first years of exile on Büyükada, 1929–33, and it was here that he began his monumental *History of the Russian Revolution*. One day in the early 1960s I was given a tour of the town by Avadis Hacınlıyan, an Armenian student of mine at Robert College who is now my colleague at the University of the Bosphorus. Avadis said that his parents were living near the Izzet Paşa mansion when Trotsky was confined there and struck up a friendship with him, but the constant presence of the secret police somewhat inhibited their conversations.

These days when I walk along Çankaya Caddesi I always stop for lunch at the cultural center there, established a few years ago by my friend Çelik Gülersoy in a handsome old mansion that he has superbly restored. Other people complain about the deterioration of Istanbul's old mansions and palaces, but Çelik Bay does something about it, restoring these venerable buildings and bringing them back into useful life again, as in the cultural center here and other places in Istanbul.

There are still three monasteries on the island: St. Nicholas, on the eastern coast; the Transfiguration, on Christos Tepe, the hill above the

town; and St. George, on Yüce Tepe, the hill above the far end of the island. All three probably date back in foundation to the Byzantine era, though the present churches and monastic buildings are from the Ottoman period. We have explored all three of these monasteries in the past, but these days when we go out to Büyükada we head straight for Yüce Tepe, taking a *phaeton* to the base of the hill. From there, donkeys can be hired to take you up to the monastery, though we still manage to do it on foot. On the feast day of St. George, April 23, hundreds of pilgrims from all over the world, Muslims as well as Christians, walk up the hill to attend a sunrise service at the monastery, many of them making the trek barefoot, tying talismanic rags to tree branches *en route*, vestiges of religious beliefs older than Christianity.

The monastery is known to the Greeks as Haghios Georgios Koudounas, St. George of the Bells. One version of the foundation legend has it that a shepherd was grazing his flock on this hill when he heard the sound of bells coming from under the ground. When he dug down he found an icon of St. George, which he and the other islanders then enshrined in a little chapel. Tradition says that first monastery here was built in 963, during the reign of Nicephorus II Phocas, though the oldest extant buildings appear to date from the mid-eighteenth century.

The building to the west of the church is a hostel for those who come to visit the monastery, particularly on the feast day of St. George. We have been joined on this pilgrimage in recent years by our grandson Alexander Baker, for April 23 is his birthday, which has prompted our Greek friends to ask why he was not named George. On that day the small café to the east of the church provides food and drink for the pilgrims, including the monastery's homemade red wine, which requires the constitution of a medieval monk. The setting is superb, with all of the other isles spread out below and the Asian coast visible as far as the Gulf of Iznik, the ancient Nicomedeia, above which one can see the summit of Ulu Dağ, Mount Olympos of Bithynia.

The two tiny islets beyond Büyükada also belong to the archipelago. The one to the east is Sedef Adası, "Mother of Pearl Island"; to the south is Tavşan Adası, "Rabbit Island." In Greek, Sedef is known as Terebinthos and Tavşan is Neandros. Tiny as they are, in Byzantine times both islets were the sites of religious establishments, with a monastery on Terebinthos and a convent on Neandros, both of them founded in the mid-ninth century by St. Ignatius, Patriarch of Constantinople.

I had thought that Büyükada was no longer a place of monastic exile, but one day in 1973 I met a character there straight out of the medieval past of Prinkipo. His name was Franz Fischer, though the locals called him Kaya Baba. He was born in Vienna in 1895, he told me, and had fought and been wounded in World War I, after which he had emigrated to the U. S. A. by way of Rumania and obtained a doctorate in micro-biology at New York University, after which he became a professor of biology at Istanbul University. Then when World War II began, he resigned his professorship, sold everything he owned, and moved to the uninhabited northern end of Büyükada, where he built a shack and retired as a hermit with his chickens and pigeons, turning his back on the world.

I accompanied Franz to his shack and he showed me the manuscripts of the two books that he had written by hand during his early years on the island, an incident that I describe in my *Stamboul Sketches*. The first volume was on pantheistic cosmology, but the second contained all the poetry he had written in the course of his lifetime, arranged chronologically. The last poem was titled "Mesons and Melons," which made me laugh because mesons were fundamental nuclear particles that I had studied at New York University. Attached to it was a letter from Professor Werner Heisenberg, the Nobel prizewinning physicist, thanking Franz for having sent him the poem, and encouraging him to keep up the good work. Since then Franz had written nothing, "because I had said all that I had to say; I am at one with the universe and I no longer feel the need to speak or write." There was an elegiac tone to his voice as he told me this, and he looked pathetically sad, but his face lit up when I promised to return and talk with him again one day.

I failed to keep my promise, however, for three years later we left Turkey before we had another opportunity to go out to Büyükada. We returned to Istanbul in September 1988, and as soon as possible we went out to Büyükada, but when I asked for Franz I was told that he had passed away. I went out to look at his shack and saw that it was no longer there; nor did anyone around remember him. And so I turned around and walked away, lighting a candle in my mind to his memory.

14

GALATA AND BEYOGLU

Galata and Beyoğlu, the oldest part of the so-called "modern city," form the north shore of the Golden Horn at its confluence with the Bosphorus. The area was anciently known as Sykai, "the Fig Trees," and during the reign of Theodosius II was made the thirteenth *regio,* or ward, of Constantinople. According to the *Notitis Urbis Constantinopolitanae,* a description of the city written c. AD 447, Sykai had a church, a forum, several public baths, a theater, and a harbor, the whole surrounded by a defense wall.

A fortress known as Kastellon ton Galatou, "the Castle of Galata" on the north shore of the Golden Horn, is believed to have been built by Tiberius II (r. 578–84). This was used to anchor one end of a huge chain which was stretched across the mouth of the inlet whenever Constantinople was attacked from the sea.

The town continued to be known as Sykai up to the seventh century, when it came to be called Galata, after the fortress built by Tiberius. The

The Galata shore of the Golden Horn after a snowstorm. On the skyline to the left is the mosque of Süleyman the Magnificent.

town was also referred to as Pera, which in Greek means "opposite," in the sense that it was across the Golden Horn from Constantinople. Later, from the seventeenth century onward, Pera referred to the district on the heights above Galata, which under the Turkish Republic became Beyoğlu, whose municipal boundaries now include Galata as well, though the latter name is still used for the port quarter at the confluence of the Golden Horn and the Bosphorus.

From about the twelfth century onwards, Galata was under the control of the Genoese. Michael VIII Palaeologos, following the 1261 Greek recapture of Constantinople from the Latins, gave Galata to the Genoese as a semi-autonomous colony with its own *podesta,* a governor who was appointed annually by the senate of Genoa. The Genoese immediately ignored the imperial directive which forbade them from fortifying the town. They continued to develop the area and its fortifications up to the end of the Byzantine era. The focal point of these fortifications was the Galata Tower, erected on the heights above the port in 1348 and still dominating the skyline on the north shore of the Golden Horn. Defense walls radiated down from the Galata Tower to both the Golden Horn and the Bosphorus, with a deep ditch outside the fortifications, while interior walls divided the town up into six fortified enceintes.

During the fourteenth and early fifteenth centuries, Genoese Galata became one of the principal ports in the Levant, handling three times as much trade as Byzantine Constantinople. The importance of the Genoese port is noted by the Muslim traveler Ibn Battuta, who visited Galata in 1334, remarking on the fact that its population was predominantly Latin, although there were Greeks and western Europeans living there as well.

The Genoese in Galata remained neutral during the Ottoman siege of Constantinople in 1453, and so when the city fell their town was not sacked. Fatih signed a peace treaty with the *podesta* of Galata on June 1, 1453, three days after the fall of Constantinople, in which the sultan recognized the rights awarded to Galata by the Byzantine emperors. But Fatih refused to recognize Genoese sovereignty over Galata, and he ordered the destruction of the defense walls as a gesture of submission to his authority, also garrisoning the Galata Tower with Turkish troops.

Fatih appointed an official known as a *voyvoda* to govern Galata. Besides the *voyvoda,* who was changed each year in March, Ottoman justice was administered by a *cadi,* or chief judge, who was paid 500 gold pieces by the townspeople. There was also a military governor, who commanded the garrison that occupied the Galata Tower and the little citadel within its barbican. Nevertheless, Galata had for a time some limited degree of autonomy over its internal affairs. The Catholic churches of Galata, as well as their religious and fraternal organizations, remained until 1683 under the control of a Christian body known as the Magnifica Comunità di Pera. Otherwise, as in the rest of Istanbul, all of the non-Muslims of Galata were under the jurisdiction of the various *millets,* or "nations," headed by the Greek Orthodox patriarch, the Armenian patriarch, and the chief rabbi.

A document of 1476 records that in Galata, besides 260 shops, there were the following number of houses owned by the various ethnic or religious groups: 535 Muslim, 592 Greek, 62 Armenian, and 332 European, the latter probably being principally Genoese. Then large numbers of Sephardic Jews were welcomed to the Ottoman Empire by Beyazit II after they were evicted from Spain in 1492 by Ferdinand and Isabella, many of them settling in Galata, along with the Moors, who had also been expelled by the Spanish rulers.

By the seventeenth century, some of the foreign powers had built palatial embassies in Pera, which was then understood to be in the heights above Galata. Under the "sanctions" negotiated by these powers with the Sublime Porte, each of their embassies formed a separate "nation," which had under its protection various churches in both Pera and Galata, as well as having its own bank, post office, and even jail.

Besides the various ethnic and religious groups, there was also a floating population of seamen and merchant adventurers from all over the Mediterranean and the Middle East, most of whom lived down by the waterfront. Evliya, in his description of Galata in the *Seyahatname,* enumerates the various groups who lived there in his time and tells of their livelihoods.

In Galata there are eighteen wards inhabited by Muslims, seventy by Greeks, three by Franks, one by Jews, and two by Armenians. In the citadel there are no infidels at all, indeed there are none until you come to the mosque of the Arabs ... The different wards of the town are patrolled day and night by watchmen to prevent disorders among the population, who are of a rebellious disposition, on account of which they have from time to time been chastised by the sword. The inhabitants are either sailors, merchants, or craftsmen such as joiners or caulkers. They dress for the most part in Algerine fashion, for a great number of them are Arabs or Moors. The Greeks keep the taverns; most of the Armenians are merchants or money-changers; the Jews are the go-betweens in amorous intrigues and their youths are the worst of all the devotees of debauchery.

It would seem that many others in Galata were "devotees of debauchery" too, as evidenced by Evliya's description of the notorious taverns there.

In Galata there are two hundred taverns and wine shops where the infidels divert themselves with music and drinking. The taverns are celebrated for the wines of Ancona, Saragossa, Mudanya, Smyrna, and Tenedos. The word günaha ["temptation"] is most particularly to be applied to the taverns of Galata because there all kinds of playing and dancing boys, mimics and fools, flock together and delight themselves day and night. When I passed through the district I saw many bareheaded and barefooted lying drunk on the streets.

Galata today has changed beyond recognition from the town of Genoese and Ottoman times. The population is now almost exclusively Muslim Turkish, including many Gypsies, with only small numbers of Greeks, Armenians, Jews, and Levantine Europeans remaining, along with the rare family of Genoese descent, for the Magnificent Community of Pera has now all but vanished.

The only Byzantine monument in Galata is opposite the ferry station in Karaköy, the area around the Galata Bridge, where one can see the minarets of two contiguous mosques, Kemankeş Mustafa Paşa Camii and Yeraltı Cami. The first of these mosques was built in 1624 by Kemankeş Kara Mustafa Paşa, grand vezir of Murat IV, who erected it on the site of the Roman Catholic church and hospital of St. Anthony, which had been demolished in 1606.

Yeraltı Cami means the Underground Mosque, and is so called because its prayer room is below street level. The mosque lies within a vaulted cellar of a Byzantine structure, the superstructure of which has now vanished but is ascertainable as the Castle of Galata erected in the late sixth century by the emperor Tiberius II.

The mosque comprises narrow passages which lie between six rows of nine square pillars supporting the low vaulting. The tombs of Abu Sufyan and Amiri Wahibi, two sainted Muslim warriors who were killed in the first Arab assault on Constantinople in the eighth century, are at the rear. In 1640, a Nakşibendi dervish claimed to have been told the location of their graves in a dream, prompting Murat IV to build the present tombs, one for each of the saints. In 1757, Köse Mustafa Paşa, who served as grand vezir under three successive sultans - Mahmut I, Osman III, and Mustafa III - converted the dungeon into a mosque.

This is one of the places that have not changed in the slightest in all the years I have been in Istanbul, as I could tell after a recent visit to

Yeraltı Cami. Now, as then, the mosque, is used primarily by women, who cluster around the tombs of the two sainted Arab warriors, rocking back and forth on their haunches as they pray as if to a departed god, a scene that can evoke biblical images.

There are ten churches of various creeds in this part of Galata, including three along Kemeraltı Caddesi, the first stretch of the main shore highway up the Bosphorus from the Galata Bridge. These three are: the Armenian Catholic church of Surp Hisis Pirgiç (Christ the Savior), built in 1834; the Roman Catholic church of San Benoit (St. Benedict), founded by the Benedictines in 1427; and the Armenian Gregorian church of Surp Kirkor Lusavoriç (St. Gregory the Illuminator), founded in 1431 and completely rebuilt in 1959 as a replica of the famous church of St. Gregory at Echmiadzin in Armenia, a seventh-century edifice considered to be one of the masterpieces of medieval Armenian architecture.

The side street beside the Armenian church leads into a labyrinthine quarter of old Galata in which it is impossible to give exact directions. When I first explored this quarter in the early 1960s, I was surprised to find three old churches that I at first thought to be Greek Orthodox, dedicated respectively to St. John the Baptist, St. Nicholas, and the Panaghia, the Blessed Virgin. The first one of these that I came upon was the Panaghia, whose courtyard gate had carved above it the name of the church and a cross with a star and crescent in its upper right quadrant, the symbol of the Turkish Orthodox Church, an emblem I later found on the other two churches. I learned that the head of the Turkish Orthodox Church was a dissident Greek Orthodox priest from Anatolia named Efthimios Karahisarides, better known as Papa Eftim, with whom I had a long conversation one Sunday in the early 1960s. The church, which is presently headed by one of Papa Eftim's sons, has now a congregation of no more than a handful of old people, as I found when I visited the Panaghia a couple of years ago, once again startled to hear the Mass sung in Turkish.

There are in this neighborhood also four Russian Orthodox chapels, whose little sky-blue onion domes can be seen from the Galata Tower. These were built in the years 1870–80 as way stations for Russian pilgrims *en route* to pilgrimages in the Holy Land. Two of the chapels are still functioning.

The lower terminus of Tünel, the funicular railway that takes passengers up to the heights of Pera in just 80 seconds, sits between the Galata Bridge and the Atatürk Bridge. When it first opened in 1875,

there was great public enthusiasm among most of those who lived in Pera, for it spared them the long and arduous climb up Yüksek Kaldırım, the Great Step Street. But there were a few old-timers who refused to use Tünel, which they contemptuously called "the Mouse's Hole," one of them saying, "Why should a man go underground before he dies?"

The entrance to a magnificent but very dilapidated old caravansarai, the Rüstem Paşa Hanı, can be found on an alley off Kardeşim Sokağı, the Street of My Brother. It was built for the grand vezir Rüstem Paşa by Sinan. Petrus Gyllius wrote that when he was in the city in 1544–50, the Latin church of St. Michael was demolished to make way for Rüstem Paşa's *han*. The first time I visited the building, I noticed a Byzantine Corinthian capital to the left of the entryway, where it serves as a wellhead, and I figured that this must be a last remnant of St. Michael's, preserved here by pure neglect.

At this point the highway becomes Tershane Caddesi, named after the great *tershane,* or naval arsenal, built by Fatih on the Golden Horn above the present Atatürk Bridge. Galata Bedesten, a covered market built by Fatih soon after the Conquest, is to the left. There is no inscription or documentation to prove this, but its similarity to the Old Bedesten in the Covered Bazaar shows that this too is a work of Fatih.

The avenue ends at Azapkapı, the Marine Gate, so called because this was once the gateway to the Ottoman *tershane*. Beside the avenue sits the Azapkapı Sebili, one of the most beautiful Ottoman street-fountains in the city. This baroque structure, founded in 1732–3 by the *valide sultan* Saliha Hatun, mother of Mahmut I, includes a *sebil* with three grilled windows, and impressive *çeşmes* on either side. Floral motifs cover the façade of the fountain. A few years ago, when I was guiding a group of my students through Galata, we found that the basins of the *çeşmes* were being used as beds by two vagrants, who slept soundly while we examined the *valide sultan's* fountain.

The handsome mosque on the shore of the Golden Horn, beside the Atatürk Bridge, is Azapkapı Camii, built by Sinan in 1577–8 for the grand vezir Sokollu Mehmet Paşa, for whom the architect had earlier built another mosque below the Hippodrome on the First Hill, which I mentioned in an earlier chapter.

Yeşildirek Hamam, a work of Sinan that was part of the Azapkapı *külliye*, is across Tershane Caddesi. The *hamam* is no longer of any architectural interest, since it appears to have been completely rebuilt in modern times, continuing in use as a public bath despite its dilapidated condition. The cul-de-sac to the right of the *hamam* is Eflatun Çıkmaz, the Dead End of Plato, a name whose origin is anyone's guess.

Yolcuzade Sokağı, the Street of the Traveler's Son, leads onto Yanık Kapı Sokağı, the Street of the Burnt Gate, which takes its name from the ancient gateway through which it passes a short way along. This is the only surviving portal in the medieval walls of Genoese Galata, dating from 1397. Above the gateway there is a tablet decorated with the cross of St. George, symbol of Genoa the Superb, between a pair of escutcheons bearing the coats of arms of the noble houses of Doria and De Meruda.

The courtyard of Arap Camii, the Mosque of the Arabs, can be approach via a passageway under its towering minaret which is actually a campanile, for this is the former Latin church of Sts. Paul and Dominic, built by the Dominican fathers during the years 1323–7. Early in the sixteenth century it was converted into a mosque and given over to the colony of Moorish refugees from Spain who had been settled in Galata by Beyazit II; hence the name Arap Camii. Due to fire, the building has been restored several times. On one occasion it was made much wider when the north wall was pushed outwards by several meters. A restoration in 1913–19 revealed the original floor and many Genoese tombstones of the late Byzantine period. Some of the tombstones, which I have examined at the Archaeological Museum, bear the date 1347, when the Black Death came to Galata aboard ships from the Genoese colony of Kaffa in the Crimea, before spreading from Constantinople and ravaging western Europe.

Perşembe Pazari Caddesi, the Avenue of the Thursday Market, named for another of the city's traveling street markets, is near Arap

Camii. The upper stretch of the street is lined with picturesque old buildings of stone and brick that were once thought to be Genoese. I myself thought that they were Genoese, since Evliya writes of the Genoese houses of this sort that he saw when walking this way, but a Cufic inscription on one of the buildings dates it to 1735–6. Current opinion is therefore that they are Ottoman buildings of the mid-eighteenth century, although I am not completely convinced, still holding out for the more romantic possibility that they are Genoese.

The upper end of the street leads into Bankalar Caddesi, formerly Voyvoda Caddesi. The present name comes from the many banks that were established along this avenue in late Ottoman and early Republican times. The most notable of these is the Ottoman Bank, whose huge neo-classical edifice is on the south side of the avenue on the second block to the right.

The building on the corner of Galata Kulesi Sokaği, which takes up the whole side of a very short block, is the ancient Podestat, the Palazzo Communale of Genoese Galata. This was erected in 1316, the only change since then being a cutting back of the façade on Bankalar Caddesi when the avenue was widened in the late nineteenth century. The building directly above this, on the opposite side of the side street to the right, Kart Çinar Sokağı, is also a Genoese building dated 1316, probably an annex of the Palazzo Communale.

The short side street to the left, Eski Banka Sokağı, is entirely bounded on its right by a huge old building known as the Han of St. Pierre. An inscription records that this was erected in 1771 by the Comte de St. Priest, French ambassador to the Sublime Porte in the reign of Mustafa III, who built it as the "lodging and bank of the French Nation." A plaque on the façade bears the coat of arms of the Comte, and another, at the angle where the street bends to the left, has the arms of the Bourbons. A third plaque above that of St. Priest notes that the *han* was erected on the site of an earlier house, where the celebrated French poet André Chenier was born on October 30, 1762. Chenier left Galata with his parents when he was only three years old and spent the rest of his short life in France. He died on the guillotine on July 25, 1794, just two days before the Terror ended on the Ninth Thermidor, with the famous remark – while pointing at his head – *"Et pourtant il y avait quelque chose là"* ("There really was something there after all"). A haunting line in one of Chenier's poems expresses his unfulfilled longing to see the lost Galata of his childhood: *"Galata, que mes yeux désiraient dès longtemps..."* ("Galata, whom my eyes have long desired").

The Roman Catholic church of Sts. Peter and Paul, founded by the Dominican fathers in 1475, is located further up Galata Kulesi Sokağı. The present church is the result of a rebuilding in 1841–3 by the Fossati brothers, who later restored Haghia Sophia.

Along the street, directly opposite the entrance to the monastery, sits the old British jail. This was part of the old British Consulate in the last years of the Ottoman era, and was probably used principally as a lock-up for obstreperous British sailors. It has been well restored by my friend Mete Göktuğ, a Turkish architect who is one of those who are trying to bring Galata back to life after the long decline that has left it a run-down slum. Mete has converted the jail into an attractive café–restaurant, where I always stop for lunch when strolling through Galata.

The Galata Tower, which looms over the whole area, is at the top of the street. This is the iconic image of Galata, and after its recent restoration it looks very much as it would have when it was erected in 1348, with its archaic conical tower once again in place.

When we first visited the tower, in the fall of 1960, it was still being used as a fire-control lookout, as it had been since the mid-nineteenth century. We ascended by a rickety wooden staircase up as far as the penultimate floor, from whence we had to climb a nearly vertical wooden ladder to reach the fire-watch station, where the fireman in charge

View of the confluence of the Bosphorus and the Golden Horn from the heights of Pera, with the Galata Tower in the right foreground. Print by William Bartlett, c.1838

offered me a glass of rakı as a restorative. Now most of the ascent is by elevator, and on the top floor there is a tawdry nightclub offering belly-dancing. But the view from the observation deck is still magnificent, with all of the city and its surrounding waters spread out below.

Part of the barbican around the tower has been restored. The beautiful rococo fountain set up against the wall of the barbican is the Bereketzade Çeşmesi. The fountain in its present form was built in 1732, but the original was erected soon after the Conquest by Bereketzade Hacı Ali Ağa, first Turkish governor of Galata, and stood beside the mosque that he founded, about 60 meters below the tower. When the mosque was demolished in 1950, the fountain was moved to its present location and subsequently restored.

Galip Dede Caddesi leads uphill from the Galata Tower to the upper terminus of Tünel. The entryway of the historic Galata Mevlevihane is near the top of the street on the right. This is a former *tekke* of the mystical brotherhood known as the Mevlevi, famous in the West as the "Whirling Dervishes." The Galata Mevlevihane was one of the sights that foreign travelers were shown in Ottoman times, as John Cam Hobhouse writes in the journal that he kept during his travels in Greece and Turkey with Byron in the years 1809–10: "the people of Constantinople run in crowds to amuse themselves (for no other motive can be assigned to them) at the exhibition of the turning ... Dervishes, to which all strangers are carried, as to the theatre or other places of entertainment in the cities of Christendom."

The *tekke* was built in 1492 by Şeyh Muhammed Semai Sultan Divani, a direct descendant of Mevlana Celaleddin Rumi, the sainted divine and mystic poet who in the thirteenth century founded the dervish brotherhood of the Mevlevi. The *tekke* was closed when all the dervish orders in Turkey were banned in 1925; it was then abandoned until it reopened in 1975 as a museum, having been restored in the interim. The central structure, which was the *semahane,* or dancing-room of the Mevlevi, now houses the Museum of Divan Literature, exhibiting the works and memorabilia of the Sufi poets and philosophers who once lived here.

Among those buried in the picturesque graveyard of the *tekke* is the celebrated Count Bonneval, known in Turkish as Kumbaraci Osman Ahmet Paşa. Bonneval was a French nobleman who joined the Ottoman army in the reign of Mahmut I and was made Commandant of the Corps of Artillery (Kumbaracıbaşı). He died in 1747, having spent the last years of his life as a dervish in the Galara Mevlevihane. A French contemporary wrote of Bonneval that he was "a man of great talent for war, intelligent, eloquent with charm and grace, very proud, a lavish spender, extremely debauched, and a great plunderer."

One day in the mid-1960s, before the *tekke* had been reopened, I had persuaded the watchmen to admit me and two friends, Michael Austin and Bill Hickman, both of whom were fluent in Turkish and could read old Ottoman script as well as Persian and Arabic. I had asked them to help me decipher the inscriptions on the tombstones, and in doing so we were surprised to find that some of them marked the grave of women who were members of the Mevlevi, the first of them that we identified being that of Derviş Emine Hatun, who died in AH 1280, or AD 1864.

While we were doing this, I noticed that there were three white-bearded old men having tea in the pergola behind the *semahane,* and one of them made a gesture inviting us to join them. When we did so they greeted us warmly, saying that they had seen us reading the inscriptions on the tombstones and were curious as to where we had learned how to do so. Michael and Bill said that they had studied Turkish, Persian, and Arabic at university and that they both taught Ottoman history and literature. This pleased the old men, who told us that they had come from Konya to gather the works of Mevlevi literature and memorabilia to be exhibited in the museum that would be opened here after the *tekke* was restored. This was the first we had heard of this project, which was completed about ten years later.

Evliya catches the free spirit of the Mevlevi in his description of their now vanished *tekke* in Beşiktaş, on the European shore of the Bosphorus.

The Mevlevi tekke in Beshiktash is only one story high. The room for the dancing and singing of the dervishes looks out toward the sea ... Their Sheikh, Hasan Dede, who was more than 110 years at the time of his death, used to mount the chair on assembly days and, falling into ecstasy, would many times interpret the verses of the Mesnevi according to the author's original meaning. His successor, Nizen Dervish Yusuf Chelebi, would at times hurl himself down from his chair among the dancing fakirs. When he sang, his voice was so inspired that his audience would remain spellbound. All the lovers of the deity would gather round him and listen to the divine chanting until they were completely out of their wits. He was a very prince of the speculative way of contemplation.

At the upper end of the street, Istiklal Caddesi, the old Grande Rue de Pera, is the main thoroughfare of Beyoğlu, just as it was of Ottoman Pera, extending from the upper terminus of Tünel to Taksim Square.

The Austrian historian Joseph van Hammer, who once, in exasperation, said "Ennui, ennui, thy name is Pera," wrote of the Grande Rue that "It is as narrow as the intellect of its inhabitants, and as long as the tapeworm of their intrigues."

Van Hammer was speaking of the polyglot Levantines who inhabited Pera in his time, the mid-nineteenth century, mostly the non-Muslim minorities and the European businessmen and those attached to the embassies along the Grande Rue. After the creation of the Turkish Republic in 1923, the European ambassadors moved to Ankara, and their old residences along the Grand Rue, now renamed Istiklal Caddesi, the Avenue of Independence, were then lowered to the status of consulates. Nevertheless, these old buildings are so historic and palatial that we continue to call them embassies.

The first street on the right is Kumbaraci Yokuşu, which at its lower end leads to the Crimean Memorial Church. Lord Stratford de Redcliffe, who was Great Britain's ambassador to the Sublime Porte from 1810 until 1856, had it built in the years 1858–68. The church was designed by G. E. Street, architect of the Royal Courts of Justice in London. When we first came to Istanbul, the church was badly dilapidated and was subsequently abandoned, but Father Ian Sherwood almost single-handedly restored it, and it is now functioning again, a large number of its congregation being refugees from Sri Lanka and other places.

The old Swedish Embassy is back on Istiklal Caddesi. The first Swedish ambassador to the Sublime Porte took up residence here in 1750 in a wooden mansion, destroyed by fire in 1818. The present building, designed by the Austrian architect D. Pulgher, was completed in 1870, the decor of its public rooms dating from the period 1790–1810.

The huge commercial building called the Narmanlı Han, distinguished by its portico of enormous Doric columns, is directly across the avenue from the Swedish Embassy. This is one of the oldest buildings along the avenue, probably dating from the late eighteenth or early nineteenth century. During the year 1831, when the present Russian Embassy further down the avenue was under construction, the Russian legation was housed here. It remained in the possession of the Russian government until after World War I, when it was acquired by the Narmanlı brothers, who converted it into an apartment house, with shops on the ground floor. The rooms on the upper floor at the curved corner of the building facing Tünel, were for many years the residence of the renowned Turkish artist Aliye Berger-Boronai (1904–1973), daughter of the famous Şakir Paşa, last Ottoman governor of Salonika, and sister of the celebrated writer Cevat Şakir Kabaağaç, the Fisherman of Halicarnassus.

Whenever I pass the Narmanlı Han I look up at Aliye's old apartment and think of her, for during our early years in Istanbul this was the focal point of Bohemian Beyoğlu, and at her madcap parties we met all of "the unpublished writers, unhung painters, and unheard poets" of that lost generation, as I described them in the first edition of *Strolling Through Istanbul*. She is gone now and her apartment has been converted to commercial uses, but Aliye's paintings survive, in museums and private collections. My own collection comprises only a single engraving but many memories, perpetuated by a treasured photograph by Sedat Pakay of Aliye looking out wistfully from a window of her apartment, which is how I see her whenever I pass the Narmanlı Han.

The Russian Embassy, built in 1837–45 by Giuseppe Fossati, lies further down the avenue. The building was damaged in the 1894 earthquake and even more by a storm in 1905, after which it was restored by the Italian architect Guglielmo Semprini. I was a guest here once in the early 1960s, when the Russian cultural attaché, who I was told was a KBG agent, invited me to have a drink, but he obtained no secrets from me, only my opinions on one of my favorite American writers, Jack London, whom he too admired.

Halfway along the next block on that side a stairway leads down to the Roman Catholic church of Santa Maria Draperis. The church was founded in 1453, just before the Conquest, its original location being near the present Sirkeci station in the old city. It then moved to Galata and later to Pera, where it was established on its present site in 1678. The current church is due to a complete rebuilding in 1904 by Semprini.

Postacılar Sokağı, the Street of the Postmen, is at the beginning of a very long block on which are the main entrances to two of the oldest embassies in Pera, first the Dutch and beyond that the French, whose gardens extend down the slope towards the Golden Horn. The first Dutch embassy was established on this site in 1612; the present building is a work of Gaspare Fossati from the mid-nineteenth century. The French embassy, the oldest in Pera, dates back to 1581, but was completely rebuilt in the years 1839–47 by the Parisian architect Paul Laurcéisque.

Istiklal Caddesi continues up to the Roman Catholic church of San Antoine. This traces its origins back to 1227, the year after the death of St. Francis of Assisi, when the Franciscans built a church in Galata. After this was destroyed by fire in 1696 the Franciscans moved to Pera, ultimately building the present neo-Gothic church in 1913, a work of the Italian architects Giulio Mongeri and Edoardo de Nari. Our son Brendan was married at San Antoine in 1987; he and his fiancée, Ann Taylor, came all the way from Boston to take their vows here, while Dolores and I came from London for the ceremony, because this was the church that we had attended most frequently during our first years in Istanbul.

The side street to the right beyond the church is Acara Sokağı. I cannot pass this street without feeling a tug on my heart, for at its lower end was the famous *Boem* (Turkish for "Bohemia"). This was the liveliest of the many Greek *tavernas* in Istanbul during our early years here, all of them now long gone. The owner, whom we knew only as Yorgo, managed to keep order even during the most spirited evenings, when the dancers sometimes seemed on the verge on extending their *syrto* out

The Roman Catholic Church of San Antoine in Beyoğlu

into the street. His most popular entertainers were the singer and guitarist Todori Negroponte and his lady, the pianist Baroness Tashkent, who continued performing at *Boem* and other Greek *tavernas* in Istanbul up into their early nineties. One anecdote will suffice to give some idea of Todori's irrepressible spirit. One evening in 1974, when Turkey and Greece almost went to war over Cyprus, a Turkish general was sitting at a front table while Todori was singing one Greek song after another. During the first intermission Todori came to sit at our table, and someone asked him if it was wise to sing Greek songs in front of a Turkish general at such a sensitive time. Todori blew a kiss to the general and said to him and everyone else, loudly and in Turkish, "I sing Greek songs in Istanbul and Turkish songs in Athens; I'm a hero of our times!"

One block beyond Acara Sokağı is Galatasaray Meydani, named for the famous Galatasaray Lisesi. Galatasaray was founded at the end of the fifteenth century by Beyazit II as an extension of the renowned Palace School in Topkapı Sarayı; its students were youths taken in the *devşirme* who were trained for careers in the various branches of the Ottoman government and army. In 1868, Sultan Abdül Aziz reestablished the school as a modern secondary on the French model. It has had an important role in the modernization of Turkey ever since then, producing many of the country's leading statesmen and intellectuals.

Meşrutiyet Caddesi leads to the old British Embassy. This is the most impressive of all the embassies that were built in Pera during the Ottoman era. It is a palatial edifice in the style of the Italian Renaissance, with a large courtyard in the front and in the rear a spacious and very English garden. The present building was originally designed by Sir Charles Barry, but it was completed in 1855 by Barry's disciple Charles Smith along somewhat different lines. We have been guests here on many occasions, both for celebrations of the Queen's birthday in the garden and at parties given in the great ballroom. On the latter occasions I am always reminded of the incident that took place at a ball given here in 1856 to celebrate the end of the Crimean War, when Florence Nightingale asked the British ambassador if she could have the linen napkins to bind up the wounds of the soldiers in her hospital. These included my great-grandfather Thomas Ashe, an Irish soldier who had been wounded in the last battle of the Crimean War.

Meşrutiyet Caddesi continues on to Tepebaşı, literally "Top of the Hill," where in the last quarter of the nineteenth century the first European-style hotels were founded. The most renowned of these, the Pera Palas, is still flourishing, catering almost entirely to the same kind of clientele as when it first opened in 1895. Once, in the mid-1960s, Dolores and I turned the children over to a babysitter and spent a four-day holiday in the Pera Palas, booking into the royal suite for 8 dollars a night, a somewhat reduced rate arranged by the Greek manager Niko, a good friend who owed me a favor. The suite is now a museum, since Atatürk always stayed there when he was in Istanbul.

To the left of the British Embassy is the famous Panos Şaraphanesi, a Greek wine tavern founded in 1892 and recently reopened after a restoration. It now caters to young people, rather than the more colorful down-and-out winos I used to see in there when I first came to Istanbul. The most famous of these was a taxi-driver named Şevki, better known as Karancaezmez, "The Man Who Does Not Step On Ants," because of the erratic way he walked when leaving the wine shop.

Here again I refer back to my *Stamboul Sketches,* in this case to remind myself of the colorful characters I knew here in times past, including two barefoot Jewish porters and Şevki, whom I compared to the saint-fools of Evliya's times. The first of these was Solomon, who "strapped to his chest a steering-wheel, gear-shift, hand-brake, and horn, which he operates like any driver as he speeds barefoot through the narrow streets of Galata, honking at those who get in his way." The second was Yakob, who "tried to outdo Solomon by attaching a helicopter propeller to his shoulders."

Karancaezmez, or Şevki, the most famous of present-day saint-fools, is a devoted supporter of the Galatasaray football team. He dresses from head to toe in their orange and yellow colors and has painted his ancient taxi in the same hues, decorating it with signs and banners glorifying Galatasaray. His children, daughters as well as sons, are all named after members of the team, and he dresses them and his poor wife in the team colors. All patrons of his taxi must swear their allegiance to Galatasaray before they are allowed in. On the night before each game he appears in Galatasaray Square holding his arms aloft in silent prayer for his team, fingering a string of huge orange and yellow prayer beads.

As Evliya wrote about the folk saints of his time: "Some are nobles, some imbeciles, some distracted men, some holy men, some poor, some walk under the dress of the common people, some as sheikhs, and some as drunkards; for the tradition says: 'My saints are all under the vaults of heaven, nobody knows them but I.'" Such are the saints of Stamboul, those of Evliya's time and of our own. They all await canonization.

Şahne Sokağı, the Street of the Theater, goes through the heart of the Galatasaray fish market. This is the single most colorful street in Istanbul, and I am happy to say that it has lost little of that color in all the years that I have known it. It is even livelier now that when I first knew it, for there are now many more *meyhanes,* or taverns, along the market and the side street to the left, Nevizade Sokaği. The *meyhanes* I frequented in times past were all in Çiçek Pasajı, the Passage of Flowers, an L-shaped passageway linking the upper end of Şahne Sokaği with Istiklal Caddesi.

The Pasaj was closed for a few years in the early 1970s after part of its structure collapsed, but then it reopened after a restoration. When it did reopen it was under new municipal rules, so that many of the colorful types who frequented it in times past were no longer allowed in, for they would have put off the more respectable clientele who now frequent the Pasaj, including women, who seldom went there in the past. So these days you no longer see sword-swallowers, fire-eaters, acrobats, dancing bears, three-card men, deformed beggars, or gypsy bands. Nor will you see Arnavut Çiçekçi, the Albanian flower-seller, who would in times past stagger through the Pasaj trying to sell the dead roses he had gathered in the cemetery where he slept at night in an unlocked tomb. They are all gone and I miss them. It is true that now my friends can take their wives to the Pasaj, but I can't imagine why they would want to, because it's just not the same without the Albanian flower-seller and the others of his type, who now exist only in my memory.

The last stretch of Istiklal Caddesi leads from Galatasaray to Taksim Meydanı, Beyoğlu's main square, if you can call it that. The side streets branching off this stretch of the avenue are lined with cafés, bars, night-clubs, and places where you can drink and listen to live music, the best of which are humble little *meyhanes* where an Anatolian bard accompanies himself on the *saz* while he sings the songs he has composed after a day working on a building site. My own tours of Beyoğlu often end in one of these places, where at evening's end I recall the lines that Evliya wrote of the *saz*-playing minstrels of his own time, probably in similar circumstances: "These players are possessed of the particular skill to evoke by their tones the remembrance of absent friends and distant countries, so that their listeners grow melancholy."

View of the old city at twilight, from the Golden Horn

15

THE BOSPHORUS

Petrus Gyllius, writing of the establishment of Byzantium in the seventh century BC, says that the true founder was the Bosphorus, by which he meant that it was the presence of this continent-dividing strait that led Byzas and his companions to build a city here. For here they could control the main crossing-point between Europe and Asia and the passageway from the Propontis, or Marmara, into the Pontus Euxinos, more simply known as the Euxine and now as the Black Sea.

Any description of the Bosphorus involves the names Rumeli and Anadolu, the first referring to places on the European side of the strait and the second to those on the Asian shore. The first of these toponyms derives from that of the old Ottoman province of Rumeli, which included Thrace and what is now southern Bulgaria. This name comes from the Turkish *Rum,* or Rome, referring to the eastern Roman dominions that later came to be called the Byzantine Empire. Anadolu is the

Waterfront houses
along the Asian shore
of the Bosphorus

Turkish for Anatolia, the Asian part of Turkey, where 97 percent of the country's land mass is located. Anatolia is the Greek for "east", more literally "the land of sunrise." The name "Asia" may originally have had the same meaning as this in both the Semitic and Indo-European families of languages, while Europe may have meant "sunset" or the "land of darkness." The distinction between those two names would have been dramatically evident to ancient navigators making their way from the Propontis to the Euxine, with Asia to the east and Europe to the west, the sun rising above one shore of the strait and then setting below the other, the deep waters of the channel clearly dividing the land of sunrise from the land of darkness.

The Bosphorus is some 32 kilometers in length, extending generally north–south, though it changes direction abruptly half a dozen times as it flows from the Black Sea to the Sea of Marmara. Its maximum width is 3,500 meters, measured along a line between Rumeli Feneri and Anadolu Feneri, the Lighthouses of Europe and Asia that mark the entrance to the strait from the Black Sea. From there the strait runs in the approximate direction northeast to southwest for the first 10 kilometers of its course, converging to a width of 1,200–1,500 meters. Over the next 10 kilometers it changes direction twice before it comes to its narrowest stretch, known in Turkish as Boğazkesen, or Cut-Throat, flowing north–south for 3 kilometers, with the opposing continental shores only 700 meters apart between Rumeli Hisarı and Anadolu Hisaı, the Castles of Europe and Asia. Beyond the castles, the Bosphorus is fed on its Anatolian side by two streams known as the Sweet Waters of Asia, in Turkish called Göksu and Küçüksu. The strait then gradually widens as it follows a meandering course in the general direction northeast–southwest for the next 9 kilometers, measuring about 2,000 meters in width when it is joined by the Golden Horn to flow into the Sea of Marmara.

The depth of the Bosphorus at the center of its channel generally ranges from about 50 to 75 meters, but at one point just below the castles it reaches a depth of 110 meters. The predominant surface current flows at a rate of 2 to 4 knots from the Black Sea to the Marmara, but, because the channel is so tortuous, eddies producing strong reverse currents flow around most of the indentations on both shores. A strong wind from the south, the dreaded *Lodos,* may also reverse the main current and make it flow toward the Black Sea, in which case the counter-eddies also change direction.

Recent studies have shown that the Bosphorus was formed quite suddenly c. 5600 BC, when the waters of the Black Sea, fed by the rivers flooded by melting glaciers of the last Ice Age, burst through a natural

earth dam at what is now the northern end of the strait and flowed
through the intervening valley into the Sea of Marmara. The best-
known myth connected with the Bosphorus is that of Jason and the
Argonauts, who passed through the straits on their way to the land of
Colchis in quest of the Golden Fleece. Petrus Gyllius identified a number of places along the Bosphorus associated with Jason's voyage, which
is probably based on an early Greek exploration of the straits and the
Euxine beyond. The travel writer Tim Severin re-enacted Jason's voyage
in the mid-1970s, and he wrote to me with an invitation to join his crew,
but we were away from Turkey at the time and so I missed the opportunity, sad to say, for I would like to have been a modern Argonaut.

On the best-known way to explore the Bosphorus is by sea, going up
the European shore and returning along the Asian side, stopping *en
route* at one or another of the villages along the strait. The seaside settle-
ments closest to the city have now became part of the urban mass of
Istanbul, but those farther up the Bosphorus still retain something of
their village-like character, though even they are fast losing their old
charm, as I see to my great regret whenever I return here after a pro-
longed absence.

On the ferry from Eminönü, the first major monument along the
European shore of the Bosphorus is Kılıç Ali Paşa Camii, which stands

Nusretiye Camii, the
Mosque of Victory.
Print by Thomas
Allom, c. 1838

beside the Bosphorus in Tophane, just beyond the former bounds of
Genoese Galata. This mosque complex was built by Sinan for Kılıç Ali
Paşa, the famous admiral who was the only hero to emerge on the

Ottoman side in the Battle of Lepanto in 1571. The mosque, which Sinan completed when he was nearly ninety, is a scaled-down version of Haghia Sophia, which continued to influence the great architect even in the twilight of his long career. The *külliye* also includes a *medrese,* a *hamam,* and the *türbe* of the founder, who died in 1587 at the age of ninety.

Tophane, "the Cannon House," takes its name from the multi-domed structure above the highway across from the mosque. This is a cannon foundry built in 1803 by Selim III for his New Army, replacing earlier foundries going back to the time of Fatih. Across the highway from the foundry is Tophane Çeşmesi, the most beautiful of the baroque street-fountains in Istanbul, built in 1732 by Mahmut I.

A short way farther along the shore highway is Nusretiye Camii, the Mosque of Victory, built in the years 1822–6 by the Armenian architect Kirkor Balyan for Mahmut II. The mosque is so named to mark Mahmut's destruction of the Janissaries in 1826, an episode known in Turkish as Vakayı Hayriye, the Auspicious Event. It is, in my opinion, the finest of the baroque mosques in the city.

A graceful classical mosque stands at the water's edge about 700 meters farther along. This is Molla Çelebi Camii, another work by Sinan. The mosque was built in 1561–2 for the Kadıasker (Chief Justice) Mehmet Efendi, a *savant* and poet of Süleyman's time. About 100 meters

A *yalı,* or waterfront mansion, at Yeniköy on the European shore of the Bosphorus

beyond the mosque there is another elegant baroque street-fountain, also dated 1732. The fountain was built by Hekimoğlu Ali Paşa, whose mosque we saw on our tour of the Seventh Hill.

The next building of interest, 400 meters away, is Dolmabahçe Camii, a baroque mosque started by the *valide sultan* Bezmialem, and completed in 1853 by her son Abdül Mecit. The architect was Nikoğos Balyan, a grandson of Kirkor Balyan, builder of Nusretiye Camii. Nikoğos also erected the clock tower beyond the mosque, both of them built by him at the same time as Dolmabahçe Sarayi, the enormous edifice of white marble that lies a short way farther along the Bosphorus.

Dolmabahçe Sarayi, meaning "filled-in garden," is the grandest imperial Ottoman palace on the Bosphorus. Ahmet I and his successor Osman II filled in what was formerly an inlet of the Bosphorus in order to create a royal park. The present palace was built for Abdül Mecit by Nikoğos Balyan and his brother Karbet. It was completed in 1854, but the sultan and his household only took up residence in 1856, when Topkapı Sarayı, which for the previous three centuries had been the principal imperial residence, was abandoned. With the exception of Abdül Hamit II, who preferred the greater tranquility of his palace at Yıldız, a short way up the Bosphorus, Dolmabahçe became the principal residence of all the later sultans. After the demise of the Ottoman empire, the palace became an important state residence. It was used by Atatürk as his presidential residence in Istanbul. The room in which he died on November 10, 1938, has been preserved as it was at the time of his passing.

Beşiktaş, once a Bosphorus village and now part of the urban mass of Istanbul, is some 200 meters beyond the palace. The Maritime Museum (Deniz Müsesi) is just beyond the south end of the park by the *iskele,* and is worth a visit if only to see the imperial *pazar caiques,* the beautiful barges in which the sultans were rowed to their palaces along the Bosphorus and the Golden Horn. When I see these caiques, I am always reminded of a verse by Nedim, the court poet of Ahmet III, the Tulip King, where he asks his love to join him in a voyage to Sa'adabad, the Palace of Eternal Happiness:

Let us give a little comfort to this heart that's wearied so,
Let us visit Sa'adabad, my swaying cypress, let us go!
Look, there is a swift caique all ready at the pier below,
Let us visit Sa'adabad, my swaying cypress, let us go!

The handsome domed structure in the park is the *türbe* of the famed Hayrettin Paşa, known to Western readers as Barbarossa. The *türbe* is a work of Sinan and was completed in 1542, four years before Barbarossa's death. The bronze statue of the celebrated pirate admiral, by the Turkish sculptor Zühtü Müridoğlu, was erected in 1946, the fourth centennial of Barbarossa's death.

Barbarossa is one of the very few Ottoman names that have survived in modern Turkey. One of his descendants, Kenan Barbarossa, was a student of mine at Robert College in the early 1960s, and one day he showed me Hayrettin Paşa's last will and testament, which is still in the family's possession, unlike the vast properties that the old admiral once owned.

The attractive brick and stone mosque on the other side of the highway is another work of Sinan. This is Sinan Paşa Camii, completed in 1556. The founder was another of Süleyman's admirals, a brother of the grand vezir Rüstem Paşa.

The Çırağan Palace Hotel is about 500 meters beyond Beşiktaş. The main building of the hotel was erected on the ruins of Çırağan Sarayı, another imperial palace built by Abdül Mecit, completed in 1874. Çırağan housed the newly reconvened Ottoman Parliament for a time after the Constitution of 1908 came into effect, but then early in January 1910 it was destroyed in a fire. When I first passed the palace, in a ferry in September 1960, it was still a fire-blackened shell, but then two decades later the Çırağan Palace Hotel was erected on its site, incorporating the few marble columns that still remained from the original palace.

A short distance beyond the hotel along the shore highway a side road leads uphill to Yıldız Park, the site of Yıldız Sarayı and its various pavilions, kiosks, and surrounding gardens.

A short way beyond the entrance to Yıldız Park a narrow road leads up from the shore highway to the shrine of Yahya Efendi, whose mother nursed his infant foster brother, Süleyman the Magnificent. Yahya became a noted divine during the reign of Süleyman, and when he died here in 1570 he was buried in a *türbe* built by Sinan. The *külliye* also includes a *medrese,* which is now enveloped in a cluster of nineteenth-century wooden buildings, including a dervish *tekke,* that have grown up around Yahya Efendi's shrine. The buildings themselves are charming, but even more picturesque is the setting, with the tombstones in the graveyard scattered apparently randomly among the trees. Beyond, one can catch an occasional glimpse of the Bosphorus. This is one of the most popular shrines in the city, and whenever I go there I find crowds of pilgrims clustering around Yahya Efendi's *türbe.*

Ortaköy, 800 meters further along the Bophorus, is now part of the urban mass of Istanbul, but it still has a village-like atmosphere, despite

the many restaurants, cafés, bars, and night-clubs that have opened in and around it in recent years. The village is dominated by Mecidiye Camii, a charming baroque mosque dramatically situated on a promontory just upstream from the ferry landing. The mosque was built for Abdül Mecit in 1854 by Nikoğos Balyan, architect of Dolmabahçe Sarayı and Dolmabahçe Camii.

Within the village there is a synagogue and a Greek Orthodox church on successive corners along the shore road, both of them still functioning. On the corner beyond the church there is a recently restored Ottoman *hamam*. This was built by Sinan for Hüsrev Kethüda, who served as steward for the grand vezir Sokollu Mehmet Paşa.

Just beyond Ortaköy, the strait flows under Atatürk Köprüsü, the first of the Bosphorus bridges, which opened on October 29, 1973, the fiftieth anniversary of the founding of the Turkish Republic. On that day Dolores and I looked on from a hillside on the Asian shore, for we thought that there was no way that we could make our way on to the bridge, as there were vast crowds heading for it from both sides of the straits. Then as we watched, we could see the great mass of humanity

above
Yalıs on the Asian shore
of the Bosphorus

above right
The upper Bosphorus
bridge, passing
directly above the
great fortress of
Rumeli Hisar

being forced off the bridge by the army and police, and I later learned that the authorities feared that the weight of the crowd would cause the structure to go into a torsional mode of vibration and collapse. The bridge has never since been open to pedestrians.

In turn beyond the bridge are Kuruçeşme, Arnavutköy, Bebek and Rumeli Hisarı, four communities along the European shore that still retain their village-like character, particularly in the side streets that lead uphill from the shore road, flanked by old wooden houses of the late Ottoman era that have all but disappeared elsewhere in the city.

Arnavutköy is the most picturesque of the villages on the European shore of the Bosphorus, particularly the row of old wooden houses along the waterfront beside the *iskele*. The village still has a Greek community, who worship in the Church of the Archangels, whose dome can be seen from passing ferries. The promontory on the upstream end of the village is known as Akinti Burnu, "Cape of the Current," because the Bosphorus flows more swiftly there than anywhere else on the European side of the strait, some 5 knots when the wind is from the north. Sailing vessels in times past had to be towed around this point, and even today small fishing boats barely make headway there.

The *iskele* in Bebek has recently been restored, and next to its ticket office and waiting room Çelik Gülersoy had opened an elegant café. Just upstream from the *iskele* in Bebek there is a charming little mosque built in 1913 by Kemalettin Bey, a leader of the so-called "neo-classical" school of Turkish architecture.

Boğaziçi University, the University of the Bosphorus, is on the hill between Bebek and Rumeli Hisarı. Established in 1971, the university is on the site of the old Robert College, founded in 1863 by the American missionary Cyrus Hamlin. The students at Robert College were originally all from the non-Muslim minorities, the first Turk to graduate being Hüseyin Pektaş of the class of 1903, who later became Turkish vice-president of the college. When I arrived in 1960, the student body, which then numbered 800, was almost exclusively Turkish, and included women, the first of whom had been admitted four years earlier. When I left in 1976, the new University of the Bosphorus was well underway, and when I returned to the faculty in 1993 it was flourishing, with an enrollment of 10,000, its graduate school granting doctorates in virtually all fields except law and medicine. The staff and graduates who attended Robert College during its 108-year history include among their number some figures of great importance. The graduates include four prime ministers: two of Bulgaria in the late nineteenth century and two of Turkey in more recent years, namely Bülent Ecevit and Tansu Çiller, the first woman to hold the office in Turkey.

Dolmabahçe Sarayi, on the European shore of the Bosphorus

The Bosphorus reaches its narrowest width between Rumeli Hisarı and Anadolu Hisarı, just beyond Bebek. In 512 BC, the Persian king Darius chose this point to span the strait while leading an army of 700,000 to fight the Scythians. The army crossed on a bridge of boats built by the king's Greek engineer, Mandrocles of Samos, a feat recorded by Herodotus, whose account includes the first mention of Byzantium in history.

The village of Rumeli Hisarı takes its name from the great Castle of Rumelia, built by Mehmet II in the summer of 1452 to cut off Constantinople from the Black Sea in preparation for his siege of the city the following year. It is a magnificent late medieval fortification, the largest ever built by the Ottoman Turks, and it still dominates the narrows of the Bosphorus, its massive towers part of the landscape of memory for those of us who have lived a large part of our lives within view of Rumeli Hisarı.

The cemetery under the walls of the fortress is the oldest Turkish burial ground on the European side of the city, its earliest grave dating to 1452. One of the interesting graves that I discovered here is that of Durmuş Dede, whose tomb is just above the Bosphorus road, the inscription recording the date of his death as 1648. Durmuş established a *tekke* on the shore of the Bosphorus here that continued in existence until the dervish orders were banned in 1925. During Ottoman times ships heading up the Bosphorus to the Black Sea would drop off supplies for the dervishes in the *tekke*, for they believed that Durmuş Dede would then give them good luck on their voyage.

The public road to the lower entrance of our university leads past this cemetery, and I always walk along it on my way to and from the Bosphorus. At the foot of the hill a new park has been created across the shore road from the Bosphorus, and at its center is a bronze statue of the Turkish poet Orhan Veli (1914–1950), who is shown here feeding seagulls, as he often did at this place. When I see his statue I am reminded of one of his poems – "Something's Up" – translated thus by my late friend David Garwood:

Is the sea this lovely every day?
Do the skies look like this all time,
Are things, this window, for instance, always as lovely as this?
No, certainly not,
I swear it.
There's something behind all this beauty.

Just upstream from the village of Rumeli Hisarı is Fatih Mehmet Sultan Köprüsü, the second Bosphorus bridge. This was opened in 1988, exactly 2,500 years after Darius had Mandrocles build his bridge of boats across this same stretch of the Bosphorus.

Beyond the second bridge there are a succession of communities on the European shore of the middle Bosphorus – Baltaliman, Boyacıköy, Emirgan, Istinye, Yeniköy, and Tarabya – all of which still retain their village-like character in their interiors. Yeniköy and Tarabya were once predominately Greek, but now most of the Greeks have departed, though their churches still continue to serve their diminishing congregations. Both Istinye and Tarabya were identified by Gyllius as sites associated with the voyage of Jason and the Argonauts, their ancient names being Sosthenion and Therapeia, respectively, but the identification with the mythical voyage of the *Argo* is very tenuous.

The next village is Büyükdere, which was also predominately Greek up until recent times, and which now has a large number of gypsies. Büyükdere, meaning "Great Valley," was known in Greek as Kalos Agros, or "Beautiful Meadow," both names stemming from the broad valley that extends inland from the bay. The knights of the First Crusade camped in this valley before they crossed the Bosphorus in 1096, and up until the late nineteenth century locals pointed out an ancient plane tree under which Godefroy de Bouillion, the leader of the expedition, pitched his tent.

Next comes Sarıyer, the last big village on the European shore of the Bosphorus. Sadberk Hanım Museum, a unique and rich collection of antiquities and Turkish works of art, superbly displayed, is by the entryway to Sarıyer. The most picturesque part of Sarıyer is its enclosed port, where the local fishermen moor their boats after long voyages in the Black Sea, spreading out their nets on the quay to dry and be mended. The fishermen were once predominately Greek, but now they are mostly Laz, from the eastern Turkish coast of the Black Sea, as I knew when I heard the wail of a *gayda,* the primitive Pontic bagpipes that they occasionally play when they are mending their nets.

The shrine of Telli Baba, whose name literally means "the Wired-Up Saint," lies on the approach to Rumeli Kavağı, the last *iskele* on the European shore. Telli Baba is one of the most popular of the Muslim folk saints of Istanbul, because he is reputed to have the power of finding suitable husbands for the young women who make pilgrimages to his tomb. After their weddings the grateful brides come here to give thanks to him, fastening coils of silvered wire to the grillework of his tomb as talismans – hence the name *telli.*

At Rumeli Kavağı there is a clear view of the mouth of the Bosphorus on the Black Sea, 7 kilometers distant. The coastal highway ends here, and those who want to drive further have to turn inland and continue along the road that runs along the crest of the ridge, ending at Rumeli Feneri, with a turn-off *en route* to the hamlet of Garipçe, the only other community on the European shore of the upper Bosphorus.

But the best way to see the upper Bosphorus is by boat, for this part of the strait is completely undeveloped, and, except for the submarine net that once barred the way, it looks exactly as it did when I first saw it in 1960. The area has a wild, desolate beauty, but there are occasional

Mecidye Camii, on the European shore of the Bosphorus at Ortaköy, with Atatürk Köprüsü, the first Bosphorus bridge, in the background

fine, secluded beaches, while the sea is enlivened by cormorants, shearwaters and schools of dolphins.

The only two villages on the European shore of the upper Bosphorus – Garipçe and Rumeli Feneri – were both identified by Gyllius with sites mentioned in the *Argonautica*. Garipçe, meaning "strange" or "curious," because of the odd contours and textures of the dark and craggy promontory on which the hamlet is built, is dominated by the ruins of an Ottoman fortress built in 1773 by Baron de Tott, a French engineer in the Ottoman service. The ancient Greek name of this place was Gyropolis, Town of Vultures. Gyllius identified it with the home of King Phineus, who advised the Argonauts on how to pass through the Symplegades, the infamous "Clashing Rocks" at the mouth of the Bosphorus.

Gyllius identified the Symplegades with the huge rock formation off the European shore at Rumeli Feneri at the mouth of the Bosphorus. The rock, which is now joined to the shore by a concrete mole, is about 20 meters high, divided by a deep fissure into two parts. On the peak of the highest part are the remains of the so-called Pillar of Pompey. The fragmentary monument is not really a column base, as Hilary Sumner-Boyd and I discovered when we made the perilous ascent. Rather, it is a very old altar, embellished with eroded reliefs including the garlanded head of a ram. Gyllius thought that the altar was probably a remnant of a shrine to Apollo, which Dionysos Byzantios says the Romans erected on one of the Clashing Rocks. The column, which featured a Corinthian capital, had disappeared by 1800, having fallen over in April 1680.

The lighthouse from which Rumeli Feneri takes its name is at the highest point of the fishing village. Since antiquity there has been a beacon here that, with the one across the way in Anadulu Feneri, marks the entrance to the Bosphorus from the Black Sea. The ruined fortress on the promontory just beyond the village dates from 1769, built by a Greek military engineer in the Ottoman service.

The ferry crosses the mouth of the Bosphorus to Anadolu Feneri, where it makes the return journey down the Asian shore of the strait. The Asian shore of the upper Bosphorus is even more scenic than the European side, for the hills are higher and steeper, at a number of places falling in sheer cliffs into the sea.

After Anadolu Feneri, a hamlet clustering around the lighthouse on the hilltop above the mouth of the Bosphorus, the next community is Poyraz, a tiny village on the heights above. Poyraz is a corruption of the Greek Boreas, mythical King of the Winds, and is the Turkish name for the cruel northwest wind that thrashes along the Bosphorus during the winter months. The long sandy beach below the village is known as Poyraz Bay, where in times past we would come to swim in the summer. The coastal stretch from there to Anadolu Kavağı, the next village, is now called Keçili Liman, Goat Bay. While we have seen goats, as well as sheep and cows, grazing on its barren slopes, is not really what one would usually call a bay as it is so rugged and sheer.

The lofty promontory on the approach to Anadolu Kavağı is the ruined fortress known as the Genoese Castle. The fortress is actually Byzantine, as evidenced by numerous inscriptions, although it may have been taken over by the Genoese during the last two centuries of Byzantium. We would occasionally picnic there in times past, commanding a magnificent view of the upper Bosphorus and its mouth on the Black Sea. The promontory is known in Turkish as Yoros, which led Gyllius to identify this as the site of the temple of Zeus Ourious, Zeus of the Favoring Wind, and the Hieron, or holy precinct, where there were shrines of the Twelve Gods. This would be the temple that Darius visited while Mandrocles was building his bridge of boats across the Bosphorus. I remember reading Herodotus' account of this incident on the occasion of our first picnic on this hilltop, in Book IV of his *Histories,* where he writes that

Darius continued his march from Susa to Chalcedon on the Bosphorus, where the bridge was, and then took ship and sailed to the Cyanean rocks – those rocks according to the Greek story used to be constantly changing their position. Here seated in the temple which stands by the straits, he looked out over the Black Sea, a sight indeed worth seeing.

Below the fortress to the south is the village of Anadolu Kavağı, the last ferry stop on the Asian shore of the Bosphorus. South of the village is Yuşa Tepesi, the Hill of Joshua, whose summit is the highest point along the Bosphorus after Büyük Çamlıca, 201 meters above sea-level. Originally known as the Bed of Hercules, the hilltop is called the Giant's Grave by Westerners. The Turkish shrine on the hilltop is dedicated to a Muslim saint known as Yuşa Baba, whose lengthy grave, marked by columns at the head and foot some 12 meters apart, has encouraged the belief that he was a giant, an Islamic reincarnation of Joshua with the stature of Hercules.

The next *iskele* is at Beykoz, by far the largest village on the upper Bosphorus. The harbor of Beykoz still has a *dalyan,* a huge fishnet suspended on poles, which the local fishermen draw up when they trap a school of fish. This is the only *dalyan* remaining on the Bosphorus, and each time I approach Beykoz I fear that it will be gone, but somehow it continues to survive.

The village square of Beykoz has a highly unusual and pretty *çeşme* in the shape of a loggia with a dome and columns. An inscription dates it to AH 1159, or AD 1746, and another source identifies its founder as one Ishak Ağa, inspector of the customs under Mahmut I.

The next *iskele* is Çubuklu, where on the hill above the village sits the former palace of the Khedive of Egypt, a characteristic landmark on this part of the Bosphorus. It was built c. 1900 by Abbas Hilmi Paşa, the last Egyptian Khedive, or hereditary Viceroy, and for a palace of that date it has considerable charm.

The *iskele* at Kanlıca has been famous for centuries for its yogurt, served at little restaurants around the ferry landing. The mosque on the far side of the square is a minor work of Sinan, built in 1560 for the vezir Iskender Paşa.

Between Kanlıca and Anadolu Hisarı, the next village, the ferry passes once again under the second Bosphorus bridge. A short way beyond the bridge are what remains of the oldest and most historic *yalı* on the Bosphorus. This was built in 1697 by Amcazade Hüseyin Paşa, the fourth member of the illustrious Köprülü family to hold the office of grand vezir. The following year Hüseyin Paşa represented Mustafa II in the negotiations with the European powers that resulted in the Peace of Carlowitz, the final articles of which were signed in this *yalı* on January 26, 1699. The original *yalı* has long since disappeared, with the exception of the remains of a once attractive room built over the sea. It is in such a terrible state that it is unlikely to be restored.

The *iskele* in Anadolu Hisarı is just north of the mouth of the Göksu, one of the two streams that make up the Sweet Waters of Asia, the second of which, Küçüksu, is a few hundred meters to the south. Just beside the *iskele,* to the north, is the little fortress of Anadolu Hisarı, one of the most romantic sights on the Bosphorus, a sea-girt medieval castle that well deserves its Turkish name of Güzelce, the Beautiful One. The fortress was built by Beyazit I in 1397, when the Ottomans first reached the Bosphorus. Beyazit soon afterwards put Constantinople under siege, but the city was spared when the sultan was defeated by Tamerlane at the Battle of Ankara in 1402.

In times past we often hired a *sandal* in Bebek and rowed across the Bosphorus to Anadolu Hisarı, where we would have a drink at the café under the bridge over the Göksu before returning. (After parties at Robert College, some of the more adventurous of our friends occasionally swam across the Bosphorus, a sobering experience.) Evliya writes of this romantic bridge in his description of the Göksu, which in Turkish means "the Heavenly Stream":

The Göksu is a river resembling the spring of life, which flows from Mount Alemdag, and is adorned on both banks with gardens and mills. It is crossed by a wooden bridge, under which pass the boats of lovers, who come here to enjoy the delicious meadows; it is a place very worth seeing.

The Sweet Waters of Asia were a favorite resort of the sultans and the Ottoman aristocracy. Two monuments remain from those days, the palace and fountain of Küçüksu. The palace, erected for Abdül Mecit in 1856–7, is a charming little rococo building designed by Nikoğos Balyan. It stands on the brink of the sea on the location of several earlier imperial pavilions. The fountain, one of the most beautiful baroque works in the city and a favorite subject for artists in the nineteenth century, was built by the *valide sultan* Mihrişah in 1796. The founder's name and the date of foundation are given in a long calligraphic chronogram of 32 lines by the poet Hatif, inscribed across all four faces of the fountain, ending with these verses:

And our course wishes us to be of this water now,
And to be as tall as a cypress tree, a fragile beauty in the meadow;
Hatif, tell us a date worthy of this soul-caressing fountain:
Küçüksu gave to this continent brilliance and light.

Just beyond the Kücüksu *iskele* is the Kıbrıslı Yalısı, the longest seaside mansion on the Bosphorus, dating from the mid-nineteenth century. It takes its name from its second owner, the grand vezir Kıbrıslı (from Cyprus) Mehmet Emin Paşa, whose descendants still live in the *yalı*. The second mansion beyond that is the Kırmızı (Red) Yalı, also dating from the mid-nineteenth century. This handsome edifice was for long the residence of the Ostrorogs, a noble French-Polish family who moved to Turkey in the late Ottoman era. The last of the line, Count Jean Ostrorog, invited us to a party at the *yalı* in 1973, when we met all of the old Ottoman aristocracy who were still living in their seaside mansions on the Asian shore of the middle Bosphorus. They are all gone now. The Count himself passed away in 1975, and whenever I pass his *yalı* I remember him sitting there on his balcony of a summer evening, waving to friends passing in a *sandal* under a full moon.

Between Küçüksu and Vaniköy, the next *iskele*, is Kandilli Burnu where the water flows at 4 to 5 knots, the so-called Devil's Current. The deepest part of the Bosphorus is in the center of the channel off Kandilli Burnu, where there is a trough 110 meters in depth.

Kuleli Officers Training College is an imposing site on the shore south of Vaniköy. The original training school and barracks here were built c. 1800 by Selim III, part of his attempted reform of the Ottoman armed forces. The present structure dates from an extensive rebuilding and enlargement by Abdül Mecit, completed in 1860. The older building served as a military hospital during the Crimean War, its nursing service supervised by Florence Nightingale, along with the hospital at the Selimiye barracks.

The next *iskele* is at Çengelköy, a picturesque village whose main square is at the ferry landing, shaded by plane trees and graced by a baroque fountain. South of the *iskele* there is the handsome Sadullah Paşa Yalısı, one of the oldest on the Bosphorus, dating from the late eighteenth century.

The ferry stops next at Beylerbey, just above the first Bosphorus bridge. Adjoining the *iskele* is Beylerbey Camii, an attractive baroque mosque built in 1778 by the architect Mehmet Tahir Ağa for Abdül Hamit I.

Beylerbey Sarayı, the largest Ottoman palace on the Bosphorus after Dolmabahçe, lies almost underneath the bridge. The first sultan to reside at Beylerbey was Mahmut II, who built a summer palace that was destroyed by fire in the mid-nineteenth century. The present Palace of Beylerbey was built by Sarkis Balyan for Abdül Aziz and was completed in 1865. Beylerbey, in my opinion, is more beautiful than Dolmabahçe, and was probably more comfortable to live in and more private.

The next *iskele* is at Kuzguncuk, which still retains its village character despite its close proximity to Üsküdar, the next stop on the ferry. Kuzguncuk was noted in times not too far past for its multi-ethnic character, but most of the non-Muslim minorities have now departed. Besides the village mosque, there are two Greek churches, an Armenian church, and two synagogues, all of them still functioning, though with much diminished congregations.

The ferry journey ends at Üsküdar, but there is more yet to be said about the Bosphorus, particularly for an observer looking back from the twenty-first century to the time when he first came to Istanbul. "What has changed?" people ask, and in lieu of an answer I sometimes refer them to a chapter of my *Stamboul Sketches* entitled "A Café on the Bosphorus," named for a now-vanished *meyhane* called Nazmi's. There a fisherman named Riza Kaptan once explained to us the unchanging cycle of seasons and their ever-recurring winds that has implanted itself deeply in the subconscious of the city, so that those of us exiled here have attuned ourselves to it just as did the departed generations who dwelt here in times past.

When I returned to Istanbul in 1993, after an absence of seventeen years, I found that Nazmi's had closed and that Riza Kaptan had passed away. I sat on a park bench on the quay opposite the site of Nazmi's, now occupied by an apartment house, and from there I could see two old fishermen sitting in a shack they had built on the bit of strand beside a seaside *yalı*. After a while one of the fishermen joined me, having no idea who I was, although I recognized him as one of Riza Kaptan's younger cronies, his beard now as white as mine. He asked me who I was, and I said that I was an American teaching at Boğaziçi University, the old Robert College. He smiled at that, saying that he remembered an American teacher from the College who used to talk with Riza Kaptan in Nazmi's—someone like me, he said, but with a reddish beard rather than a white one. Then I realized that he was talking about me, but I let it pass, so that he could think of me as I was, just as I remember the Istanbul that I first knew, looking back on it from the twenty-first century.

INDEX

Figures in italics indicate captions